The *Enola Gay* and the Smithsonian Institution

The *Enola Gay* and the Smithsonian Institution

CHARLES T. O'REILLY *and*
WILLIAM A. ROONEY

McFarland & Company, Inc., Publishers
Jefferson, North Carolina, and London

LIBRARY OF CONGRESS CATALOGUING-IN-PUBLICATION DATA

O'Reilly, Charles T., 1921–
  The *Enola Gay* and the Smithsonian Institution / Charles T.
O'Reilly and William A. Rooney.
      p.   cm.
  Includes bibliographical references and index.

  ISBN 0-7864-2008-1 (softcover : 50# alkaline paper)

  1. Enola Gay (Bomber) — Exhibitions — Political aspects.
  2. National Air and Space Museum — Exhibitions — Political aspects.
  3. Hiroshima-shi (Japan) — History — Bombardment, 1945.
  4. Atomic bomb — Moral and ethical aspects.   I. Rooney,
William A.   II. Title.
  D767.25.H6O74   2005
  940.54'2521954'074753 — dc22   2004028964

British Library cataloguing data are available

Cover: background ©2005 Photospin; inset B-29 Bomber, article number 67-6775, Truman Presidential Library

Manufactured in the United States of America

McFarland & Company, Inc., Publishers
  Box 611, Jefferson, North Carolina 28640
    www.mcfarlandpub.com

To the memory of
W. Burr Bennett
and to his colleagues.
In the name of historical integrity
they challenged the Smithsonian.

Acknowledgments

Our thanks to the archivists at the National Archives in College Park, Maryland, the Air Force Association, and especially Mr. John Correll, editor of *Air Force Magazine* for his leadership role in the controversey and sharing the AFA collection of material about the *Enola Gay* controversy. Thanks also to the librarians of Loyola University, Chicago.

A debt of gratitude also is due to the countless scholars and others who have written about the end of World War II. Whether or not one agrees with them, all those whose work was used in preparing these essays contributed to our understanding of the *Enola Gay* controversy. And no matter how heavily credentialed, it is not always the scholar whose insights were the most instructive. The suggestions of readers of several drafts of the manuscript are gratefully acknowledged.

Contents

It was clear that the official Hiroshima narrative would be put on trial.

— Robert Jay Lifton and Greg Mitchell, 1995

The history wars in America burst into full force when it appeared that World War II might be deconstructed and reassembled in possible irreverent ways at the National Air and Space Museum.

— Tom Englehardt and Edward T. Linenthal, 1996

With "continuing Democratic majorities surely the original Enola Gay exhibit would have opened on schedule."

— Otto Mayr, 1998

To smuggle in elements of a later knowledge when describing the mental patterns of people in an earlier period is a common temptation to writers, which should be resisted.

— Arthur Koestler, 1941

Preface

Enough has been written about the dramatic end to World War II with the bombing of Hiroshima and Nagasaki to thoroughly confuse anyone, whether scholar or general reader. The confusion was exacerbated in 1995 by the controversy that erupted over plans for an exhibit by the National Air and Space Museum (NASM) of the Smithsonian Institution to mark the 50th anniversary of the end of World War II. This book examines several important issues raised by the proposed exhibit.

The NASM and the exhibit's defenders portrayed the controversy as a debate between nostalgic veterans and authentic historians (as defined by the NASM and its staff). The controversy was much more than that. It was about a strange version of history that veterans and others knew misrepresented the facts. A review of the *original* proposal for the exhibit shows why the veterans objected to that misrepresentation of the end of World War II.

The controversy began as a small cloud on the Smithsonian's horizon several years earlier when veterans asked about the status of the restoration of the *Enola Gay*, the B-29 that carried the atomic bomb to Hiroshima. According to Martin Harwit, then the NASM's director, "Over the years, a handful of men persistently wrote to anyone they thought would listen and might act. In one of his letters, a member of this group referred to himself and his comrades as 'only five old men.' But those five were to prove remarkably influential on the fate of the exhibition." For years the letter writers had asked the NASM to restore the *Enola Gay*, which had been stored outdoors and allowed to deteriorate. The veterans wanted something done in their lifetime, before deterioration made the aircraft irreparable.

The NASM finally agreed to the restoration, but decided to present the aircraft in the context of a strange interpretation of why it flew its fateful mission. In 1994 it prepared *The Crossroads*, a book-length description

1

of the exhibit. That sparked the criticism of veterans and others, who gained important supporters as the debate became public. In response, many prominent historians came to the defense of the NASM. Criticism led to the *original* proposal's being modified several times and finally the exhibit was canceled. Unfortunately, the cancellation came only after the acrimonious "Battle of the *Enola Gay*," which was revived in December 2003 when NASM's new annex was dedicated near Dulles Airport.

William Rooney was one of the original letter writers asking for the *Enola Gay's* restoration. He read *The Crossroads*, told Charles O'Reilly about it, and they began to think about this book. As veterans of World War II they share a status some historians believe disqualifies them as critics of what the NASM staff argued was mainstream history. In the staff's opinion, the field should have been left to the more credentialed supporters of the *original* version of the proposed exhibit and not cluttered by the opinions of veterans. However, just as war can be too important to be left to the generals, history sometimes is too important to be left to historians.

Our study of *The Crossroads* led to the sources on which it was based, mostly books and articles in professional journals that are readily available. However, there was a noticeable lack of other readily available sources that did not agree with the NASM's version of a racist war of vengeance. While we have tried to present both sides of the debate, we are clear about what we believe are indisputable facts about what happened as the war was ending in the summer of 1945.

That the debate was important can be seen from the amount of media attention both sides received over a period of several months. At times partisans on each side became shrill, exchanging charges of political correctness and McCarthyism. Even academics, most of whom supported *The Crossroads* as part of mainstream history, too often lacked civility as they portrayed the NASM's critics as conservatives threatening free speech and academic freedom, and currying favor with emotionally involved veterans. It was surprising to find that historians who rallied to the defense of the exhibit failed to confront the issues raised by its critics, which led us to wonder if they bothered to read *The Crossroads* before they joined the fray. Some commentators saw the controversy as a skirmish in the history wars in which historians countered the myths of the "good war." We prefer to see the controversy as one in which revisionist ideology was going to trump the factual record and ought to be challenged.

Readers should know that in the preparation of this book no financial support was received from foundations or from any other source, including individual donors. Distant archives and libraries were used during travel to visit friends and relatives or attend reunions. It may be noted that William Rooney, a former advertising executive, has written a book about architectural decoration and Charles O'Reilly, who was a professor and university administrator, has written on research methodology, social work history and the Italian Campaign of 1943–1945. William Rooney served as an intelligence officer with the 40th Bomber Group in India and China during World War II. Charles O'Reilly was an interpreter with Italian Service Units in World War II and a counter-intelligence officer during the Korean conflict.

Charles T. O'Reilly
William A. Rooney
November 2004

I

*The NASM Plans
an Exhibit*

At the approach of the 50th anniversary of the end of World War II in the Pacific, the Smithsonian Institution's National Air and Space Museum (NASM) planned an exhibit with its centerpiece the *Enola Gay*, the B-29 that dropped the atomic bomb on Hiroshima on August 6, 1945. The exhibit was to be called *The Crossroads: The End of World War II, the Atomic Bomb and the Origins of the Cold War*. When what the NASM intended to present to the public became known, a heated controversy developed resulting in books, articles in historical journals and a multitude of articles in the media that chronicled the debates over the proposed exhibit. The debates escalated into a controversy over how the war ended that involved more than military and political history, becoming a flashpoint in the so-called "culture wars." Why that happened is beyond the scope of this book, although we touch on it in the chapters that follow. Because of the controversy the much revised exhibit was canceled early in 1995 by Ira Michael Heyman, the new Secretary of the Smithsonian.

The NASM's account of how and why war in the Pacific ended contrasts with excellent overviews of what happened in Thomas Allen and Norman Polmar's *Code Name Downfall*, and in Richard Frank's *Downfall*. Although we cover some of the same ground, as well as that in Robert Newman's *Truman and the Hiroshima Cult*, the focus of these essays is more limited: by examining key elements in what was proposed by the *original* version off the exhibit, we hope to foster a better understanding of the issues raised by the NASM regarding the end of World War II. Those issues included whether Japan was on the brink of surrender in the summer of 1945, whether American racism led to Hiroshima and Nagasaki, and whether President Truman lied about the number of casualties expected if there was an invasion of Japan. Without responding to the heated rhetoric of those who saw any criticism of the exhibit as a threat to free speech or worse, we hope that these essays can provide a dispassionate examination of why the controversy began.

Not everyone at the Smithsonian was in favor of including the *Enola Gay* in an exhibit marking the end of the war. Peace groups and others considered the aircraft a symbol of American criminality and its display a sign of obscene triumphalism. In 1987 a NASM committee had discussed the pros and cons of an exhibit incorporating the *Enola Gay*. Admiral Noel Gayler, a World War II naval aviator who later commanded United States naval forces in the Pacific and then headed the National Security Agency, opposed the idea because it gave the impression of glorifying or taking pride in the aircraft's mission. Dr. David Challinor, the Smithsonian's assistant secretary for science, agreed with the Admiral, adding that for the last 15 years he had been saying, "The *Enola Gay* will never be on an exhibit while I'm here." Challinor's remark revealed some internal staff resistance to such an exhibit.

Later, however, it was decided to go ahead with the exhibit, and after initial discussions by the NASM staff, active planning for an exhibit showcasing the *Enola Gay* began in 1990. A proposed outline gave rise to several in-house concept papers in response to observations made by internal reviewers. Finally by July 1993, NASM's sixteen page "Exhibition Planning Document" for the exhibit was ready. After reviewing the document the then Smithsonian Secretary, Robert Adams, told the NASM's Director, Martin Harwit, that much of it was "compelling" but he took exception to the title, thought the document moved too quickly to the atomic bomb, and objected to the wording that it would be "an exhibit about the wartime development of the atomic bomb, the decision to use it against Japan and the aftermath of the bombings. This should be an exhibit commemorating the end of World War II, taking appropriate note of the atom bomb's central role in one theater."

Curator Thomas Crouch took exception to Secretary Adams' criticism. "That is," he told Director Harwit, "precisely what the exhibit outlined in the document *is* all about" (emphasis in original). Crouch went on to say that he thought what worried Adams "is the fact that any morally responsible exhibition on the atomic bombing of Japan has to include a treatment of the victims.... He knows that any exhibition including an honest discussion of that topic is most certainly going to upset a lot of visitors." Crouch ended by asking Harwit if he wanted an exhibition that made veterans feel good, or one that made visitors think about the consequences of the atomic bombing of Japan. Crouch won the argument and NASM went on to develop an exhibit shaped by planning, which, according to a 1994 story in the *Washington Post*, cautioned against "the dogmatic belief in the official explanation that dropping the bomb prevented a bloody invasion." Supporters of the exhibit were frank to say that it challenged the dominant memory of the end of the war and as word drifted out in Washington fashion, questions began to be asked about the exhibit's direction.[1]

The answer came from a book length script (or detailed outline) for the exhibit, *The Crossroads: The End of World War II, the Atomic Bomb and the Origins of the Cold War,* dated January 12, 1994. For several reasons, one of which was because it said America's Pacific War was one of vengeance, while Japan defended itself against Western Imperialism, it provoked a firestorm of criticism leading to what would become known as "The Battle of the *Enola Gay*." When outside criticism of *The Crossroads* began, Director Harwit complained that critics concentrated on the written word and copies of photographs, drawing conclusions about "an exhibition medium whose main impact derives, not from words on labels, but from an apt juxtaposition of objects, documents, film, sound and lighting. Nor was the text they analyzed a final script, but rather the first of many drafts that normally follow — and that did, in fact follow." He also regretted that the videos intended for the exhibit could not be seen and that critics relied on the written script whose words, he said, "struck most as cold and analytical, devoid of the human elements the veterans most wished to see."[2]

Martin Harwit had been the director of the NASM for six years, and, according to Robert Jay Lifton and Greg Mitchell, was taking the museum "in a new direction, rejecting the notion that history is the winner's version of what happened, as Howard Zinn once put it." They went on to say "it was clear that the official Hiroshima narrative would be put on trial." Director Harwit went to some length to describe why and how numerous groups in and out of government, including Japanese museums, the Japanese Foreign Ministry, and six American national veteran organizations, were apprised of the coming exhibit. A full planning document was ready in July 1993, according to Harwit, with "a first draft of the script available for distribution to an ad hoc advisory committee in January 1994. Thereafter, we expected to make significant revisions for a full year." That contrasts with what John Correll said he was told by Harwit at a meeting on June 21, 1994. Harwit reportedly said that the museum had declared the exhibit plan final. However, at a subsequent meeting on August 17, Director Harwit said the museum intended to revise the exhibit. That happened some time after intense criticism erupted.

Although supporters of the exhibit have implied that the original January script was a tentative first draft, and possibly subject to major revisions, it seems evident that as of the end of February 1994 the NASM believed the original script would substantially structure what the public would see in 1995. That is because on February 28, 1994, the Smithsonian Institution provided the NASM $250,000 for the exhibit, in addition to the $300,000 the NASM had allocated for the exhibit from its own funds. It is hard to imagine that the Smithsonian funding would have been provided unless the proposed exhibit had been reviewed and approved by top authorities at the Smithsonian. Such funding probably meant that, at the end of February 1994, the NASM was committed to the exhibit described in the *original* January script. Although the Smithsonian's allocation appeared to be final approval of the proposal, soon afterward, matters began to unravel both inside the Smithsonian and in the community — a sorry sequence outlined in great detail in his book by Director Harwit. Because we focus on the *original* script, it is important to remember that the Smithsonian's funding for the exhibit signaled that what Harwit and the curators prepared had received approval and, at that time, the NASM was prepared to produce an exhibit based on the January script. Perhaps with "fine tuning," that script was what the NASM intended to present to the public. Apart from the exaggerated rhetoric that flourished on both sides of the controversy, the importance of the content of the *original* script should be kept in mind. It contained an ideological bias that was as historically inexcusable as it would have been had the staff presented a glorification of the A-Bomb for ending the war.

Unfortunately, the curators and their supporters are dedicated to historical "revisionism." It also is unfortunate that the words "revisionism" and "revisionist" have become pejorative. Revising our understanding of the past when new facts become available is a continuing and unexceptional process in many fields, including history. What led to the negative sense in which the words are used today is the confrontational interpretation of history pursued by many contemporary historians. Typically educated during the 1960s and 1970s, they ascribe malign motives to policy makers in the area of foreign policy, are hyper critical of American diplomacy as an arm of imperialism, and see the United States as culpable of neocolonial treatment of the third world. Their historiography indicts the U. S. for causing the Cold War, overlooks or minimizes Soviet policies that enslaved Eastern Europe, and is dedicated to imposing a conspiratorial vision of the American past that would shape a future based on their ideological agenda. In pursuing that agenda the *Enola Gay* was a convenient stalking horse.

There is no dispute that the sins committed by American policies need reporting and analysis, but the analysis must be based on facts and not speculation about motives, such as the revisionist assertions that racism led to using the A-Bomb against Japan. That interpretation could be reached only by the denial of the situation and the facts available to policy makers in the days leading up to August 6, 1945. Those facts have been well known for years, even to revisionist historians. Facts never speak for themselves, however. We must explain what they mean, and that is where our backgrounds can lead us astray, whether revisionists or not. When we speak about facts we must do so honestly, keeping in mind their time and place in the past, and not force them onto a Procrustean bed that satisfies the current fashion in revisionist history.[3]

A general overview of the proposed exhibit had been given to the Air Force Association (AFA) and other groups by NASM staff in November 1993. However, until the January 1994 script was ready, those outside the NASM, including its own advisory committee, were not aware of how the exhibit was to be presented to the public. Harwit sent a copy of the script to the Air Force Association at the end of January 1994, and in early February the advisory committee met with NASM staff to discuss the exhibit. Harwit was disappointed that the AFA copied the script and shared it with reporters and other interested parties. However, the AFA had received a copy informally two weeks before the NASM's copy arrived. To stop what it considered unauthorized reproduction and the sharing of subsequent versions of the scripts, the NASM copyrighted the five subsequent revisions. A lightly edited but essentially complete copy of the script's text minus the visual elements of the exhibit can be found in Philip Nobile's *Judgment at the Smithsonian*.[4]

When defending the exhibit, Professor Michael Hogan contended that *The Crossroads* was an "early and incomplete version of the exhibit script." However, both John Correll's report of Director Harwit's statement in June 1994 that the exhibit plan was complete, and the funding by the Smithsonian, strongly suggest that *The Crossroads* was essentially complete. Hogan's comment is a spin on the sequence that evolved through several "concept papers" to a "full planning document" in July 1993, then to the book length script in January 1994. In addition, persons close to *The Crossroads* script thought it needed only "fine tuning." Stanley Goldberg, a member of the exhibit's advisory committee, believed that "the curators had presented a solid script rooted in the latest historical scholarship." He also believed that the questioned sentences about the "war of vengeance" were well documented and gave "the lie to those who accused the curators of distorting history or pandering to the Japanese." Director Harwit admitted that changes were made only after a copy of the original script surfaced outside the NASM. Had that not happened, and without the reaction it created, it is questionable whether there would have been any advice sought from interested parties other than the advisory committee. The five subsequent scripts that were modified only in response to criticism mask the significance of the *original* vision of the end of World War II. Professor Hogan also claimed that "the curators had been willing to share their work with the Air Force Association and other interested parties, had sought their advice, and made adjustments accordingly." That happened only after the furor created by the original script. The convoluted story of what happened at the NASM because of the exhibit makes an excellent case study of aberrant organizational behavior that had a disastrous outcome for a priceless national institution.[5]

How defenders of the exhibit saw the controversy can be gauged from a comment in *History on Trial*: "the Air Force Association and other veterans' groups censured the exhibition script, complaining that the curators planned to ask visitors to consider the moral and political dimensions of Truman's decision to drop the bomb and to look at photographs of charred women and children in Hiroshima. This, the veterans said, would arouse the idea that the Japanese were victims rather than military aggressors in World War II." Unfortunately, wrote one member of the exhibit's advisory committee, "the eagerness of critics to demonize the Smithsonian obscured a central issue: the inevitable tension between the commemorative voice and the historical voice when history becomes the focus of a public exhibit or ceremony. 'The Last Act' was caught between memory and history." Finally, "no doubt, in the first draft the curators and advisory board were inadequately sensitive to the emotional and moral concerns of Americans who fought in the war, but they were not obdurate about sticking to the original plan." Harwit, however, found the curators remained obdurately committed to the original script to the bitter end.[6]

According to Tom Englehardt and Edward T. Linenthal, "the history wars in America burst into full force when it appeared that World War II might be deconstructed and reassembled in possibly irreverent ways at the National Air and Space Museum — and that the bombing of Hiroshima and Nagasaki might be used to pry open the 'Good War'; indeed to further destabilize a larger sacred myth of the country's origins and development." If anyone knew how the exhibit intended to pry open the "Good War," and deconstruct World War II in irreverent ways, it would be Linenthal, a member of the NASM's advisory committee for the exhibit. He had already done that when writing about the 50th anniversary of the attack on Pearl Harbor, sarcastically referring to how "memories of Pearl Harbor were kept alive in the aftermath of the attack via celebrations of the triumph of the forces of righteousness in the great moral drama of World War II." He also noted that the National Park Service premiered composer John Duffy's *Time for Remembrance* during the ceremonies for the 50th anniversary "to break dramatically with the stereotypical all-military format of bands, banners and bombast."

Richard Kohn, another member of the advisory committee who defended the exhibit, summed up the exhibit's initial purpose as not a historical investigation of what happened, why it happened, and what it meant, but to revisit the American decision to use the bomb in 1945, and to ask whether the bomb was justified. It was to suggest "an uncertain, potentially dangerous future for all of civilization." The exhibit would conclude, as it began, he said, by "noting the debatable character of the atomic bombing." Further, Kohn said: "Taken as a whole and read with the emotional impact on viewers in mind, the exhibition was in fact unbalanced; possessed a very clear and potent point of view ... its message could be read to be tendentious and moralizing; the exhibition script could be read to condemn American behavior at the end of World War II." Whether one was pro or con about the exhibit, after reading the original script it would be difficult to disagree with Kohn's assessment.[7]

Exhibiting Dilemmas, a 1997 book by the Smithsonian Press, can help one understand why the exhibit took its special form. Although referred to in several places, the *Enola Gay* exhibit was not among the seven recent Smithsonian exhibits discussed in detail by Smithsonian curators. However, those discussions reveal how the "Battle of the *Enola Gay*" touched a curatorial nerve. When William Yeingst and Ionnie Bunch asked if museums should explore questions in which the public seems to have little interest, and if so, how, they said, "Finding answers to these questions is problematic even in the best of times but today, in an age of uncertainty, in the politicized era of the '*Enola Gay*,' it is difficult to find the civil discourse and institutional support needed with these issues. As museums are drawn into the current 'culture wars' the debates over the role of museums in our society and, more specifically over how recent history should best be remembered, preserved, and interpreted become less academic and more acrimonious. There is a tendency ... in some quarters to think that museums have raised the wrong questions and pushed too hard or too fast to examine the rough edges of history. Yet if curators are to explore these issues—and we think that it is essential that they do—exhibits and collections must challenge as well as celebrate, educate as well as entertain, and stimulate thought as well as tradition."

They went on to say that, "after all, presenting the history of the living means treading on dreams and wrestling with recollections both cherished and painful." In addition, "because those who remember have a sense of ownership of memory, visitors to an exhibit may be unwilling to 'defer to curatorial prerogative.'" Although listening to conflicting viewpoints, curators needed to make sure that those with different opinions "understood that as historians we held the ultimate responsibility for.... interpretation." Believing that their role was to interpret the past and keep a public trust in their work, on one exhibit they "found that deconstructing the historical and curatorial process" could answer a questioner's concerns. "It is essential," they said, "that we help the public — visitors, politicians, and funders— to better understand that what curators do is based less on whim and personal ideology than on scholarship, research, and considered reflection." The authors enjoined curators to "continue to conceptualize the past in order to give visitors the tools to use to manipulate history so that they might deal better with the present."

With such modest goals in mind *The Crossroads* script was developed by relying on the curators' version of history. The manner in which it was done can be summarized in the words of Smithsonian staffers Amy Henderson and Adrienne Kappler: "within the last two decades, the curatorial advocacy of popular culture as an integral part of the museum's responsibility had transformed the public's perception from a temple into a virtual branch of popular entertainment itself." Many visitors to an exhibit that was a virtual branch of popular entertainment, who were under the age of fifty, would not be aware of the complex events of 1945; and they would not be disposed to question what seemed to be a thoughtful, authoritative version of the end of World War II. That made it imperative that the curators avoid a simplistic, unbalanced account. They failed that professional challenge to their intellectual integrity.[8]

The exhibit's journey from concept to the January script and afterwards was carefully documented by the Air Force Association, which publishes *Air Force Magazine*. Director Martin Harwit recounted his side of the story in a book published in 1996. Another somewhat less detailed review is in Michael Hogan's *Hiroshima in History and Memory*, and Edward Linenthal devoted a chapter to his interpretation of the controversy in *History Wars*.[9] Robert Jay Lifton and Greg Mitchell also devoted a chapter to the Smithsonian controversy, calling the lost exhibit, with some slight exaggeration, "what may be the most tragic, contested, and foreboding single act in our entire history." When the exhibit was canceled they said, "this was an exhibit the demands of conscience required but nobody wanted."[10]

Writing in *Japan Quarterly*, Martin Harwit reported that, in addition to the cancellation of the proposed exhibit, Congressman Sam Johnson of Texas demanded the suppression of the exhibition's catalog "which reproduced word for word the text of every label in the original exhibition as it would have stood at its planned opening in May.... Antagonists and the media had made so many false allegations and quoted so much out of context that we wished to have a record of the exact wording." The catalog was withdrawn from publication and, "In burning the catalog, Johnson and Heyman made sure that the American people would never know what the museum had actually planned to display." Harwit is correct in regretting that the catalog, and especially the genuine original script, are not available to the public. Then scholars and anyone else would be able to observe first hand the intended distortion of history by the NASM.[11]

Those in favor of the exhibit adopted the tactic of characterizing the exhibit's critics as defenders of secular myths, and constantly referred to those so-called myths as they wrote about the controversy. There are many meanings of the word "myth," but the meaning they intended is that of something imagined, false or at least deceptive, and in conflict with reality. As used by Tom Englehart and Edward Linenthal the word is pejorative. It also was pejorative in a 1995 Smithsonian Press book by G. Kurt Piehler about how Americans have memorialized their war dead. After World War I, he said, "National leaders conceived of the overseas cemeteries and monuments, the Tomb of the Unknown Soldier, and Armistice Day ceremonies as a way of mythologizing America's first European war as a time when Americans of all regions, classes and ethnic groups united behind a common goal." Piehler's use of the word suggests manipulation of the past, much as the word was used during the *Enola Gay* controversy.

Geoffrey Smith put the background for this tactic succinctly. In the last twenty years, he said, "spurred by Ronald Reagan's (and Hollywood's) tendency to dismiss the messy realities of history in favor of nostalgic celluloid repackaging, an idealized popular memory of past American greatness emerged." History, according to Smith, "remains singularly profane when compared with the core of myths and traditions constructed over time by privileged Americans to ennoble their history." He explained that the Republic's national creed has its own public values that are taught in civics classes, by popular magazines, and movies and myths like George Washington's cherry tree. Tension exists between "avowedly objective history, with its emphasis upon the complex relationship between cause and effect and change over time, and 'subjective, selective, and present-minded collective memory.'" Smith then went on to contrast the "know-nothing-ism" of the detractors of the exhibit to the "learned rebuttals" of scholars such as Martin Sherwin, Kai Bird, Edward Linenthal and Michael Kammen.[12] Continuing in that vein, J. Samuel Walker referred to "the mythological explanations for the use of the bomb" and the public reliance on that myth despite the findings of scholars.

A useful explanation of why there are such myths was offered by Professor George Mosse: "Those concerned with the image and the continuing appeal of the nation worked at constructing a myth which would draw the sting from death in war and emphasize the meaningfulness of the fighting and sacrifice.... The aim was to make an inherently unpalatable past acceptable, important not just for the purpose of consolation but above all for the justification of the nation in whose name the war had been fought. The reality of the war experience came to be transformed into what one might call the Myth of the War Experience, which looked back upon the war as a meaningful and even sacred event.... The Myth of the War Experience was designed to mask war and to legitimize war experience; it was meant to displace the reality of war."

When allocating responsibility for the troubles of the ill-fated exhibit, David Thelen, the editor of the *Journal of American History,* portrayed the controversy as one that "pitted veterans' desire to commemorate their sacrifices ... against scholars' desire to uncover truth and curators' desire to present what curator Tom Crouch called an 'honest and balanced' narrative." Thelen concluded, "in my judgment, the first script for this exhibition did all these things—and many more." Critics of the exhibit were placed on notice by Otto Mayr, a former curator of the Smithsonian's National Museum of History and Technology, when he said, "The opposition forces who brought down the project lost, for history will view them poorly: the resulting literature will see to that." Mayr may be correct that closing the exhibit gave the critics a Pyrrhic victory. The *Journal of American History* was one academic powerhouse that rallied to the defense of *The Crossroads* without considering the specific criticism leveled at the exhibit. Other academic associations that control access to the academic media closed ranks with the NASM. Long after the controversy, *The New York Times* reported "a fierce debate over the National Air and Space Museum's exhibition on the 50th anniversary of the destruction of Hiroshima," thus recognizing that the NASM designed the exhibit less to mark the end of the Pacific War than as an opportunity to condemn the bombing of Japan and the opening of the Cold War.

Thanks to casting the critics as sentimentalists who viewed the exhibit with what Steven Dubin called "generational fidelity," while others considered them ignoramuses when it came to authentic knowledge of the war, it is not surprising that some exhibit critics responded in kind, although their rhetoric was not always as genteel as that of the academics who defended the exhibit. Protagonists like Steven Dubin may have been more genteel, but he was adept at skewering one of the exhibit's opponents who was a curator elsewhere, remarking that he allowed "generational fidelity" to overcome his professional identity.

Although historian James Miller was not referring to the *Enola Gay* controversy when he made a more general criticism of veterans who write about war, he captured the attitude of his contemporaries. "Anyone who has met veterans of the war will recognize the mind set. It deserves a careful hearing, for historians brought up in the postwar era tend to play Monday morning quarterback. However, once we have done our homework, including paying attention to the reminiscences of veterans, we are duty bound to interpret." He added, "history is not immutable but constantly reinterpreted to fit society's requirements ... history is an art, not a science, as so many fervently but mistakenly believe." One can share Professor Miller's conclusion that history is an art but also ask why the veterans' mind set condemns them to misrepresent the past, unlike "duty bound" historians who reinterpret the past to fit society's mutable requirements. If Miller meant that in order to communicate with the reader, the language and knowledge, the analogies and understandings of the 1900s differed from those that of the 1800s, and in turn from those of 2000, and that those ought to be explained in the text, that would be unexceptional. But that is not what he said. What he said echoed the spirit of Soviet and Fascist historians who rewrote history to meet their patrons' mutable requirements. That led to dire results for the historian's art, and more important, corrupted their readers' knowledge of reality.[13]

The present work examines the *original* January 1994 script and also some books and the articles that defended the exhibit as well as some that provided background for the script. As originally conceived, the script revealed an ideological fixation about how the war ended, reflecting the revisionist perspective that Hiroshima was a crime against humanity of a piece with American imperialism. The curators believed that an uncritical "celebration" of World War II would contribute to militarism, and preferred to show the public a war crime that began the Cold War. Criticism of the A-Bomb that appeared shortly after World War II was offered mainly on ethical or moral grounds, while the ideological strain of the criticism became popular in the 1960s and 1970s, when revisionist historians began their ascendancy in academic history. For many of that generation, opposition to the Vietnam war was the common currency they carried into an academic career.

According to Bryan Hubbard and Marouf Hasian, the new generation of curators, which they described as revisionists, joined the NASM in the 1980s with "vastly different ideas of their role as curators and brought with them new motivations and styles of intellectual inquiry. Many had grown up during the volatile 1960s and worried that the nation's uncritical historical celebration contributed to forms of militarism and patriotism that fueled international colonialism, racism, global weapons proliferation, and environmental deterioration." Such a background was typical of how the Smithsonian's staff saw the *Enola Gay* exhibit. From a psycho-social perspective it is as important to recognize that background as it is to recognize that Elvis Presley and the Beatles played a role in transforming American youth culture.[14]

While some partisans of the exhibit misunderstood what happened at the war's end, perhaps due to ignorance of readily available facts, some twisted interpretations of the historical record to meet their agenda. Many of the contested facts were not mere differences of opinion or the debated interpretations commonly found in history books. Facts were taken out of context in a manner alien to authentic history. A constant refrain by defenders of the exhibit was that the consensus of historians was on their side, as if history was decided by a majority vote. Another mantra was the alleged academic freedom of the Smithsonian staff to present whatever, in their opinion, was an appropriate display. Although a former professor who should have known the meaning of "academic freedom," Martin Harwit denied that the changes in the script made in response to criticism were violations of the academic freedom of the curators, thus crediting them with having academic freedom. Later he viewed the cancellation of the exhibit as a violation of the curators' academic freedom. Because the concept of academic freedom as defined by the American Association of University Professors applies to college and university faculty and researchers, the argument that it was enjoyed by the curators, or Harwit, had no basis in reality. However, it was a useful ploy intended to attract support from the academic community.

No strangers to hyperbole, Lawrence Lifschultz and Kai Bird made an even stronger statement in their *Hiroshima's Shadow:* "the cancellation will stand as one of the great intellectual scandals of American History."

That was matched by Gore Vidal who Bird said called the controversy "the most debated event in our stormy history." A similar characterization was provided by Professor Michael Sherry, who reported that some curators and historians saw the controversy as an assault on intellectuals and on truth itself, "carried out by patriotic bullies who used words like liberal a bit the way Nazis had once used *Jew*." After trivializing what the Nazis did to the Jews with that comparison he went on to recall that little in the assault was unprecedented, as historians of the McCarthy era could have told them. That reckless invective did not encourage reasonable discourse with other parties to the controversy.[15]

Several names are mentioned frequently in our essays. Some were advisors to the NASM whose ideas about the war's end inspired the curators. Despite some differences in emphasis insofar as *The Crossroads* was concerned, the composition of the advisory committee insured that the members were on essentially the same wave length when it came to indicting the United States for its crimes. There was nothing unusual in this widely used practice when forming advisory committees that provide a predictable outcome whether for public or private entities. Other individuals who are mentioned frequently were stalwart defenders of the exhibit whose ideas also paralleled those of the curators. Referring often to a so-called "scholarly consensus" about their version of events in the spring and summer of 1945, the defenders of the "deconstruction" of accounts of those events belonged to a small self referential coterie of academics, with each relying on the writing of the others. Essentially, deconstruction asserts that texts have no definitive meaning. The "indeterminacy" of the narrative makes objectivity nonexistent. Texts can be analyzed in any way that the investigator wishes and thus given new meaning. Largely unchallenged by their peers, those defending the exhibit promoted the idea that there was a genuine consensus among students of the events of the summer of 1945 for so long that the repetition created an illusion of its reality.

Had the advisory committee included a naysayer or two, perhaps someone like Robert Newman, or Robert Maddox, although many others were available, it would have alerted the exhibit's planners to the minefield they were entering. However, there already were members of the NASM staff who could have provided balance to the exhibit, something that became clear with the review of *The Crossroads* by the NASM'S "Tiger Team" found in the appendix. As a Smithsonian insider (Director of the Smithsonian's Center for Folklife Programs and Cultural Studies), Richard Kurin's comments resonate with those of the Tiger Team. He may have resented the name calling and shrillness of both sides during the controversy, but was critical of how Director Harwit, the curators and the Smithsonian handled the controversy. Referring to *The Crossroads,* he said, "To have a script that was perceived and reported as putting the onus of guilt upon Americans, blaming American servicemen for dropping the bomb on innocent women and children, and putting on their shoulders the start of the cold war, nuclear waste, nuclear terrorism, and other horrors was too much of a stretch."

Relating *The Crossroads* script to the writings of its partisans reveals the relationship between what the latter wrote about the end of the war and the content of the script. When the curators stacked the deck against differing interpretations about the war's end they lacked intellectual integrity and contributed to the debacle at the NASM. The *Enola Gay* exhibit was not the first to provoke controversy about the Smithsonian's vision of American history, nor will it be the last. With a staff sympathetic to revisionism this public institution can hardly do otherwise, as shown by earlier controversies over exhibits about other aspects of American history. Kenneth Cmiel provided an example of institutional tilt when he reviewed Richard Wightman Fox and Robert B. Westbrook's *In Face of the Facts,* a collection of papers given at the Woodrow Wilson Center of the Smithsonian. He noted that several of the contributors spoke of the importance of "moral conversations" when considering issues, and then made the interesting point that while the contributors spanned a political range from center to left, the editors didn't do anything so "crazy" as to include a Republican. "Several of the essays ritually flog the right, indicating who wasn't invited to the party.... It makes the goal of comity a harder one to inclusively implement." The Smithsonian's precedents for not conversing with contrarian opinions insures that it will enjoy no end of controversy.[16]

Critics of the exhibit were pitted against academic historians like Gar Alperovitz who asserted that the bomb preventing a great loss of lives "is now known to be false." That was because the alleged consensus among scholars is that the bomb was not needed to avoid an invasion of Japan. In another place when discussing the story of the A-Bomb, Alperovitz found "there is a rapidly expanding gap between what the expert scholarly community now knows and what the public has been taught." Further, he said, there is "a steady narrowing of the questions in dispute in the most sophisticated studies that has sharpened some of the truly controversial issues in the historical debate." It was this approach that infused the content of the original script.

There was some grumbling by historians about various aspects of the exhibit, and later complaints about the supine capitulation of the NASM to the forces of right wing conservatism, but many historians agreed that the exhibit should have been displayed as originally conceived. Whether they actually saw the original script is open to question. Apparently not many copies of the *original* script were distributed by the NASM, and we do not know whether any were sent to the Organization of American Historians (OAH) and other groups for review and comment. According to Michael Hogan, Director Harwit sent a copy of a revised script late in August or early in September 1994 to Michael Kammen, president-elect of the OAH and a member of the Smithsonian Council, thus hardly a disinterested party. That timing suggests that Kammen, "who was impressed by the historical veracity and quality" of the revised exhibit, and the OAH may not have seen the *original* script. By the time the script mentioned by Hogan was sent to the OAH the controversy was in full flower. If indeed it was the revised script that was reviewed and not the *original* script, the reader would not have been fully aware of how the controversy began. Ordinarily one expects professional historians to seek an original source before jumping to conclusions.

Defenders of the exhibit received major media attention. Gar Alperovitz appeared on a national television special about the exhibit and had a story in *The New York Times*. Robert Lifton appeared on several television talk shows, and Ronald Takaki made a five city book tour and appeared on television programs in fifteen other cities via satellite. On the other hand criticisms, which often were heated denunciations of the exhibit, came from many newspapers and radio talk shows, but seldom from academics for reasons that will be discussed later.[17]

When reporting the *Enola Gay* controversy, National Public Radio (NPR) had several exhibit critics and exhibit defenders on its programs. The latter, however, received much more time to present their case, and often were the only ones heard on a program. In addition, NPR clearly stated its approval of the exhibit on more than one occasion. News analyst Daniel Schorr compared the controversy to the disputes over the Confederate flag and asserted: "The sharpest confrontation over people's history versus academic history came in the flap over the Smithsonian Institution's exhibit of the *Enola Gay*." After noting that Dwight Eisenhower wrote that it was not necessary to use the A-Bomb against Japan, Schorr added that some historians believe it was used as a warning to the Soviet Union rather than for its military effect in Japan. "But the people—

in this case, veterans organizations—were outraged that anyone should question the need to end the war quickly and spare the American lives that would be lost in an invasion of Japan." The Smithsonian gave up, and "Score one more for people's history versus academics' history—the people's history that doesn't care too much about other civilizations or the feeling of the Japanese about the atomic bomb, the history that reflects the popular passions of the moment." Because National Public Radio deals not with history but with politically correct opinion, it refused to present both sides of the controversy.

The controversy was summarized by the American Broadcasting Company's (ABC's) popular "Nightline" in the summer of 1995. "Nightline" followed the line taken by the NASM, posing it as a conflict between history and the veterans' desire for a commemorative memorial. While the program's bias was evident in its earlier coverage of the story, the clearest example of its slanted coverage appeared on July 27, 1995, in a "special report" by Peter Jennings under the heading "News: Domestic."

According to Jennings, "In 1946, facing a rising tide of questions and criticism, the atomic decision makers would feel obliged to rewrite history." He added "it is clear there are people who don't want to contemplate the moral questions that are also part of the bomb's legacy." Jennings concluded the program with "It's unfortunate, we think, that some veterans' organizations and some politicians felt the need to bully our most important national museum, so the whole story of Hiroshima is not represented here. That is not fair to history or to the rest of us. After all, freedom of discussion was one of the ideals that Americans fought and died for." It is paradoxical that Jennings claimed that the critics were against freedom of discussion when in reality the NASM and Jennings would suppress the freedom of the critics to protest the excesses of the Smithsonian.[18] How did Jennings reach those conclusions? When a program is built on the opinions of Barton Bernstein, John Dower, William Lanouette, Samuel Walker, Robert Messer, Martin Sherwin, Gar Alperovitz, and Leon Sigal, several of whom were quoted more than once in the program, without anyone to counter their claims, Jennings' overwhelming bias is on the record.

Tortured interpretations of the ending of the Pacific War are such a part of the conventional history that a virtual caricature of what actually happened has emerged. As a result many ostensibly well informed people share the doubts expressed by one World War II veteran. "The difficulty is that so much of our knowledge of that period is rooted in conjecture and surrounded by imponderables. We will never know, for example, whether if it (the bomb) had been built two years earlier, it would have been dropped on Germany. We will never know, for sure, if Japan was on the verge of surrender in August 1945. We will also never know whether the oft-mentioned 'one million estimated casualties' was only a convenient after-the-fact justification. And we will never know, as some revisionist historians have claimed, whether the secondary target of the Hiroshima bomb was Moscow, i.e., the first shot of the Cold War."

There are good answers to those questions that are not rooted in conjecture but in solid facts that are known to many revisionists who chose to ignore them.[19] Although the present authors have tried to be objective herein, we are not neutral in regard to the facts. Jack Davis is among those who would differ with our approach. He found that "The mere selection of truths, an unavoidable process of doing history, jeopardizes the objectivity of even the most conscientious historian." He joins those belittling "fact fetishists" who allow facts to get in the way of discerning what they believe really happened, and others who scoff at the idea of objectivity, claiming that the meaning of events depends on the subjective understanding of the commentator. Followers of postmodernism contend that there can be no independent standard for determining which of several interpretations of an event is the true one. Allegedly, because the true meaning of a narrative can never be found, writers can impose their own meaning on the events they study. This is not the place for an in-depth exploration of the implications of such ideas for how some historians approach the past, but readers should be aware of their approach. When added to revisionism there is an inversion of reality of the kind described by Kenneth Werrell, who said that "Japanese attitudes, along with the aid of revisionist historians, antinuclear activists, antiwar proponents, American guilt, and historical amnesia, have led many Japanese and some Americans to see the vanquished as victims and the victors as villains." Among those who inverted history in this manner were the curators at the NASM and their defenders.

Why this inversion of reality happens was pointed out by C. Behan McCullagh. "It has been a shock for us to learn that we do not perceive the world just as it is, and that our knowledge of the world is inescapably framed by the concepts and language of our culture. It is little wonder that these two discoveries have led many philosophers to deny that we can possibly know anything about the world beyond us. I hope to have shown a sense in which we can." McCullagh's book is a practical discussion of the problems of authenticating accounts of the past as well as the possibility of doing so, to the extent fallible humans make a genuine effort to do so by guarding against their interests and biases. In the process he emphasizes the importance of balance and fairness in interpreting the past, characteristics that too often are missing in the work of revisionist historians.[20]

Our intention has been to provide a reasoned understanding of events in the summer of 1945 based on facts attested to by evidence. Without advocating for the use of the A-Bomb, we believe that an honest appraisal of the situation confronting President Truman in late July 1945 shows that he felt compelled to use it, primarily (although not exclusively) for military reasons. Those who know the American political system are aware that in 1945 as today, like it or not, domestic political considerations as well as foreign policy considerations have always played a legitimate role in presidential decisions. In 1965, Len Giovannetti and Fred Freed made it clear that they opposed the use of the A-Bomb, but they concluded, "Until and unless new evidence is uncovered to prove otherwise, it is our belief that the decision to use the bomb was taken in good faith, not to unleash a weapon of vengeance against a ruthless enemy, but primarily to bring a quick end to a barbaric war and secondarily to derive the benefits of a timely victory."

Dan van der Vat was not unaware of the role played by Western exploitation of Asia in the background of the Pacific war, but he placed what happened there in perspective: "in telling this tale as it has not been told before—from both viewpoints, with the accounts of participants set in a framework of historical analysis and narrative—the rapacious and brutal Japan of the generals is not equated with the United States, which did not want war yet became the avenging 'arsenal of democracy.' There was no comparison: there was only naked aggression met by irresistible force. No less morally than militarily, no less ethically than economically, it was a most unequal fight which Japan should never have begun."

Echoing that conclusion, in 1995 historian Donald Kagan said, "Americans certainly share the same weaknesses as the rest of the human race. They need not, however, shrink from a confrontation of the 'fundamental questions' surrounding Hiroshima. An honest examination of the evidence reveals that their leaders, in the tragic predicament common to all who have engaged in wars that reach the point where every choice is repugnant, chose the least bad course. Americans may look back on that decision with sadness, but without shame." Although postmodernist revisionists have worked hard to prove otherwise, we believe that verdict stands.[21]

II

Why the Battle of the Enola Gay?

The public "Battle of the *Enola Gay*" began with a letter from W. Burr Bennett to *Air Force Magazine* on August 6, 1993. However, it was preceded by skirmishes that began in the mid 1980s between the Smithsonian and a small group of B-29 veterans who wanted to see the *Enola Gay* restored and appropriately displayed. The Smithsonian's patrician Secretary, Robert McCormick Adams, could not have imagined what he and the Smithsonian were getting into in 1984 when he replied to a veteran who asked what the Smithsonian intended to do about the *Enola Gay*. To explain what happened, one has to go back some years and ask why "the five old men" badgered the NASM about the *Enola Gay*. Their efforts are described in a chapter in Director Martin Harwit's version of the battle. The men, veterans who served in B-29 units, believed that the *Enola Gay* was historically significant and that it deserved a better fate than deteriorating in obscurity.

In 1828, lack of official interest in the *USS Constitution,* "Old Ironsides," almost led to it being scrapped. Public outrage that began with a poem by Oliver Wendell Holmes convinced Congress to have the frigate restored, and today it remains an important symbol of our history for the public to view in Boston Harbor.[1] What motivated Oliver Wendell Holmes also motivated the veterans who wanted the *Enola Gay* restored for public viewing, because of the role it played in ending the war. Without any desire to glorify the use of atomic weapons, they feared that restoration of the aircraft would be deferred until it was physically impossible to restore it, thus eliminating any chance that it could become what some considered a "national shrine" and interfere with relations with Japan. Harwit frankly said "I wanted to avoid the semblance of erecting a shrine." That statement might be misunderstood by some people as anti-*Enola Gay,* but

23

for many veterans restoration and appropriate display had nothing to do with creating a shrine, and they would have agreed with him. In a letter to John Correll, the editor of *Air Force Magazine,* W. Burr Bennett mentioned a summary of the NASM's plans for the exhibit that lacked any reference to Pearl Harbor but referred to the debatable character of the atomic bombing. He also said, "*I can assure you that we would not attack the decision to drop the bomb. Nor, on the other hand would we celebrate the event.*" (Italics in original.) A further indication that the veterans sought no confrontation comes from the fact they had suggested sending the aircraft to another site, perhaps the Air Force Museum in Dayton, Ohio, to join *Bockscar,* the B-29 that bombed Nagasaki.

After the war the *Enola Gay* continued in service until the test drop of the third A-bomb at Bikini in 1946, but not with its original crew. The plane returned to the United States in July 1946 and was placed in storage at the Davis Mothan Air Force Base in Arizona as an historic artifact. When the Air Force decided to present the historic aircraft to the Smithsonian Institution it was removed from storage (it had only 700 hours of flying time in its log) and made ready for presentation to the Smithsonian. In recognition of Paul Tibbets, who piloted the plane to Hiroshima, the Air Force ordered that he would be the only person to fly the plane. Tibbets, Theodore Van Kirk, the aircraft's navigator, and General Emmett O'Donnell, who represented the Air Force, flew to Chicago for the presentation, which took place on July 3, 1949, at what is now Chicago's O'Hare Airfield (then Orchard Field). The *Enola Gay* remained there until January 1952, when it was flown to the Pyote Air Force Base in Texas. It was moved to Andrews Air Force Base, Maryland, on December 2, 1953. At Andrews the plane remained outside for years next to the base golf course, exposed to the weather and vandals. Souvenir seekers stripped the plane of memorabilia, golf balls hit the fuselage and birds built nests in the engine nacelles while tires were unable to carry the load of the plane as they deteriorated. The plane remained at Andrews until July 1961, when it was disassembled and moved to the Smithsonian's Paul Garber Facility in Suitland, Maryland. In 1980, according to Director Harwit, "The *Enola Gay* was a wreck." After more than twenty years of neglect by the Smithsonian, actual restoration began in December 1984 and was expected to last seven to ten years. In a 1989 memo during restoration Harwit was told that the tail gunner's compartment, for example, was badly corroded because of exposure to the weather while outdoors. This allowed "weather, birds and mice to wreak havoc in this area." Eventually the *Enola Gay* was to be displayed in a new museum at Dulles Airport miles outside of Washington, a place not easily accessible to many of the visitors to the nation's capital.

In August 1984 an article by Joseph Persico appeared in *Modern Maturity* magazine about the *Enola Gay* and the Hiroshima mission. This triggered new interest in the plane, its whereabouts and its status. William Rooney wrote to the Secretary of the Smithsonian asking about the museum's intentions for its restoration. Secretary Adams' reply contained some major inaccuracies, such as when the Smithsonian received the aircraft. Adams said that the plane would be displayed at Dulles when it was restored, adding that it was of great symbolic importance and "we will need to think through very carefully how our manner of presentation will go over with a friendly and important nation that has a powerful set of its own symbolic associations with the *Enola Gay*.... 'A decent respect for the opinions of mankind,' to use a famous old phrase, requires us also to touch on the demonstrated horror and yawning future risk of the Age that the *Enola Gay* helped to inaugurate." Rooney saw Adams' letter as trivializing the aircraft's role in ending the war and it led him to search for more information about the aircraft. From General Tibbets he received information about when the Smithsonian received ownership of the aircraft and how it had deteriorated since the Smithsonian took possession. In 1986 a former Air Force B-29 crew chief visited the Garber facility and observed the progress of restoration. At that time only the forward part was under restoration and it was estimated that it would take at least five years to complete the restoration, and perhaps much longer.

As concern about the intentions of the Smithsonian developed, in 1987 a group of Air Force veterans formed the "*Enola Gay* Restoration Association. (EGRA)" The EGRA met with NASM officials to obtain information, and sought an accommodation with the museum, without success. By 1991 the EGRA decided that it could not influence the NASM.[2] It became clear from the exchange between the Smithsonian and the EGRA that the only way the plane would be restored in a reasonable time was through public pressure. Members began writing to print, radio and TV media in 1986 about the NASM's treatment of the *Enola Gay*, hoping to arouse their interest and their help to get the plane restored and displayed. When none of the media were persuaded to take up the cause, W. Burr Bennett suggested collecting signatures supporting restoration, and some 25,000 signatures were gathered, some from as far away as Germany.

The breakthrough for the small group of concerned veterans came when the Smithsonian announced plans to commemorate the end of the Pacific War with an exhibit in 1995. When information about what was planned surfaced, Bennett's letter to John Correll expressed his concern about the nature of the proposed exhibit. Correll's first impression was that Bennett's concerns might be overblown, but as he delved into the exhibit's proposal he concluded that Bennett's concerns had merit and he launched a series of critical articles that ultimately won the "Battle of the *Enola Gay*."

The NASM's curators had been admirably up front as they presented their version of what the Pacific war was about. The eighth and ninth sentences of the opening page of their *original* script said, "For most Americans, this war was fundamentally different than the one waged against Germany and Italy — it was a war of vengeance. For most Japanese, it was a war to defend their unique culture against Western Imperialism." This essay examines how those sentences, and the rest of *The Crossroads* script, were seen by the critics and the defenders of the exhibit. Mike Wallace, who was one of the latter, said, "These were not great sentences — not wrong, in context, but easily misrepresented." Stanley Goldberg, a member of the exhibit's advisory committee, believed the quotation had been ripped out of context but he also agreed that it needed "fine tuning." As the controversy went on Goldberg said that he believed that the demands for changes in the exhibit were a kind of thought control and akin to McCarthyism. Others argued that the statement was merely descriptive and did not represent the opinion of the curators.

A variation of that strained interpretation came from Lisa Yoneyama: "This phrase appeared in the script as an ironic summary of Japanese officials' gross justification for atrocities committed during the war." She added that although the curators revised the phrase, critics cited it out of context. However, there was nothing in the script, before or after that statement, to indicate that it was intended ironically or in any sense other than as a simple declarative statement. Perhaps somehow the reader was supposed to intuit the irony. Yoneyama went on to say that "Historian Martin Sherwin was one of those who called for the need to contextualize this phrase, particularly for a Japanese audience. Sherwin placed Japanese aggression within the broader historical context of the Western imperialist expansion into Asia and other parts of the world that preceded it.... Sherwin's cautionary remarks to a Japanese audience sought to deter yet another warping of critical discourses by obstructing the dovetailing of the U. S. revisionist historians' progressive position with that of the Japanese conservatives."

Although the vengeance statement was dropped from subsequent versions of the script, that theme showed how the curators saw America's role in the Pacific War. Far from misrepresenting *The Crossroads*, those sentences fairly represented the NASM's point of view. The vengeance theme was not new, having appeared in a 1991 book by NASM advisor Edward Linenthal: "The language of righteous vengeance was frequently used during and after the war to justify U. S. military action." That theme was repeated more than once by Linenthal. In an inimitable ironic manner he wrote, "If America had been forced to invade Japan, it would have lost hundreds of thousands of men. Instead, thanks to modern science a weapon of benevolent destruction, the atomic bomb, had been created. Although it was unfortunate that two such bombs had to be dropped, they *did* (sic) end the war; and they also served as a final act of righteous revenge for the 'Day of Infamy.' For many Americans the atomic bomb balanced the scales of justice." As an advisor to the exhibit he could be pleased that his theme was highlighted in the script.

Linenthal also said that for the curators "the war was but prelude to the use of the bomb, which drew back a curtain on a new age, revealing Japanese who were not so much the last civilian victims of World War II as the first victims of the nuclear age." That was an old charge originating with the Nobel laureate and Marxist P. M. S. Blackett, who decried the bombing of Hiroshima and Nagasaki. Soon after the war he said, "the dropping of the atomic bombs was not so much the last military act of the Second World War, as the first major operation of the cold diplomatic war with Russia now in progress." As a student of Blackett's work, Gar Alperovitz said, "Although the suggestion that there was a relationship between the U.S. diplomatic strategy and the destruction of Hiroshima and Nagaski was not something most people took seriously in the early postwar decades, this is no longer the case." This had been confirmed, according to Alperovitz, by the work of Professors Bernstein, Gaddis Smith and J. Samuel Walker, who had reviewed the "expert literature." The patrimony of P. M. S. Blackett is evident in the work of these authors and others who subscribe to what Alperovitz called "left-leaning" Blackett's explanation for the Cold War.

The Crossroads aligned itself with those who accused President Harry Truman of making at least a serious mistake, and according to some, committing a war crime, by dropping the A-Bomb on Japan. In a case study of the perversion of history, the script portrayed the Japanese as victims of a racist America and showcased the revisionists' conventional wisdom about the role of racism in the decision to drop the A-Bomb. The heading for page 13 of *The Crossroads* on the battle of Okinawa was "WAR WITHOUT MERCY," the title of Professor John Dower's book that emphasized what he saw as the racist character of the Pacific war. Because of the importance of this theme in *The Crossroads*, it is one of the issues discussed later.

Until it was challenged, the Smithsonian was prepared to cooperate in such intemperate trashing of history. However, what happened at the Smithsonian is only one example of how the past has been rewritten by those with an ideological agenda alien to honest history. History should acknowledge any and all the warts and wrinkles of the past, but be true to the facts. The NASM's revision of history wanted to give a new generation of students and the general public a false picture of a significant episode in the nation's past. That distortion of the historical record was a serious disservice to history and to the public. For a generation of readers far removed from the events of August 1945, the horrors of Hiroshima are only too real. What happened there helped to define much of the world's history well into the 21st century. Questions will linger about why and how the A-Bomb was used, its morality and whether it signaled the beginning of the Cold War. Those questions could not be answered during the debate over the *Enola Gay*'s mission to Japan. What can be answered are some of the distortions of the historical record made by those who prepared and defended the exhibit.

There simply is no way to adequately deal with the countless small and large errors and misinformation that were used to defend the exhibit. To parse every sentence in the script and in books and articles defending the exhibit is impossible. The following is just one example in the dispute about the number of possible casualties if there was an invasion of Japan. According to Professor Mike Wallace, "The conventional popular wisdom on this subject is that perhaps half a million would have fallen. But this was a postwar judgement."[4] Wallace was mistaken and easily could have found that the half a million figure was used months *before* the war ended. That figure was disputed at the time and can be debated at length as to its accuracy and importance, but as we show later, the number existed and was known to exist before the bombs were dropped, and could and should have been acknowledged.

During the controversy there were calls for apologies to the Japanese for the alleged war crimes committed at Hiroshima and Nagasaki. One writer said dropping the A-Bomb cried out "for repentance and reconciliation, for apologies and pleas for forgiveness," and went on to say, "it is understandable that a U.S. president will not apologize for the dropping of the atomic bomb as long as one U.S. veteran lives who believes it saved his life." Others have compared the sufferings of the bomb victims to the Holocaust as did the poet Robert Frost who wrote, "Having invented a new Holocaust And been the first with it to win a war."[5]

The real story, according to the exhibit defenders, was that the A-Bomb was used to intimidate the Soviet Union and was the opening salvo of the Cold War, forcing an insecure and defensive Soviet Union to develop its own atomic weapons—and so began years in which the world lived under the threat of atomic annihilation. Professor Barton Bernstein, who Michael

Hogan said "had probably written more on the atomic bombing of Japan than any other scholar," had stated his view of post war American policy in an earlier book: "My own essay on American foreign policy emphasizes that American leaders sought to reshape much of the world according to American needs and standards, and thereby contributed significantly to the origins of the Cold War…. Failures to reach agreement on international control of atomic energy, efforts to use economic aid to coerce the Soviet Union, and disagreements on Germany contributed to the antagonisms even before Truman, in seeking aid for Greece and Turkey, declared a war of ideology in his 'Truman Doctrine' speech of March 1947. Blinded by their own ideology to evidence of indigenous revolution in Greece, American policymakers wrongly interpreted it as a Soviet plot." His view of American foreign policy was a pervasive influence on the script, so it is useful to be aware of where he comes from intellectually. Because he has written so much about the atomic bomb and Truman, his name appears frequently in these pages.[6]

To support the theory that the A-Bomb was unnecessary, assertions about a smaller number of expected casualties if there had been an invasion and the readiness of Japan to surrender have become staples of revisionist history. They were given credence by *The Crossroads,* following the lead of Professor Alperovitz who argued that as early as April 1945, Washington knew that an invasion was "only a remote possibility." Further, "by June it was clear to American leaders that either a Russian declaration of war or a change in the surrender terms was likely to bring capitulation. Almost certainly a combination of the two measures would stop the fighting immediately." He added, "As each day of the spring passed, it became more and more doubtful that an invasion would be needed to force Japanese capitulation." On the other hand it is important to note that when the Japanese approached Moscow in June 1945, they sought to *negotiate* peace, not obtain surrender terms. By couching his discussion of that episode as moves toward surrender, Alperovitz misleads the reader. It is difficult to understand why that distinction was not obvious to those involved in his elaborately researched book.[7]

Presumably in an effort to understand opposition to the exhibit Michael Hogan wondered why critics of the exhibit did not view the curators or their historical consultants as disinterested experts. Perhaps, he said, it was because the curators' and consultants' "version of history contrasted so sharply with the lived experience of American veterans, whose personal narratives, according to the critics, constituted a collective memory of unimpeachable authority." Hogan continued, "the memories of American veterans became weapons not only in a vigorous anti-intellectual assault on the practice of professional history but also on the principle of free speech and the tradition of academic freedom." Comparing the knowledge of "disinterested" experts with the personal narratives of witnesses whose memories had suffered the erosion of time, and who knew little if anything about the larger war in which they played so small a role, was a recurrent theme by the defenders of the exhibit. Other themes found in articles by the "disinterested" experts were the anti-intellectualism of critics and the violation of academic freedom and free speech, all specters paraded to enlist academic and media support for the exhibit.[8]

The tenor of the script was not surprising if one reviews the professional literature about the role of museum curators in contemporary society. They are to confront the illusions and misconceptions about the past held by the public. That was the stance of the Smithsonian's staff. Tom Crouch, who was one of the principal authors of the *original* script, said, "it is not enough for an exhibition planner to provide an accurate description of individual objects and images. The curator must always be aware of the big picture — the basic message that is being communicated by the gallery as a whole." And Michael Neufeld, one of the curators for the exhibit, suggested "great pains should be taken to insure that the exhibit not be celebratory." We will see what basic message Crouch and his colleagues wanted to communicate, and ask whether apart from artifacts and images, if the basic message was accurate.

As time went on, discussing the exhibit posed problems for both sides of the controversy because there was not a common basis for conversation, let alone debate. Thoughtful debates can occur only when the participants agree on its terms. Many contemporary historians argue that there is no such thing as objective history and that events in the past meant only what dominant elites imposed on them. The historian's role is seen as demolishing the myths and falsehoods that bedevil past "history." Interpretations of the past seem to become acceptable in professional circles when they counter those made earlier, and preferably shock the public into an acceptance of the revised version of their gospel. Thus history becomes an Oliver Stone docudrama that mixes fact and fiction presented as authentic history and accepted as such by many who view his films. This was applauded by Paul Buhle when reviewing a book about Stone's films, as "fictionalized postmodern versions have appeared merely more imaginative, not less persuasive."[9]

The exhibit's critics believed that history, honestly and objectively written, insofar as that can be done by fallible individuals, is not about preferred outcomes or today's conventional wisdom, but consists of examining facts in context as dispassionately as possible, and interpreting their meaning. They contended that the exhibit ignored important facts, and that sometimes its defenders did so in order to score points in favor of the exhibit and indict the United States for using the atomic bomb. They believed that distortion of history was unfair to the public, to future generations and to those who had the terrible responsibility of sanctioning the use of the bomb.

Those who objected to the Smithsonian exhibit did so because it intended to erase from public memory, not myths but the vivid reality of actual events. That reality existed in the casualty lists that appeared in hometown newspapers, in the ordered headstones and lists of the missing in military cemeteries, and in the evidence taken in war crimes trials in the Far East after the war. That reality was minimized by *The Crossroads* and so were the horrendous experiences of those who became POWs as well as other victims of the Japanese. There would be little point in revisiting the pattern of behavior of the Japanese military in the places they occupied and their treatment of captives, had *The Crossroads* made a genuine effort to account for them. However, except for a few comments about POWs, the curators virtually ignored what happened to Americans in Japanese hands. The barbarity they suffered was equaled by the suffering of other Allied POWs and civilians throughout Asia.

That failure aroused critics of an exhibit that could ignore what happened on the infamous Burma-Siam railroad that cost the lives of 250,000 men. Eric Lomax wrote: "I have tried not to anticipate, to use hindsight too much in my telling of this story so far, but the fate of these already half-addled men deserves recording here. 'F' and 'H' Forces had the highest casualty rates of all the POW drafts on the railway. They were to give the work a final boost, to complete the line earlier than planned — a kind of expendable shock force. Some of them would walk two hundred miles up into the hills; one in three of them would die, and many of the rest be crippled for the rest of their lives by illness or injury." The fate of our allies was ignored in favor of stressing the fate of the unfortunate victims of Hiroshima. At least some semblance of parity would have been appropriate.

As did all the combatants during World War II, the Japanese conducted bacteriological warfare research. But Unit 731 outside of Harbin in Manchuria tested bacteria on prisoners, and the staff performed experiments similar to those conducted by the Germans on concentration camp inmates. Some details of those experiments are found in *Japan at War*, which also has interviews with soldiers who beheaded and bayoneted Chinese prisoners as part of their training, one of whom reported cutting off the heads of forty Chinese prisoners. Shortly before the war ended, eight captured B-29 airmen were subjected to vivisection at Kyushu Imperial University. What happened was described in chilling detail by Saburo Ienaga. In addition, according to Yuri Tanaka, "It seems that dissection of live prisoners for the purpose of medical training was widely practiced by Japanese military doctors throughout the Asia-Pacific region." That was confirmed by a Japanese physician who participated in several such training demonstrations. The script and its defenders did not believe such events needed telling as part of "contextualizing" the Pacific war.

As Sheldon Harris showed in *Factories of Death,* claims that American POWs were among the victims of experimentation are tenable. Not only Americans but other Allied POWs and large numbers of Chinese perished in this manner. It should be recognized that such brutality was only an extension of the basic cruelty that characterized Japanese treatment of POWs, regardless of race. Not only POWs but thousands of Chinese civilians died as unwitting subjects of Japanese field testing of plague and other biological weapons. Although such examples should not have dominated the exhibit, their subordination to other appropriate elements of the exhibit such as an emotionally wrenching child's lunch box from Hiroshima, with all that it implied, was a reason for fairly criticizing the NASM for a lack of balance in its presentation of what happened during the Pacific war.

If the NASM actually sought the balance it claimed in the exhibit, it could have consulted Yuki Tanaka's accounts of atrocities, in an effort to understand the system that indoctrinated the Japanese military to willingly engage in them. Unlike Daniel Goldenhagen's simplistic attribution of a centuries-old persistent strain of anti-Semitism in German society as what led to the Nazi effort to exterminate European Jewry, Tanaka explored the political and social aspects of Japanese military behavior. The result is a chilling recitation of horrors, many of which were known not long after the war. Cases recounted by Tanaka have the virtue of coming from someone with command of the Japanese sources as well as American and Australian sources.

Tanaka stated frankly that he considered the war crimes trials unfair because they "did not deal with any war crimes committed by Allied forces, the most obvious example of war crimes committed by the United States was the dropping of the atomic bombs on Hiroshima and Nagasaki. Of course, the unfairness of the tribunal itself does not invalidate the criminality of the various atrocities that the Japanese forces committed during the Asian-Pacific War." That he is frank about his opinion, and that he documents violent behavior by American and Australian troops in Japan does not lead to an equivalence theory. Writers in Germany, Italy and Japan point to the bombing of Dresden as balancing a Rotterdam, or Hiroshima for Nanking, suggesting that everybody committed atrocities and the Axis was no worse than the Allies. Does a My Lai balance the German massacre at Lidice or the Japanese massacres in Manila, and can other examples be found to balance the books? Criminal behavior has always existed in armies and ought not be condoned. What is important to remember, however, is that the scale and kind of atrocities committed by the Japanese Imperial Forces *as a matter of policy* was incalculably beyond any by the Allies in the Pacific war.

Professor John Dower proposed an interesting counterfactual when he asked, if the Japanese won the war, what war crimes might they have charged against the Americans and British. He assembled what he considered four reasonable accusations, including the use of atomic bombs (leaving unsaid how Japan might have won after the bombs were used). How should one view the implications of these "reasonable" answers to the question of Allied culpability? Dower would not be alone in implying that the Japanese not only felt their survival threatened by the United States, but objectively had reason to react to that threat. While not condoning Japan's reaction to America's hegemonic assault, in this plague on both your houses view from Olympus he implied that their case was not unreasonable. What any rebuttal to that case might be is left unsaid.[10]

The Crossroads and its defenders also overlooked the fact that, as part of the last ditch defense of their homeland, the Japanese military ordered the killing of Allied prisoners if there was an invasion. Although the *Enola Gay* symbolized America's role in ending the war, the A-Bomb ended the war for about 300,000 Allied POWs and internees who were liberated from 200 prison camps where they had endured brutal treatment and were condemned to death. Unfortunately, Hirohito's surrender announcement did not save several hundred Allied POWs from execution by the Japanese after the surrender.[11]

The evidence of the Japanese intention to eliminate all their prisoners is not anecdotal. Tom Moon described what it was like for the men in a POW camp. "It was from the OSS men the prisoners learned of the A-bombs that had ended the terrible war. The prisoners now realized why the Japanese had carried gasoline cans out to the air-raid trenches a few days earlier. News of the A-bomb had reached the guards. Orders had been given to kill all prisoners at a later date in order to release troops for the defense of the home islands. They wanted to burn their captives and get it over with. An officer named Odera, however, had convinced his superiors that the game was up and that they would be held responsible for their actions. Unfortunately, the Japanese Commander in the Philippines had carried out the horrible task of dousing American POW's with gasoline and setting them on fire. Many of the dying Americans pleaded with the Japanese to shoot them and end their suffering." Perhaps to avoid offending more sensitive visitors to the exhibit, the curators decided to overlook such matters.

A common and to some extent valid point is often made by historians: that the memories of those "who were there" can be faulty, or circumscribed, and that what they recall has to be taken in the context of the big picture. To ignore or depreciate that kind of experience returns us to only the arid statistics of war, which, although important, must be coupled proportionately with the experience of those who were there, otherwise there is no possibility of truly understanding what happened in times past. Historian Gerda Lerner, who escaped from Europe in 1939 and lost relatives in the Holocaust, said that it is extremely painful to think about that time, but "If we don't, then the eyewitness primary account is lost, and the only people who will interpret this period are people who don't have a clue. They weren't there." If there is validity to social history, or history from the bottom up, to understand the lives of French peasants, 19th century English miners or the American labor movement as seen through the lives of New England textile workers, then it is no less important to understand the war through the experiences of those who were there.[12]

It was easy but unfair to tar critics of the exhibit as driven by hatred or hostility toward the Japanese or engaged in Japan bashing. For veterans the war was over and the Japanese had paid a high price for their adventure. If veterans could not forget what happened, they could, and most did, forgive the Japanese people. They did not want to reopen old wounds; the Smithsonian did that by presenting a falsified version of history. Veterans called for an honest account of what actually happened, and why it happened, so it would be understood by a generation fortunate enough to only read about the travail of their elders who endured and won a brutal war.

One defender of the exhibit carried the veteran bashing to an obscene extreme by equating Nazi SS behavior with that of an American pilot. According to Philip Nobile, "the parallel statements of two soldiers, one German and one American, one judged, one unjudged, can elucidate the original sin." One statement was by Rudolph Hoess, the commandant of

Auschwitz at his trial before the Nuremberg Tribunal in 1946, that the thought of disobeying an order never would have occurred to anybody. The other was by General Paul Tibbets who piloted the *Enola Gay*, who said that he was doing what he could to bring the war to a victorious conclusion.

If interested in what happened in August 1945, and why, one can find, uncolored by an ideological mindcast, solid, carefully documented, honest answers to the claims of the revisionists. The hard work of documentation has been done by competent historians who went back to the sources and did what undergraduate history majors ought to be taught about studying the past. Unfortunately, the overwhelming number of articles and books on the subject are based on the work of writers such as Barton Bernstein, Kai Bird, John Dower, Michael Sherry and Gar Alperovitz, all of whom were prominent in the defense of the NASM. These and other writers continue to ignore evidence that contradicts their theories and offer conclusions that misrepresent what happened over Japan and why. That leaves students in high schools and universities at the mercy of misinformation, both by inclusion and omission, implying or accusing the United States of a war crime.

There is general agreement that, for many reasons, a sea change occurred in the historical profession in the 1960s and 1970s. Building on what had been learned from the social sciences, developments in political philosophy, literary criticism and new fields in history, interest in the Cold War and the generational tensions that marked the period, historians sought new venues. According to Professor Eric Foner, who would become the president of the American Historical Association, "In the past twenty years AMERICAN HISTORY (caps in original) has been remade. Inspired initially by the social movements of the 1960s and 1970s—which shattered the 'consensus' vision that had dominated historical writing—and influenced by new methods borrowed from other disciplines, American historians redefined the very nature of historical study.... The study of American history today looks far different than it did a generation ago." What resulted with regard to World War II, according to David Farber, was that "historians have pushed even harder at the basic narrative of the war years. Professor Dower cogently argues that 'race hate' both undergirded the Japanese and the American war efforts and explains the course and nature of the war in the Pacific. Michael Sherry ... similarly foregrounds the cultural understandings that made the fire bombing and atomic bombing of civilian targets seem reasonable to Americans." Inspired by the shattering of the consensus vision, Farber, Sherry and others added their vivid imaginations to the time honored tools of their profession and created a truly mythical end of the Pacific war that parades as a scholarly consensus.[13]

A not atypical example of how history has been distorted was created by a writer who said: "clouds hid the Mitsubishi iron works so the pilot targeted the Catholic Cathedral in the Urakami district." Because Nagasaki was where Catholicism began in Japan hundreds of years earlier, deliberately aiming at a cathedral or any religious building would show American callousness and strengthen the argument about American barbarity. Although the cathedral was not the aiming point, it suffered the fate of the factories and the rest of the city. Charles Sweeney, who piloted the aircraft that dropped the bomb, said that when a hole in the clouds appeared midway between the two large Mitsubishi armament plants in the industrial Urakami valley, the aircraft was two miles north of the assigned aiming point and away from the residential area. The bombardier locked onto a racetrack reference point and dropped the bomb at 10:01 A.M. It exploded almost dead center between armament plants and a steelworks. "This spot was only 500 yards north of the edge of the sprawling arms plant, or .75 miles from its center, and .80 miles from the center of another Mitsubishi complex." That information was available long before the story about aiming at the cathedral was written, but it would not have supported the notion that there were no limits to American barbarity.

How someone else pushed at the former narrative is found in Sanho Tree's review of a book by Robert Maddox, *The Hiroshima Decision Fifty Years Later*. According to Maddox neither MAGIC nor ULTRA, the intercepts of the Japanese and German codes, "gave reason to believe that surrender was imminent before the bombs were used." Tree rebutted this, claiming that evidence directly contradicted him and referred to Truman's journal entry on July 18, 1945, about an intercept of a telegram from the Japanese Emperor asking for peace. That intercept was one of several cables that went from Tokyo to Moscow telling the Japanese ambassador to press for Soviet mediation. Tree misinterpreted the cables as indicating that *surrender* was imminent. Truman's note has to be understood in the context of what was known about Japan's situation from other sources. That cable did not in any way contradict Maddox. Tree was not alone in relying on such a fragile reed to ignore the significant difference between a request for mediation for a negotiated peace and an offer to surrender. The cables referred to the former and not the latter, and failing to distinguish between them misrepresents what actually was happening.

Tree also claimed that, while the authors of the books he reviewed emphasized the buildup of Japanese defenses in the summer of 1945, it was simplistic to extrapolate from this and compare it to what the Japanese hoped to have by the time of the November invasion of Kyushu, one of Japan's home islands. Tree went on to describe the plight of the Japanese population, but was unaware or did not understand that the defenses and troop level in the summer of 1945 had so impressed the Joint Chiefs that they considered exploring alternatives to invading Kyushu. In common with others who stress the deterioration of Japan's situation in the summer of 1945, implying that it meant Japan was about to surrender, Tree misrepresented the situation as it was known at the time in Washington and ignored what is known about the defiant mood of the Japanese military.[14]

In the preface to Kai Bird and Lawrence Lifschultz' *Hiroshima's Shadow,* Joseph Rotblat, who had worked on the Manhattan Project and was a Nobel Laureate, repeated a number of the misrepresentations one expects from revisionists. Claiming that the bomb was built to deter Hitler, he made the surprising claim that "We needed the bomb so that it would not be used." Further, "Japan was the designated target for the atom bomb almost from the beginning of the Manhattan Project." He also believed that the scientists who initiated the work never thought of Japan as the target. In addition, he made the extraordinary accusation that Truman continued the war until the bombs were ready for use because "the bomb was seen from the beginning as a powerful instrument in the ideological struggle between the United States and the Soviet Union." That is why Rothblat believed that Hiroshima and Nagasaki marked not so much the end of World War II but the beginning of the Cold War. He also quoted General Leslie Groves, who headed the Manhattan Project, as saying that the bomb was always expected to be used on Japan. Later Groves was to say that from the time he began the project he had no illusion "but that Russia was our enemy and that the project was conducted on that basis."

Some may be impressed by the comments of a Nobel laureate, even when they contradict the historical record. However, President Roosevelt was unequivocal about using the bomb against Germany if necessary. Furthermore, there is no evidence to support the oxymoronic claim that a weapon not advertised to the Germans was developed to deter Germany from using the bomb it was attempting to create. Calling Japan the designated target from the beginning leaves the impression that Germany was not a target, an impression that feeds the canard that the bomb was dropped on Japan for racist reasons. The "evidence" for using the bomb against Japan came from a conversation Rotblat supposedly had with General Leslie Groves, an excellent administrator and a blunt, opinionated individual who obviously was not in a decision making position about the ultimate use of the bomb. At best Groves' remarks represented his opinion, certainly one not shared by President Roosevelt and the small circle that knew about the Manhattan Project. As Lifschultz and Bird mentioned in referring to President Truman, "Memoirs by definition represent a subjective form of historical evidence." The same caution should be applied to Rothblat's recollection of his conversation with Groves.[15]

The strangest of Rothblat's charges was that Truman continued the war until the bombs were ready. That meant Truman could have ended the war, perhaps in April during the battle of Okinawa, but marked time while men died there until the bomb was ready. Although one becomes accustomed to wild ideas from revisionists, that one raises the question of whether the author can be taken seriously in other than his narrow scientific specialty. With a combination of carefully phrased statements by carefully selected contributors and carefully selected documents, *Hiroshima's Shadow* is an invaluable resource for discovering the revisionist wisdom about the end of World War II.

It is impossible to understand the *Enola Gay* controversy without considering the context of the decisions made in 1945 that are at the roots of the controversy. Two elements of that context help to show the genuine complexity of the environment in which the Truman administration had to function. One has to do with the fact that Washington officials have been faulted for considering domestic politics when dealing with wartime strategy. But partisanship did not stop on December 8, 1941. The president led the nation, but with a wary eye on Congress and a sometimes restive press. Truman's concern with Congressional efforts to end Lend Lease and begin industrial reconversion after Germany's defeat, reveals the importance of domestic policy matters even at such a critical moment in the war as the summer of 1945. Domestic pressure for demobilization of the troops who defeated Germany was accompanied by morale problems among troops who resisted the thought of transfer to the Pacific. Such issues had to be factored into how to end the Pacific war.[16]

Junior high school students are introduced to a sanitized version of what happens in Washington, but by the time one has a doctorate in history one ought to understand how national policy happens in Washington in peace and war. That is why it is surprising to find revisionists conveying their unease that public opinion and Congressional concern received a hearing when momentous decisions were to be made. They either fail to understand the democratic process or would prefer to have it otherwise. Although all the actors in those decisions may have been mistaken, and the final decision even been wrong, in the 1940s the messy American system had operated that way for over a century and a half, and continues to do so today.

In the area of foreign policy Washington had to deal with a problem that continues to bother the revisionists who see it as contributing to the Cold War. It is only one example of the misinformation that takes time to counter. For example, Professor Alperovitz believed that Stalin wanted to take only a token surrender of the Japanese in northern Hokkaido, one of the Japanese home islands, but acceded to Truman's refusal, thus increasing tension between the United States and the Soviets. Actually the record is clear that the Soviets wanted more than a ceremony; they intended to occupy Hokkaido, and had forces ready to invade Hokkaido after they took Sakhalin island.[17]

On August 19 Marshall Vasilevskii ordered the Ist Far Eastern Front, obviously on Stalin's orders, to occupy the northern half of Hokkaido as well as the southern Kuriles. However, on August 22, Vasilevskii rescinded the order about Hokkaido although the occupation of the southern Kuriles went ahead. Evidently Stalin concluded that the attempt to land forces on Hokkaido would cause a political row and perhaps even an armed clash with the United States. Stalin chose to be satisfied with securing the concessions he had obtained at Yalta.

The invasion of Sakhalin was strongly resisted by the Japanese and the island was not secured until August 25, long after the Emperor called for an end to hostilities on August 15. Although Robert Messer thought that the refusal to accept Soviet occupation of Hokkaido, as the Allies had done in the case of Italy, legitimized Soviet unilateral control over Eastern Europe, he overlooked that the Soviets began to control Eastern Europe before Italy was occupied by the Allies. After meeting with Stalin on May 28, 1945, Harry Hopkins, President Roosevelt's aide, reported that Stalin wanted to share in the occupation of Japan equally with the United States. The War Department recognized that Soviet participation in the occupation of Japan would reduce American military requirements for the occupation, but experience in Germany suggested that it might be best to restrict the occupation of Japan to American forces.[18]

That Truman wanted to preempt a possible Soviet occupation of the Japanese home islands was eminently reasonable. Aware of what was happening in Eastern Europe, and what Tito was trying to do in Trieste and Venezia Giulia, Truman would have been remiss not to take account of the strong possibility that if Hokkaido came under Soviet control, it would end as a satellite like North Korea. For revisionists to intimate that this was a furtive, Machiavellian maneuver raises the question of whether they would have preferred it if Truman did otherwise and if so, suggests that they would be content to live with the consequences of more residents of our global village trapped behind an Asian Iron Curtain.[19]

Historians call events that might have happened "counterfactuals," and the conventional wisdom about the A-Bomb is replete with them. The result is a history akin to what was foisted on the Russians by Stalin when the Soviets had a virtual loose leaf history because of the many revisions of events and personalities made by the regime, with the latter literally erased from history. Because revisionists follow this unhallowed practice, students of World War II often must rely on essentially counterfactual accounts that distort and debase the historical record. Professor Bernstein is a bold advocate of their use, saying that although Truman counseled against "Monday-morning quarter backing," "such admonitions should not bar counterfactual analysis, block the consideration of alternative pasts, nor prohibit people from applying moral principles that were sometimes asserted, and more often eroded in World War II."[20]

Counterfactuals cannot be dismissed as unimportant because at times they have been used to change the history books. A notorious example after World War I was the German effort to salvage something from the ruins of a catastrophic defeat by claiming that the war was lost, not on the battlefield but at home. That counterfactual fueled a new political party that in a decade reversed Germany's fortunes, led to another war and testified to the power of a lie that led to renewed ruin. The Nazis changed not only the history books; they changed the history of the century.

Weaving counterfactuals is an engaging hobby for some historians, but it does little to enhance our understanding of specific historical events. Writing about the European war, I. S. O. Playfair suggested avoiding "the cloudy land of might-have-been, and not mistake our desks for the battlefield. History at times may assume an air of certainty, but sure it is that nothing is certain in war." The Pacific war ended in a certain way and despite its success it cannot be immunized from criticism. However, the critics might consider that, had their favorite alternative been adopted, the outcome might not have been as sanguine as what actually happened.

In a lengthy evaluation of the *Enola Gay* controversy, Otto Mayr, a former museum director, severely criticized the manner in which the NASM developed and promoted the Enola Gay exhibit and faulted Martin Harwit and his superiors for failures in leadership. Comparing an academic book with a museum exhibit he noted that the first is complex, while of necessity the museum simplifies. The book's author accepts responsibility for the work and has freedom of expression to which the reader can respond. An exhibit is the product of an anonymous team effort and although there is collective responsibility, there is no way for the visitor to express reactions or join in a discussion with them. Thus while an exhibit can be controversial, it must be balanced and non-judgmental.

Describing the usual steps taken in developing an exhibit, Mayr was critical of how Martin Harwit developed the proposal and became too involved in the project at the expense of his role as NASM director. Mayr also said, "The decision to drop the bomb, for example, should have been reconstructed exclusively from documents dating before the day of Hiroshima." Although he thought *The Crossroads* script contained some malapropisms that were criticized by the AFA which "the NASM had shown the association in confidence," Mayr expressed surprise that the exhibit's opponents used angry language and that there was "a suspension of civilized behavior." The critics squabbled about details and the specific language of the exhibit. They resorted to "epithets like 'liberal historians' and 'political correctness.'" But Mayr failed to mention that the defenders also resorted to epithets, and called the critics conservatives and ignorant.

Although lamenting the intrusion of politics, he noted that during decades of stable liberal majorities in Congress, the Smithsonian found it safe to present exhibits to liberal audiences. A new Republican majority in Congress made that impossible, he said, but had there been "continuing Democratic majorities surely the original *Enola Gay* exhibit would have opened on schedule." That was an unexpected admission from a former insider that under the "liberal" Smithsonian administration and a liberal Congress, and apart from the historical merits of the exhibit, *The Crossroads* as originally conceived would have been hostage to a politically correct version of history. After complaining about the behavior of the exhibit's critics, Mayr continued to say that the NASM had a duty to defend its position, and in doing so, "It should have listened to advice and criticism in an open-minded, self-critical attitude. In its pronouncements, especially to hostile special-interest groups, the museum should have been courteous and precise." Although basically on the side of *The Crossroads*, Mayr left no doubt that among the many failures he listed at the beginning of his article (although he did not call them such), the NASM failed to listen to critics, whether or not they were hostile, and ended with a public relations disaster.[22]

Revisionists argued that the *Enola Gay* controversy had implications far beyond those of the immediate exhibit, portraying it as a dispute between myth and reality and an attack on intellectual freedom. Those defending the exhibit were the alleged realists while its opponents defended a myth based on ancient memories and falsehoods. In one sense the defenders were right about the controversy's more fundamental implication. It was and remains: what does it mean that practitioners of the historian's craft so adamantly defended the distortion of history by an exhibit that falsified the story of what happened in the summer of 1945? Although there always will be differing opinions about what happened in the past, that was not the case with the script for the exhibit. One can agree or disagree about the use of the A-Bomb on several grounds. Those who believe that unconditional surrender contributed to Japanese intransigence or that the A-Bomb was immoral are entitled to their opinions. But why the Allies remained committed to unconditional surrender, and what preceded the decision to use the A-Bomb must be fairly stated, whether one agrees with them or not. The facts about anticipated casualties that influenced actions in the summer of 1945 and other contested matters exist beyond the realm of opinion and should be treated as part of the nation's authentic patrimony and not manipulated in the service of ideology.

III

Was Japan Ready to Surrender?

According to *The Crossroads*, "By the summer of 1945, Japan was a nation on the brink of collapse." The Allied blockade had reduced civilian and military supplies (including food), many large cities were rubble, civilian morale was ebbing and further resistance seemed futile. Thanks to MAGIC and other intelligence sources, the Allies knew of Japan's desperate situation. The Japanese were already seeking peace and soon would have surrendered, saving countless lives." As told by the curators, the clear implication of this brink of collapse theory was that, had President Truman waited a little longer instead of dropping the A-Bomb on August 6, 1945, in a short time Japan would have capitulated.*

If the curators saw Japan on the brink of collapse, they were not alone, because General Douglas MacArthur shared that opinion in the spring of 1945: "My staff was unanimous in believing Japan was on the point of collapse and surrender. I even directed that plans be drawn 'for a possible peaceful occupation' without further military operations." However, unlike the curators and MacArthur, who later changed his mind, the Combined Chiefs were less optimistic at their meeting in Potsdam on July 19, 1945, and "set the target date for forcing the unconditional surrender of Japan for November 15, 1946," eighteen months after Germany's surrender. That date was set by well-informed men who, despite Trinity, still had only a potential weapon, and were anxious to end the war, but realized that it could be an arduous battle to subdue Japan. That they considered the war could continue into November 1946 formed part of the context for presidential decision making that some historians lightly dismiss. Whatever

---

Japanese peace feelers, and unconditional surrender which is intertwined with the status of the emperor, are closely related but deserve individual attention. That is why a chapter is devoted to each.

the NASM's curators believed about Japan being on the edge of collapse, that belief was not acted on by the Japanese government, and that determined the course of the war, not the curator's speculative hindsight.[1]

There had been peace feelers from Japanese diplomats in Sweden and Switzerland seeking to explore peace terms, but such unofficial contacts were what Edwin Reischauer called "vain efforts at starting peace negotiations by minor Japanese officials whose perception and daring exceeded their authority." Those feelers had no results other than to confirm what Washington knew through MAGIC. In *The Crossroads*' view, "It is possible to say, at least in hindsight, that the United States should have paid closer attention to these signals from Japan. Like so many aspects of the 'decision to drop the bomb,' this matter will remain forever speculative and controversial."[2] Of course it is possible to say anything in hindsight, no matter how historically irrelevant, but despite the polite disclaimer about the statement being speculative, the curator's message was clear: the president should have waited.

The Crossroads also concluded that the Potsdam Declaration was not effective in changing the position of the Japanese government because Secretary of State James Byrnes had eliminated any reference to the retention of Emperor Hirohito on the throne, as well as any direct references to the atomic bomb or Soviet entry into the war. "As a result of these changes, the Proclamation was not effective in changing the position of the Japanese government. The reaction of the military was especially hostile. On July 28, Premier Suzuki announced that his government would ignore ('mokusatsu') the proclamation. This word was translated in the West as 'to treat with silent contempt,' making the Japanese look even more arrogant. Nothing further stood in the way of using the atomic bomb on Japan." That *The Crossroads* would accuse Byrnes of failing to tell Japan about the A-Bomb or Soviet intervention reveals its appalling naivete. The nuanced account of Byrnes' actions at Potsdam by David Robertson contradicted *The Crossroads*. After reviewing the revisionist interpretation of Byrnes' actions at Potsdam, and especially the interpretations of Professor Alperovitz, Robertson concluded: "Thus, by the standards of both good investigative reporting and good legal pleading, the supposed attempt by Secretary Byrnes before and after Potsdam to keep the U. S. public, in Alperovitz's phrase, 'prisoners of officials who have an interest in withholding evidence,' was an abysmal failure." Newspapers had carried stories about events at Potsdam, which leads to the question: if that was known at the time, years later, why did Alperovitz claim information was suppressed?[3]

Tokyo wanted Moscow to mediate peace terms with the Allies. The

Suzuki cabinet had been charged both to continue the war and to seek peace terms which would include the retention of some of Japan's territorial gains, although the Soviets were assured Japan would not insist on retaining all the territory it had occupied. It also was intimated that there might be a possible alliance with Moscow. A "special envoy" was sent to Moscow about July 12 to explore whether the Soviets would assume the role of mediator, but Moscow dandled the Japanese emissary and never reacted to the Japanese approach. Many writers have grossly misinterpreted the meaning of such actions by Tokyo. Robert James Maddox made clear what revisionist have conveniently misunderstood, misrepresented or ignored, mentioning as an example: "Martin J. Sherwin, in *A World Destroyed*, repeatedly confused Japan's desire to obtain a negotiated peace with its willingness to surrender. Seeking peace on its own terms was Japan's not unreasonable goal, from its own point of view, but it did not meet the goals of the Allies."[4]

The only officially sanctioned, formal Japanese overture seeking mediation was made to Moscow on August 7, the day before Stalin declared war on Japan. Even then the Japanese government wanted to talk about negotiating for peace, but on its terms. Only after the second A-Bomb and the Soviet declaration of war was Japan ready to surrender. Whether war with the Soviets tipped the scales toward surrender is debatable. It surely played a part in Hirohito's decision, but the Soviet action came after the A-Bomb, and there is every reason to believe that Hirohito was candid when he gave credit to that terrible weapon as his reason for ending the war. That is why it is difficult to understand Richard Minear's extravagant claim, "No serious student accepts the claim that the bomb changed the minds of Japan's leaders."

Japanese reliance on the approach to Moscow for mediation led them to ignore a peace proposal from their ambassador at the Vatican. In late May 1945, Martin Quigley, an American Office of Strategic Service (OSS) agent in Rome, spoke to Msgr. Egidio Vagnozzi of the Vatican diplomatic service about attempting to open a discussion about peace through the Japanese ambassador to the Vatican. Vagnozzi did so and although skeptical, the Japanese ambassador to the Vatican, Ambassador Ken Harada, informed Tokyo about the overture on June 3, 1945.[5]

Through MAGIC, Washington was aware of the matter as soon as Tokyo. For five days Ambassador Harada vainly waited for a reply from Tokyo and then on his own initiative asked Vagnozzi to contact Quigley about possible surrender terms. On his own Quigley outlined some terms and they were sent to Tokyo on June 12. Again, MAGIC told Washington of Harada's cable to Tokyo. That the two cables were received in Tokyo was confirmed in 1972 in a letter to Quigley from Harada. The latter said that the effort came to naught because Tokyo was determined to seek peace through the mediation of Moscow, an effort that he said began on July 12, as well as the intransigence of the Japanese Army, which still refused to surrender.

Quigley provided an interesting footnote to the history of the A-Bomb, although he probably would have been the first to agree that his contacts were unofficial and tentative. Whether his reports to OSS in Washington received much attention is doubtful. They came at the same time the OSS began to question the VESSEL messages about events in the Vatican. These had received much attention but now were suspected of being spurious, which indeed they were. Tokyo's failure to follow up on Harada's messages was known to Washington and could reasonably be interpreted as Japanese disinterest in the messages sent by Harada. Quigley's book is an interesting addition to our knowledge of the last days of the war but its title, *Peace Without Hiroshima*, is typical of the "what ifs" and "might have beens" of events in 1945.[6]

Another counterfactual, one that revisionists prefer not to explore, is what would have happened had Stalin responded to Japan's overture in July for Soviet mediation. Might the war have ended without the A-Bomb? Either explicitly or implicitly the revisionists show commendable understanding and tolerance of Soviet actions in Eastern Europe that they believed were intended to defend against American hegemony. That attitude seems to have limited their exploration of why Stalin failed to act to prevent Hiroshima. He had an avenue to Tokyo denied to Washington and had he wanted to mediate, there would have been no use of the A-Bomb. "Some guilt for Hiroshima and Nagasaki," Stephen Harper said, "must surely attach to Stalin and his aides for their cynical, self-seeking rebuff to Japan's persistent appeals for their mediation to end the war. Also, and more particularly, for the slaughter on both sides in their seven-day offensive — a heavy toll in lives for Soviet territorial gains already agreed to by the Allies." Surely the Soviets who could talk directly with Tokyo bear more of a burden than revisionists find it possible to explore.

But speculation about what might have happened had Stalin acted as an honest broker is pointless because he had no intention of doing so. Whatever the merit of the Japanese effort in mid July, it was doomed by Stalin's realpolitik. Although Gar Alperovitz and others make much of information that became available after the war about the effort of the Japanese peace party to end the war, the outcome of that effort was uncertain until August 7, when Japan formally asked Moscow's intervention, not to surrender but seeking to negotiate peace terms. Insofar as anyone knew at the time, Japan was determined to continue hostilities until its terms were met. The belated and abortive peace feelers reveal that Japan did not entertain seeking an end to the war until it was compelled to do so by overwhelming force. It should be obvious to sophisticated historians that there is a vast difference between seeking peace terms and surrender, but that distinction escapes too many revisionists to be accidental.[7]

It is useful to place the events of the summer of 1945 in a broader context, remembering that decisions in Washington were not made in a vacuum. A global conflict was the context within which decisions were made about fighting Japan. The Allies had experienced long years of war during which hopes were raised, and then dashed. They were ready to believe in a Japanese surrender when it happened. Those who thought Japan was ready to surrender in the summer of 1945 replayed what happened in Europe in the summer of 1944, when it seemed Germany was almost defeated. Success in France in the summer of 1944 fed Allied optimism about an early end to the war. Noel Annan, who served in the British Joint Intelligence Staff, recalled that Britain's Joint Intelligence Committee believed that Germany would be out of the war by Christmas. Paul Nitze, who served in the U.S. Strategic Bombing Survey, said that it "was the expectation of many, from President Roosevelt on down, that the war in Europe would be over before the end of the year." Many in the U.S. Congress also assumed that, with the war in Europe in its last phase, there was no need for additional military manpower or high-level production of war materiel. Not only headquarters but troops in the field were optimistic. J. Glenn Gray, who was at the front, wrote in his journal on July 6, 1944: "Today we return to the front! A great change of mood has come over us all ... peace is in sight, or the illusion of peace ... that there will be no more weary winters to spend on war torn fronts."[8]

Front line troops paid a high price for that optimism. Vernon Walters, who served as a liaison officer with the Brazilian division in Italy, saw how, although facing a strongly entrenched enemy that winter on the Gothic Line, scarce ammunition had to be strictly rationed. General Andrew Goodpaster, who was wounded in the battle of Cassino, also was harshly critical of the cutbacks in the induction and training of men for the American forces and the premature reductions in the production of ammunition.[9] An overextended and overburdened Allied supply system, and German recovery thanks to shorter lines of communication and supply, caused hope for an early end of the fighting to ebb by the autumn. All optimism ended on December 16 with Hitler's winter offensive and the Battle of the Bulge.

Advocates of industrial reconversion were opposed by the military and by "dollar a year men" in the administration who were on leave from major corporations. Arguing that the war was not over, they were against disrupting production vital for the military. John Ohl's biography of General Brehon Somerell, who headed the Army Service Forces and was the top logistics expert for the army, reviewed the tension in Washington between those who wanted early industrial reconversion and Somervell's demand that it wait until the war ended. Congressmen who were more interested in politics as usual argued for reconversion to benefit the domestic economy and maintain employment; others cited the continuing need for weapons and supplies for the military. Political considerations, long term policy issues, and the needs of the military were involved in a debate that ultimately was decided in favor of the military. Richard Polenberg aptly summarized the high level maneuvering that accompanied the debates over the timing and rate of reconversion to a peace-time economy. Despite some understandable concerns about dealing with unemployment that might follow the end of war production, the army held firm about its priorities. During that debate some production suffered and ammunition and other material often were in short supply, at a cost to operations and to the safety of troops in the field.[10]

The Allies were understandably concerned that optimism about a swift end to the Pacific war could create a situation similar to what happened earlier in Europe. War weariness was rampant and the new Labor government in Britain was already withdrawing troops from the Pacific although fighting continued. The Allies knew that the Japanese army had powerful forces on the home islands and, after Okinawa, knew that future Japanese resistance could be fierce. The American navy lost almost 5,000 men killed and another 5,000 wounded at Okinawa while the ground forces had 7,600 men killed or missing and almost 33,000 wounded in addition to almost as many non-battle casualties. It was against that background that the Joint Chiefs of Staff issued their directive for "OPERATION OLYMPIC" on May 14, 1945 and scheduled an invasion of the island of Kyushu for November 1, 1945. Plans for the invasion proceeded without knowledge of the existence of the A-Bomb, which was not tested until July. From the intelligence available to the JCS, and they had access to MAGIC and ULTRA as well as other sources, there was evidence of Japan's increasingly desperate situation but little evidence that Japan was ready to surrender.[11] The Japanese were not alone in continuing to fight what most observers would consider a lost war. Germany did the same. The shrinking German forces were caught between the advancing Allies on the west and the Soviets in the east. Germany's large cities were in rubble, civilian morale was shattered, there was hardly any food and virtually no fuel or munitions, but Germany continued to fight until Hitler was dead.

One can speculate about the cultural, internal political or other reasons that cause seemingly rational arguments for surrender to falter. The fact remains that intelligent people resisted seemingly rational arguments and persisted in bringing disaster on their countries. To understand what happened in Japan in the summer of 1945, one must examine what happened there without imposing a definition of what would be "rational" or "reasonable" behavior in the extreme crisis that faced the Japanese government. The British philosopher Bertrand Russell believed that men are sufficiently rational to acquiesce to their own survival. That agrees with the theory in political science that rational choice is the dominant motive. However, any policeman can attest to the fact that if rational choice ruled, fewer prisons would be needed; in any event, the theory was developed too late to persuade the Japanese to be rational as the B-29s reduced their cities to ruin. For their own complex reasons the Japanese leaders compromised their nation's survival by adamantly refusing to surrender.

When Barbara Tuchman considered the problem of ending a conflict, she wrote: "Ending a war is a difficult and delicate business. Even intelligent rulers, when they exist, often find themselves unable to terminate a war, should they want to." Americans need not go abroad for an example of a refusal to accept defeat. Late in the Civil War it became clear, at least to the North, that the South was defeated. Knowing it could not win in battle the Southern strategy was to persist in the hope that political pressure in the war weary North would force the government to move towards a negotiated peace on terms favorable to the Confederacy. After the national elections of 1864 that hope faded. By the end of 1864 any reasonable appreciation of the situation facing the Confederacy would have counseled surrender, but General Lee continued to fight General Grant for another three months with disastrous results for the South. Like the South's leaders, and although certainly intelligent, leaders in Tokyo clearly did not want to end the war, unless on their terms, and they continued their doomed struggle.[12]

The tortuous path Japan took toward surrender was traced by Professor Herbert Bix who found that the government engaged in tactical delays for internal and external reasons, and he noted that Japanese Premier Suzuki twice publicly and officially rejected the Allied call to surrender in the Potsdam Declaration of July 26. A Japanese radio broadcast said, "Unconditional surrender for the Japanese people is impossible.... The Japanese Imperial Government will ignore this joint declaration and will adopt a policy to strive toward completion of the Greater East Asia War in conformity to the hitherto established basic principles." That sounded like a rejection. On July 28, according to David Rees, Suzuki said that he considered the Potsdam Declaration a rehash of the Cairo Declaration and "the government will just ignore it." Despite the debate over the exact meaning of the word mokusatsu, Rees said that Foreign Minister Togo did not question the meaning it was given by American translators and that it would be understood by the Japanese man in the street. Basically the same meaning of a policy of mokusatsu [lit. to kill with silence] was given by Nakamura Masanori. The Acting Secretary of State, Joseph Grew, who had been ambassador to Japan from 1931 to 1941, said, "The action of Prime Minister Suzuki in rejecting the Potsdam ultimatum by announcing on July 28, 1945, that it was 'unworthy of public notice' was most unfortunate."

However, Professor Akira Iriye, who was one of the advisors to the exhibit, said that the British Foreign Office regarded Suzuki's statement as intended for domestic consumption and not a rejection of the Allied surrender terms. "But the United States so interpreted it, decided to use the atomic bomb, and, ... when Japanese peace overtures were finally received on August 10, acted unilaterally to bring about Japan's surrender." Professor Alperovitz and others also have argued that the wording of the rejection was ambiguous and should have been seen as such by Washington, because failing to do so led to dropping the bomb. That argument lacks credibility, because they reasoned backwards, seeking to justify why the A-Bomb should not have been used. In *Japan's Longest Day*, the primary dictionary definition of the word was given as to ignore with silent contempt. Subtle minds might argue about shades of meaning in the word; it clearly meant rejection of the Potsdam Declaration and was understood as such by the Japanese press. Tokyo did not lack translators familiar with the nuances of their language, and of English, and of the importance of conveying meaning in another language. And there was no lack of Japanese linguists in Washington who were aware of the same obligation to convey what words meant. Whether for domestic political reasons or otherwise, Suzuki was read as he intended the message to be understood in a worldwide broadcast, as effectively rejecting the Allied demand for surrender.[13]

Hyoe Murakami told how the Japanese government acted in this crisis. "As the situation on Okinawa deteriorated, the army began to call for a final battle on the main Japanese islands. Even the army was aware that the situation was hopeless, but despite this, or rather precisely because of it, it hoped at once to inflict grave losses on the American forces.... And thereby achieve an honorable peace settlement." Throughout July the army remained "implacable" in opposing negotiations. From May into August, according to Robert Butow, "the army insisted that mediation must not be based on the assumption that Japan was proposing peace because she was beaten. Since the army maintained that Japan was not defeated, it was impossible to reach any agreement on peace terms." Professor Akira Iriye has written extensively on Japanese-American relations, and believed that Prime Minister Suzuki had an exaggerated notion of military resistance to surrender and wanted to reassure the people that the nation was not defeated. As a result he publically depreciated the Potsdam Declaration. However, Iriye said, "The Potsdam Declaration should have been accepted immediately and unequivocally by the Japanese government, for it gave them just what they were seeking, 'peace on the basis of something other than unconditional surrender.'"[14]

The stalemate in Tokyo continued into August. At a meeting of the Supreme Council for the Conduct of the War on August 9, War Minister Anami Korechika continued to oppose acceptance of the Potsdam Declaration, despite the Soviet declaration of war and the bombing of Nagasaki. Recourse then was made to the Emperor at a meeting later that night. At that meeting Anami continued to oppose surrender but the Emperor decided that the war should be ended. On August 10, the United States informed the Japanese that the Emperor would be subject to the Supreme Commander of the Allied Powers, the formula that allowed the Emperor's retention. Another meeting to finalize the surrender decision waited until August 13 with the war party still strongly in opposition, however, again the Emperor decided that the war should end. Continuing debate required yet another meeting with the Emperor on August 14, when he reaffirmed his decision to end the war. Finally, on the night of August 14, the Suzuki government told the Allies it accepted the Potsdam Declaration. Despite an abortive putsch by some officers, Hirohito finally announced the surrender to his nation at noon on August 15, 1945.

It is difficult to understand the argument that Japan was on the brink of surrender before Hiroshima if one consults Robert Butow and others who have provided detailed accounts of what happened in the final days before Hirohito announced Japan's capitulation. In those eight days after the initial A-Bomb and three days after the future of the Emperor was assured, thousands more died on both sides. The emperor's final decision was made in an atmosphere of extreme hostility to the "peace party" that led to the assassination of several of its members by hard liners. There also was the serious attempt of a coup by hard line army officers who wanted to continue to fight and were ready to seize the Emperor. Had the coup succeeded, there would not have been the Emperor's surrender announcement, and hopeless fighting would have continued for some days with more casualties. Although virtually all of the Japanese military followed the Emperor's order to surrender, some did not. POWs were executed and isolated detachments continued to resist. The determination to resist, even beyond the last hope of staving off invasion, was shown by Admiral Matome Ugaki's suicide flight with a squadron of young fliers as the surrender was announced. They made a kamikaze attack on American ships and all were shot down.[15] Why capitulation took so long is an important question, but more important is the fact that it took two A-Bombs and Soviet entry in the war before the Japanese surrendered.

Speculation about whether the Japanese would have ended the war had the Allies waited a little longer and continued conventional bombing without using the A-Bomb relies heavily on the conclusions of the United States Strategic Bombing Survey, led by Paul Nitze, that was completed shortly after the war. In Professor Dower's opinion, "analysts for the prestigious U. S. Strategic Bombing Survey ... concluded that pre-surrender estimates of Japan's capacity for continuing the war had been greatly exaggerated. This is an ex post facto conjecture, but it reflected a common observation that Japan at war's end was vastly weaker than anyone outside the country had imagined — or anyone inside it had acknowledged." In the report, of which he was the principal author, Paul Nitze contended that conventional bombing would have ended the war in a short time. Long afterwards in his 1989 memoirs, he argued, "Even without the attacks on Hiroshima and Nagasaki, it seemed highly unlikely, given what we found to have been the mood of the Japanese government, that a U. S. invasion of the islands would have been necessary." Herbert Feis contended that "There cannot be a well-grounded dissent from the conclusions reached as early as 1945 by members of the U.S. Strategic Bombing Survey ... certainly prior to 31 December 1945, and in all probability prior to 1 November 1945, Japan would have surrendered even if the atomic bombs had not been dropped."

To buttress his argument against the use of the atomic bombs, Professor Alperovitz used excerpts from an April 1946 U.S. Army intelligence report that concluded that the Emperor and his advisors, "the Cabinet and presumably the majority of the people knew how impossible it was to continue the war without all of Japan being destroyed.... The war almost certainly would have terminated when Russia entered the war against Japan." The naivete of the report is apparent when it is realized that it found that the majority of the people knew the war was lost, as if that made a difference in authoritarian Japan. Essentially the report was a reprise of Nitze's Strategic Bombing Survey. As evidence, even if post facto, against using the atomic bombs, it is subject to the same caveats expressed by Robert Newman, who has a devastating criticism of what Professor Dower called a "prestigious" survey. The survey was prestigious in its leadership but Newman showed that it was hastily conducted and lasted only about two months, ending by December 1, 1945. Calling Nitze's report "counterfactual," Newman called attention to its sloppy methodology and flawed research, saying that it supported a preexistent conclusion that more conventional bombing and blockade would force the Japanese to surrender to avoid starvation. Nitze ignored the behavior of Japan's leaders when confronted by the awesome destruction of Hiroshima. It is important to know that despite his conclusions in the Survey, Nitze approved the use of the A-Bomb. Years later in his memoirs he did change the conclusions he reached in the SBS report. Another who was critical of the USSBS's striking conclusion that in "all probability" Japan would have surrendered without the A-Bomb before November 1, 1945, was Professor Bernstein, who also called that conclusion counterfactual. There can be no doubt that the bombing of Japan made a significant contribution to that country's defeat. However, there can be little if any reliance on the USSB's seemingly authoritative conclusions after one reads the mutually reinforcing accounts of Newman and Bernstein.[16]

Yet another who had believed the second bomb, if not the first, was unnecessary was Edwin Reischauer, a Japanese expert and the ambassador to Japan from 1961 to 1966. At the time he thought dropping the bomb was a mistake. "The Americans, without stopping to think fully about what they were doing, proceeded on August 6 and 9, 1945, to drop on the cities of Hiroshima and Nagasaki the two atom bombs.... An argument could be made for using the first atom bomb on Hiroshima in order to shock the Japanese leaders into surrender, because the decision then hung precariously in the balance, but there was certainly no justification for using the second bomb."

Reischauer, who served in the Pentagon during the war, held that opinion because "Even in February of 1945 it was beginning to become clear that Japan could be defeated without Soviet aid, and as events worked out, the Soviet entry into the war on August 8, like the dropping of atomic bombs on Hiroshima and Nagasaki on August 6 and August 9, was only a minor incident, perhaps hastening the Japanese surrender by a few days but not determining it." However, he hedged and countered that opinion a paragraph later, saying, "Certainly there was no assurance in February

1945 that the Japanese would ever surrender, and up to the very end many American leaders retained their doubts as to whether the Japanese forces overseas would respect a surrender made by the Tokyo authorities. While our ultimate victory was already assured, our government made the Yalta agreement with the hope of saving American lives which might otherwise be expended in rooting out bitter-end resistance in Manchuria, Korea and North China. The bargain proved to be based on inaccurate premises, but these premises seemed reasonable enough when it was made." Later he said, "The Japanese would have had to go on fighting, and there would have been an absolute massacre with attendant starvation. I feel that many people would have died."[17]

For the sake of argument, one could assume, as Nitze did, that the conclusions of the SBS are accurate and that the Emperor and the so-called peace party were willing to surrender in May. The SBS assumption was that without the bombs and Soviet entry into the war, because of food shortages, slipping morale, continued conventional bombing, etc., a surrender would have come without the bombs or an invasion, although it was not sure of exactly when. In other words, the blockade, and conventional bombing had so reduced the nation's ability and willingness to fight that surrender was inevitable. On the other hand, after May there were three critical incidents, two A-bombs and Soviet entry into the war, which at least would seem to have been highly correlated with the surrender. Even if the SBS analysis is accepted as accurate, which is not unchallenged, its observations were not available to the president, so its conclusion is essentially an interesting counterfactual that is irrelevant to the decision made to drop the bomb in August 1945.

With regard to the SBS emphasis upon conventional bombing, it is useful to learn from John Skates that the SBS commissioners were chosen, and the study was sponsored, from within the Army Air Forces. Then Strobe Talbot, a sympathetic chronicler of Paul Nitze, weighed in with this conclusion: "Most subsequent analysis of the course of events within the Japanese government in August 1945, contradicted the survey's conclusion: the nuclear attack had indeed been 'war-decisive.' The very day after the attack on Nagasaki, the Japanese government issued a statement substantially agreeing to unconditional surrender. Whatever Nitze's eyes, instincts, and instruments told him on the scene, and whatever his report told the world, the Bomb had indeed ended the war."[18]

A confusing argument against the A-Bomb in an excellent book was made by Leon Sigal. "The accepted wisdom on the end of the war between the United States and Japan is that the atomic bombings shocked Japan into surrendering unconditionally. That is wrong." He continued, "The emperor himself seems to have seen the bomb too as providing the context for intervening in the policy process. In the end it was his intervention, not the atomic bombings or Soviet entry, that was decisive." Sigal believed that only if the bomb shocked the army into surrender could the bomb be said to have ended the war and since the army was not "shocked" into surrender and wanted to fight on, the bombs were not decisive. Unlike the army, the bombs shocked the Emperor enough, or so he said, that he ordered the surrender. Although on his own terms Sigal found the bombs unnecessary, in the final analysis he splits hairs about the role of the bombs in a way that makes no sense. If the bomb caused Hirohito to intervene, how can anyone reasonably deny that the bomb led to the surrender? Without that intervention the war would have continued. One may disagree with Sigal's conclusion but his account of the political process in Tokyo is must reading for anyone interested in an in-depth analysis of what was happening there in the final months of the war.

A similar argument was made much earlier by Joseph Marx: "The bombing of Nagasaki did not end the war. It did give the Emperor a means by which to convince the military that the Potsdam terms had to be accepted. It gave some of the military a way out — accept surrender because the atomic bomb was not a weapon to which a people, no matter how brave or how full of patriotism, could stand up. In effect, it became a method of saving face for the military. It gave them an excuse to follow the Emperor's wishes to surrender." Marx had no doubt about the necessity of using the second bomb to force the surrender.

Both of these arguments repeat the much earlier one of Robert Butow. "The atomic bombing of Hiroshima and Nagasaki and the Soviet Union's declaration of war did not produce Japan's decision to surrender, for that decision — in embryo— had long been taking shape. What these events did do was to create that unusual atmosphere in which the theretofore static factor of the Emperor could be made active in such an extraordinary way as to work what was virtually a political miracle."[19] These writers quibbled about the efficacy of the bombs, whether directly or indirectly, as an inducement to surrender. Had the three events mentioned by Butow not occurred, what would Hirohito have done, and when? And at what cost to both sides?

With a balanced straddle of the issue that eventually agreed with the "scholarly consensus," J. Samuel Walker asked, was the A-Bomb necessary? "The fundamental question that has triggered debate about Truman's decision since shortly after the end of World War II is, was the bomb necessary? In view of the evidence now available, the answer is yes ... and no. Yes, the bomb was necessary to end the war at the earliest possible moment.

And yes, the bomb was necessary to save the lives of American troops, perhaps numbering in the several thousands. But no, the bomb was probably not necessary to end the war within a fairly short time without an invasion of Japan. And no, the bomb was not necessary to save the lives of hundreds of thousands of American troops." Fortunately for Japan, Hirohito did not agree with Walker.

Speculation about what precipitated the Emperor's decision to surrender ranged from contending that it was Soviet entry into the war, to others crediting the A-Bombs, to Japan's war weariness. In a lengthy examination of the events leading to Japan's surrender, Sadao Asada considered the alternatives to the A-Bomb, such as conventional bombing and blockade, as well as the impact of the Soviet attack. The conclusion was, "In the end, Japan needed 'external pressure' in the form of the atomic bombs for its government to decide to surrender."[20]

That the brink of surrender theory actually was an unsubstantiated *ex post facto* hypothesis finds confirmation in Herbert Bix' conclusion: "Generally speaking, it is true that any demand for surrender without prior negotiation has some retarding effect on the process of ending a war. But in this case it was not so much the Allied policy of unconditional surrender or 'absolute victory' that prolonged the Asian-Pacific war, as it was the unrealistic and incompetent actions of Japan's highest leaders." Bix ascribed to Hirohito much more influence on policy than most writers. For example, Edward Drea described Hirohito as one who consistently reacted to military operations; he did not initiate them and he came across as a cautious procrastinator, willing to let events take their course. "In the face of total defeat, he valued the imperial institution more than his people, his army, and his empire." Drea might have been describing King Victor Emanuel of Italy, also a master procrastinator, whose dithering about firing Mussolini, delay in authorizing Armistice negotiations and delay in declaring war on Germany prolonged the suffering of his people.

Until the final decision by Hirohito, the Japanese military wanted to fight and were willing to sacrifice the lives of their compatriots in a Gotterdammerung ending to the war. *The Crossroads* seemed to concede that Japan was prepared to fight to the bitter end. "By the summer of 1945, every man and woman in Japan over the age of 13 was a member of the People's Volunteer Army, and subject to military discipline. They were drilled with spears and makeshift weapons for the final battles on the beaches." However, reinforcing the earlier picture of the nation actually on the brink of surrender, it added, "But the ability of the Japanese people to fight was increasingly undermined by blockade, starvation, overwhelming Allied air power and the collapse of industrial production." *The Crossroads* was not as definitive as Lisle Rose who earlier said that Japan "simply could not have continued the war beyond mid-autumn." Despite that fact, he said, the United States refused "to rise above wartime emotionalism and the momentum of unrestrained militarism to consider realistically or humanely the plight of Japan." As the Warners had discovered, however, despite blockade and bombing, the Japanese had been able to reinforce Kyushu with men, weapons and supplies to an extent deemed impossible by American intelligence because of the interdiction of the sea lanes and presumed loss of weapons and inability to replace them. If that was the case, then where did all that materiel come from? Without the bombs and Soviet entry into the war the possibility of continued Japanese resistance was more than a guesstimate and something to be seriously considered by the Allies, who knew much more than Lisle Rose and who, at the highest level, were singularly unemotional in conducting the war.

If history was truly based on evidence, then the fictional endings of the war presented by the curators and the revisionists would be given short shrift. Richard Frank told about the actual ending of a tragic time in twentieth century history when he wrote: "Without atomic weapons the Emperor's intervention would have been delayed. His action was essential to obtain an organized surrender, and it caught Japan on the edge of a precipice of a series of events that would have plunged its people into catastrophe. The decisions made by Truman and his subordinates to add nuclear weapons to the campaign of blockade and bombardment cost the lives of between 100,000 and 200,000 Japanese at Hiroshima and Nagasaki, on top of the many tens of thousands of others who died in the incendiary raids or due to the ultimate effects of the blockade. Those Japanese noncombatants, however, held no stronger right not to be slaughtered than did the vast numbers of Chinese and other Asian noncombatants ... alternatives to the atomic bombs carried no guarantee that they would end the war or reduce the amount of human death and suffering ... the deaths actually incurred in ending the war were not gratuitous. American goals were not simply victory but peace. Had American leaders in 1945 been assured that Japan and the United States would pass two generations in tranquility and still look forward with no prospect of future conflict, they would have believed their hard choices had been vindicated — and so should we."

Against the evidence, revisionists continue to depict the events of July and early August 1945 in terms of how, at the time, a few Americans saw the situation in Japan, which was not how the Japanese government behaved. MAGIC told Washington about Japan's peace feelers and desire for Moscow's mediation, on Japanese terms. Unfortunately for the Japanese people those were gestures, some intended to buy time for a negotiated peace, and were not substantial moves toward ending the war. Only wishful thinking, or a deliberate denial of what happened in Japan in August 1945, can lead to believing that Japan was on brink of surrender before the A-Bomb fell on August 6, 1945. The direct responsibility for opening the door to Hiroshima and Nagasaki and the atomic era rests squarely with Japan's leaders.[21]

IV

Unconditional Surrender

There has been an interminable debate about the wisdom of the Allied call for unconditional surrender by the Axis. In the case of Japan *The Crossroads* claimed that in hindsight it is clear that Japan might have surrendered had the United States modified its demands and guaranteed the retention of the emperor. This essay examines a policy announced at the Casablanca Conference in January 1943 that was attended by Churchill and Roosevelt and questions the clarity of the curators' hindsight about how the war might have ended.

The policy of unconditional surrender has been criticized as too harsh and as contributing to the intransigence of the Japanese and reluctance of the Germans to consider deposing Hitler. Seeking to explain the failure of the German generals to oppose Hitler, General Hans Spiedel said: "It would have been easier for our best military commanders had it not been for the agreement at the Casablanca Conference to demand unconditional surrender."[1] As late as April 26, 1945, after Himmler approached the Swedish government with a conditional offer to surrender, the Allied reply was that there could be no question of anything but unconditional surrender simultaneously to the three major powers.[2] The policy remained after Germany's surrender and proved a sticking point for the Japanese.

Critics of Allied intrangiesence about this policy sometimes look to the Italian surrender as a precedent for modifying the demand for unconditional surrender. However, Italy's case was quite different from Japan's because Italy officially, although belatedly, initiated surrender talks with the Allies. It should be remembered that peace talks with Italy did not begin until after the war and a peace treaty was not signed until February 10, 1947, becoming effective on September 15, 1947. Unlike in Japan, the Italian military was aware of the futility of continuing to fight long before its defeat in North Africa, and played a leading role in Mussolini's ouster on July 25, 1943. His successor Marshal Pietro Badoglio was anxious to end the alliance with Germany and to leave the war. Like Emperor Hirohito, however, King Vittorio Emmanuel III was a procrastinator who waited until mid August to begin negotiations with the Allies. The Italians balked at the term "unconditional surrender" and reluctantly signed a "short form" military armistice on September 3rd that did not refer to unconditional surrender. The Armistice took effect on September 8, 1943. A later "Instrument of surrender of Italy," called the "long form," demanded that Italy's armed forces surrender "unconditionally." The Italians negotiated the deletion of the word "unconditionally" although that word was inserted in the preamble to the long form to say that Marshal Badoglio accepted its terms unconditionally.[3] If the concept of unconditional surrender was so objectionable to Western European Italians, one can surmise its importance to the Japanese. There can be no doubt that the policy hardened the resolution of Germany and Japan to resist.

On July 13, 1945, Navy Secretary James Forrestal recorded in his diary the first real evidence of a Japanese desire to get out of the war, thanks to intercepts of messages from Foreign Minister Togo to Ambassador Sato in Moscow. Sato was to tell the Russians that Japan wanted to remain at peace with Russia and did not want permanent annexation of territories it conquered in Manchuria. He added that the unconditional surrender terms of the Allies was about the only thing in the way of termination of the war and that if this was insisted upon, the Japanese would continue the fight. Sato said Tokyo's proposals were unrealistic and that Russia could not be divided from its Allies. Togo insisted that the proposals go to the Russians, but there was no response from the Russians. The impasse continued until it was resolved by the atomic bombs with an assist from Soviet intervention. In the opinion of John Skates, "Those who still search for an explanation of why the atomic bombs were used against an already defeated Japan need look no further than the conflict between America's rigorous insistence on unconditional surrender and the irrational, suicidal, and hopeless nature of Japan's last defenses."

An overriding justification for the unconditional surrender policy was to avoid the problem that surfaced in Germany after World War I when the Germans contended that their army had not lost the war in battle but on the home front. There could be no doubt that by the Allies continuing the war to the bitter end in 1945, both Germany and Japan knew they were utterly defeated in the war they confidently began. President Roosevelt made this clear when he said, "it is of the utmost importance that every person in Germany should realize that this time Germany is a defeated nation.... The fact that they are a defeated nation, collectively and individually, must be so impressed upon them that they will hesitate to start any new war." When Admiral Louis Mountbatten, the Allied commander in Southeast Asia, was told about the A-Bomb he regretted its use because he believed that unless the Japanese were defeated in the field they would make the same claim as the Germans after World War I. The Soviets also favored unconditional surrender. In his meeting with Marshal Stalin on May 28, 1945, Harry Hopkins was told that the Soviet Union preferred to "go through with unconditional surrender and destroy the military might and forces of Japan once and for all." If milder peace terms were agreed to, Stalin suggested "giving them the works once we get into Japan."[4]

Professor Michael Walzer, a philosopher who writes about the "just war," and politics from a self proclaimed "left" perspective, accepted the policy of unconditional surrender for Germany. He agreed with George Kennan that a peace compromise with Hitler was impracticable and unthinkable. However, he believed that the "Japanese case is sufficiently different from the German so that unconditional surrender should never have been asked." Professor Michael Sherry held that Truman's failure at Potsdam to clearly state that the Emperor could be retained "was rightly condemned as the most tragic blunder in American surrender policy." He agreed, "there can be no certainty that Japan would have accepted in July what it submitted to in August, but the chance was there." Then he approved Professor Walzer's statement, "the victorious Americans owed the Japanese people an experiment in negotiation. To use the atomic bomb, to kill and terrorize civilians, without attempting such an experiment was a double crime." Walzer had gone on to say, "Some restraint upon their war-making power might be justified, but their domestic authority was a matter of concern only to the Japanese people." McGeorge Bundy shared Walzer's concerns about unconditional surrender but said, "I think he may be insensitive to the strength of the case for the severe defeat, extended occupation, and imposed constitutional change, as means to prevent renewed Japanese militarism."[5]

What Bundy characterized as Walzer's "insensitivity" meant that, had his position been followed, Japan would not have been occupied and reforms would have been left to whatever evolved in Japanese politics. But according to Edwin Reischauer, "In any country in wartime a few men inevitably must make grave decisions for their countrymen, but for Japan the decisions were particularly crucial and the men participating in them unusually few." Apparently Professor Walzer was not aware of that fact or of the authoritarian militaristic state described by Saburo Ienaga, one without civil rights that ruthlessly suppressed dissent. After fighting to end its brutal policies it would have been absurd to accept Walzer's fatuous suggestion and risk allowing a military dictatorship to retain the reins of power. The Allies intended that Japan's surrender would mean more than having troops lay down their arms. Japan would forfeit its overseas empire and be forced to cooperate with an occupation that required the acceptance of unprecedented economic, political and social changes in Japanese society, with or without the Emperor.

Notwithstanding the accommodations that were made, first to Italy and then to Japan, latter day critics of the policy ignore or dismiss the fact that contemporary British and American public opinion, and legislative opinion, were committed to the Casablanca policy. In these democracies Roosevelt and Churchill would have found it difficult to renounce a goal that had been so firmly stated as Allied policy. Even Churchill bowed to political reality. In 1943 he had objected to imposing unconditional surrender on Italy, but when his war cabinet objected to Italy's exclusion he dropped his objection.

Admiral William Leahy was one of those who expressed his opposition to the policy, as did Secretary Stimson, who believed the Japanese should be told that they could keep the Emperor. According to Alonzo Hamby, "Truman seemed somewhat sympathetic, said he had left the door open for Congress to alter the unconditional surrender policy, but felt he could not take action to change public opinion." Brian Villa has a good account of the military's reservations about the wisdom of unconditional surrender compared to that of hard liners in the State Department. He reveals the complexity of the issues involved in formulating a policy that was responsive to domestic realities, the future of the occupation of Japan and the potential cost of an invasion. The military knew the ultimate cost of the policy if it was adamantly pursued and succeeded in getting it modified, although the final decision was left to their elected officials. Churchill and Truman shared the military's reservations, but once unconditional surrender was endorsed by their constituents, for better or worse in the case of Japan it became a virtually unalterable Allied policy until the very last moment.[6]

When comparing various opinions about the policy, J. Samuel Walker noted that Professor Alperovitz held that public opinion did not demand rigid adherence to the policy. On the other hand, polls at the time suggested that there was a risk to a change in policy. Then Walker summed up the situation facing Truman: "As a president who was still unsure in his position, unsure of his public standing, committed to carrying out Roosevelt's legacy, and most importantly, seeking a way to end the war decisively at the lowest possible cost to American lives, the potential drawback of softening the demand for unconditional surrender had to be balanced against the potential (but far from certain) benefits." In an article on how textbooks deal with the Cold War, Walker referred approvingly to some books that contained sketches of Truman's personality that implicitly took issue with the "heroic image" of him that flourished in what he would consider popular mythology. Revisionist mythology presents Truman as a weak and insecure person unable to face the challenges of the presidency to the satisfaction of Walker, Bernstein, Alperovitz and others who seek to redefine Truman and history on their terms.

Because politicians, commentators, religious figures, newspapers, and private citizens criticized the policy, Professor John Chappell intimated that it was opposed by a significant number of Americans, an idea contradicted by contemporary polling data. As Professor Chappell described the opposition, at the same time he claimed that "The U.S. government endeavored to discourage public interest in reports of Japanese peace feelers," and naively faulted U.S. leaders for discussing unconditional surrender "in forums isolated from public input." Unfortunately, he failed to explain how, since the press and members of Congress were far from silent about the policy, the government had discouraged public interest in the policy. Nor did he explain why the criticism of the policy by the press and members of Congress did not qualify as traditional public forums. Following Professor Bernstein and others, he regretted that "American leaders thought almost exclusively in military terms when they discussed methods of ending the war, even though many citizens and commentators believed that diplomacy might end it just as expeditiously and preclude further combat." Presenting the final act of the conflict from the perspective of well intentioned Americans who saw Japan on the brink of surrender and believed diplomacy would bring about surrender conveys a skewed view of what was happening in Japan. That is where the Supreme War Council made American hopes for a diplomatic resolution of the war an impossibility.[7]

Long after the fact, it is well to remember that debates about the policy of unconditional surrender did not take place in university seminars. The debates took place in the real world of 1945, by people who, as did Abraham Lincoln in his time, understood the temper of a people, press and Congress tired of war, reluctant to make more sacrifices and anxious to have their sons come home. That must be factored into interpretations of why the president held to the policy stated in paragraph 13 of the Potsdam Proclamation: "We call upon the government of Japan to proclaim

now the unconditional surrender of all Japanese armed forces, and to provide proper and adequate assurances of their good faith in such action.
The alternative for Japan is prompt and utter destruction." On August 10
the Japanese indicated acceptance of the Potsdam terms with the understanding that the emperor could remain. Even after what seemed an
ambiguous answer allowing his retention, the Supreme Council split three
to three on the question of surrender until Hirohito made the decision to
capitulate. Those who continue to believe that Japan was on the brink of
surrender should remember that vote.[8]

Related to unconditional surrender was the question of the status of
the Emperor. According to *The Crossroads*, "To many Americans Hirohito
was a hated symbol of Japanese military aggression," and "public hostility greatly restricted the maneuvering room of President Truman and his
advisors."[9] Joseph Grew, Acting Secretary of State and former ambassador
to Japan, unsuccessfully urged that the Japanese be told that they would
be allowed to retain the Emperor. On May 28, Grew recommended that
the president mention the Emperor's retention in his speech on May 31,
but in a meeting with Archibald MacLeish and Dean Acheson they strongly
opposed the idea. Nevertheless Grew presented the idea to Truman, who
told him to discuss it with the Secretaries of War and Navy, and General
George Marshall and Admiral Ernest King, but for military reasons they
all rejected Grew's proposal. Although Grew continued to press his idea
on June 18, Truman decided to wait until the meeting at Potsdam. The
sequence of Grew's efforts show that top officials in the administration as
well as the president heard and considered Grew's recommendation and
did not believe it was a viable policy.

With Allied public hostility to Hirohito running high, it is understandable that internal political reasons contributed to Allied reluctance
to issuing a statement about the Emperor's status. Forrestal's diary for
May 29, 1945, reported a meeting to respond to the president's request for
the military's view of what he should say in a message to Congress on the
conduct of the war. "It had been proposed that he say something to indicate that our objectives toward Japan did not include necessarily the
destruction of their political concepts, of their religion, and particularly
of the Emperor as a symbol of their religion. It was agreed that the time
was not appropriate for him to make such a pronouncement."[10]

When *The Crossroads* asked "Would the war have ended sooner if the
United States had guaranteed the Emperor's position?" its answer was, "In
hindsight, it is clear that American and Japanese leaders might have reached
an agreement on Japanese surrender, if the United States had made such
an offer and if the Suzuki government had been willing to communicate

directly with President Truman through a neutral power. In effect, that is what happened after the atomic bombing." The staggering oversimplification of this "it is clear" statement, in the face of what has been known for decades about what happened in Japan in August 1945, is unfortunately not a unique example of the distorted version of history *The Crossroads* intended to present to the public.

After the war the former Acting Secretary of State Joseph Grew continued to believe that, had there been a categorical statement that the Emperor could be retained, the Japanese might have surrendered. However, on the basis of available Japanese records Herbert Feis said, "I find that they indicate that the Japanese government would not have surrendered before July, either in response to such a statement of policies in explanation of our call for unconditional surrender as the State Department urged the President to make, or such a statement about the dynasty as Grew had in mind." What the curators claimed was clear in the 1990s had been contradicted by the documents available to Feis in the 1960s.[10]

Although it has been argued that the atomic bombings and Soviet declaration of war were needed to shock the Japanese and allow Hirohito to save face and force a surrender, *The Crossroads* proposed another counterfactual, one that echoed Professor Bernstein: "it is possible that there was a lost opportunity to end the war without either atomic bombings or an invasion of Japan, if Grew's advice had been accepted." Herbert Bix, who had the advantage of careful study of the Japanese documents of the day, and did not believe the A-Bomb was needed to compel surrender, looked to Japan's future and refuted that feel good counterfactual: "If Grew and the Japan crowd had gotten their way, and the principle of unconditional surrender had been contravened, it is highly unlikely that Japan's post-surrender leaders, now the "moderates" around the throne, would ever have discarded the Meji Constitution and democratized their political institutions." Furthermore, according to Bix, while Grew was ambassador in Japan, he relied on the opinions of men he believed to be Western style liberals and "failed to understand that the court had formed an alliance with the military at the start of the 1940s that made the Pacific War possible."[12] Bix also asked, "Would Japan's leaders have surrendered more promptly if the Truman administration had 'clarified' the status of the emperor prior to the cataclysmic double shocks of the first atomic bomb and Soviet entry into the war?" His answer was succinct: "Probably not."[13]

Japanese reluctance to accept even the concept of surrender, let alone unconditional surrender, found expression in the words used by Hirohito in telling the Japanese that the war was over. Japan entered the war, he said, for the welfare of all nations, had not sought aggrandizement but only the security of East Asia, and had submitted to a cruel bomb. The emperor did not explicitly mention the word surrender or defeat. That reluctance to admit surrender continued long after the war. When asking for the return of islands off her northern coast that were still occupied by the Soviet Union in 1974, Japan argued that she did not, in fact, surrender unconditionally. A 1974 document that dealt with Japan's Northern Territories contended that "Japan lost the war, to be sure, but did not surrender unconditionally. It surrendered on the terms of the Potsdam Proclamation, through which it also accepted the Cairo Declaration." (The Cairo Declaration [paragraph 8 of the Potsdam Proclamation] stated that Japan would be stripped of all territories taken by force.) Whether there was any merit to that contention under international law is less important than the fact that the Japanese government continued to hold that position long after the war.

Richard Frank agreed with Herbert Bix that the fundamental political reality was that Japanese, not American, leaders decided when the war would end. Asserting that there was no alternate credible evidence from the eight men who effectively controlled Japan's destiny, he said that relevant documents were lacking that suggested "Japan would have surrendered on modified terms, coupled to Soviet intervention or some other combination of events, excluding the use of atomic bombs." As a final statement on the merits of the unconditional surrender policy, listen to an historian who was hyper critical of the manner in which the Pacific war was fought. According to Professor Dower, "To argue that Truman should have abandoned the 'unconditional surrender' policy at the last minute minimizes the political uproar that would have provoked not only in the United States but in the Allied camp generally." He argued that if the United States offered a conditional surrender, Japan would have attempted to negotiate to preserve as much as possible of their system and their gains, as they had done earlier in offers to Moscow. Further, after reciting changes that the occupation forced on Japan, such as popular sovereignty and extensive human rights, Professor Dower added, "None of this would have been possible had the Americans agreed to a conditional surrender."[14]

With leisure to speculate, and knowing more than any of the principals could have known at the time, it is as easy to write about the might-have-been alternatives to unconditional surrender, and just as irrelevant as it would be to wonder whether a dry field at Waterloo would have changed European history, or what would have happened if General Washington's boat capsized while crossing the Delaware to visit the Hessians on the day after Christmas in 1776.[15]

V

Was Germany an A-Bomb Target?

We ask whether Germany would have been subjected to the A-Bomb because the assumption of many revisionists is that it would not have been used against fellow whites. While *The Crossroads* did not explicitly mention this, many far from subtle references to American racism throughout the text made it an obvious inference. That is why this essay examines the issue of racism in the Pacific War, and especially in the decision to use the A-Bomb on Japan. *The Crossroads* accepted that President Roosevelt intended that the A-Bomb be used against both countries, but strongly implied that America was driven to use the A-Bomb on Japan because of racism and a desire for vengeance. "The distance separating Japan and the United States underscored the cultural gulf separating the two societies. Ignorance about the other's culture, combined with racism, desire for revenge, and the strain of total war produced virulent hatred on both sides." The script quoted historian Allan Nevins: "Probably in all our history, no foe has been so detested as were the Japanese." There is plenty of evidence of American racial prejudice against Asians, from the Chinese exclusion legislation to what could be found in the Hearst newspapers in the 1930s when they ran lurid stories about the "Yellow Peril," while during the war American propaganda portrayed the Japanese as bestial. In addition, during the war some Americans unquestionably were guilty of individual and collective acts of barbarism; ergo, it is argued that the Pacific war was racist and that led to Hiroshima. The clear message conveyed in *The Crossroads* was that an A-bomb would not have been used against fellow members of the white race.

Perhaps Professor John Dower has been the most influential voice promoting the idea that racism led to "war without mercy" by both sides in the Pacific and that the use of the atom bombs was the result of a racist culture. Referring to Allan Nevins' statement about the detested Japanese, he found virtual equivalence between the Japanese and American conduct of the war. Because *The Crossroads* saw the Pacific war through the same lens as Professor Dower, it is useful to examine his version of the war. When defending *The Crossroads* Professor Dower gave a virtual reprise of the topics found in the original NASM script. Two examples that illustrate his selectivity in presenting them are mentioned here. Asking why the haste in bombing Nagasaki before the Japanese could assess the impact of Hiroshima and Soviet entry into the war after those events, he implied that the Japanese did not realize their changed situation. But historians of that period know, and certainly Professor Dower ought to have known, because it is amply documented, that after those events the Japanese military knew what they meant but insisted on continuing the war. He also asked how we should respond to the position of some Japanese that while Hiroshima may have been needed to change the position of the militarists, Nagasaki was a war crime. That question was left up in the air to make the point that indeed it was a war crime. Could it be that he was unaware of the well documented fact that even after Nagasaki only Hirohito's intervention finally overrode the military's desire to continue fighting? It is puzzling that someone so skilled in making a case would prefer not to let the reader know that there were well known answers to such questions, even if he disagreed with them.[1]

Recycling the so-called alternatives to the bomb, Professor Dower claimed that they complicate the "simple story line of the heroic narrative." However, that the alternatives had been studied is given short shrift in his heavily documented but over simplified narrative. He agreed that "No one denies that these policy makers desired to hasten the war's end and to save American lives, but no serious historian regards those as the sole considerations driving the use of the bombs on Japanese cities." In his opinion the principal other reason was that "Sheer visceral hatred abetted this early targeting of Japan for nuclear destruction." Was that an overriding reason for using the A-Bomb? Given his selective reporting of the events of the summer of 1945, readers are set up for that conclusion. However, the reader is not told the weight of the other considerations driving the decision to use the bomb, or how they were factored into the avowed purpose of saving lives. The mere assertion that they entered the decision making process is not enough.

Any group can be demonized by stringing together accounts of atrocities, as Professor Dower did to support his hypothesis. "It was the common observation among Western war correspondents that the fighting in the Pacific was more savage than in the European theater. Kill or be killed.

No quarter, no surrender. Take no prisoners. Fight to the bitter end ... such attitudes contributed to an orgy of bloodletting that neither side could conceive of avoiding, even though by mid-1944 Japan's defeat was inevitable and plain to see." Professor Dower failed to say that, regrettably, Japanese troops did not surrender, even though to him it seemed clear Japan was defeated. Lacking his sensitivity, for GIs it was a case of kill or be killed. Unlike in the Pacific, there were no Western journalists on the steppes of Russia, or in Poland to document the behavior of the Soviet Army and the German Army. If he were aware of post war accounts of what both sides did in the Eastern war, he would know that they would qualify as what he called "war without mercy." Most would agree with Dower's implicit advocacy of kinder and gentler wars, perhaps like those staged by "condottieri," the mercenary captains who fought for Milan and Florence in Renaissance Italy. Unfortunately, they have not been accepted as models for warfare.

In a multidisciplinary approach explaining the war, Professor Dower included a 1945 article that traced Japanese behavior to child rearing practices. That hypothesis overlooked the fact that racism played no role in brutalities that happened in wars between armies of the same race in Europe and Asia, indicating that racism is not a necessary element in atrocious behavior. There were racists in the American military and at home, but extrapolating from no matter how many anecdotes to indict an entire army and a society based on such shaky "evidence" does not qualify as a reasonable interpretation of the character of the war conducted by the United States. It does show how the loose use of a word can complicate genuine understanding of the sociological and psychological factors that operated during the war. That the word racism was politicized will not disabuse revisionist true believers in American guilt, but if those who insist on the importance of archival evidence followed precedent, they would have to question the lack of a genuine, authoritative paper trail to indict Americans while one does exist to indict Germany and Japan in the many volumes of the Nuremberg trials and in what surfaced in the Tokyo trials and elsewhere. To rest an extraordinary conclusion about an event as enormous as a war on instances of depraved behavior and off the cuff statements in order to indict a society suggests the talent of a pop culture pundit rather than an historian interested in authenticity.

The irrationality of the Allied approach to the war was shown in Professor Dower's counterfactual exercise contrasting the combat soldiers' attitudes toward the Japanese with those of academics and Asia specialists who, presumably, had a more objective and rational understanding of the Japanese. "In Western eyes, fixed on the war in Asia, madness itself became culture bound, as the lingo of the battlefield revealed. In Marine jargon, GIs who suffered shell shock and battle fatigue and went out of their minds were said to have 'gone Asiatic.' What the academics and Asia specialists tried to do was put things in better perspective — to call attention to a web of fundamentally cultural forces that contributed to Japanese violence and tightly regimented group behavior; to demonstrate that even the war fanaticism was not inevitable, and rational appeals could be made to the Japanese to surrender; and to point out that Japanese culture contained within itself the potential for change and constructive peace. This was a notable accomplishment in such a caldron of intense race hate, although on purely intellectual grounds the fundamentally anthropological and psychological approach to the problem left a great deal of territory still thinly covered: serious analysis from the perspectives of history and political economy, for example; questions of class and state power; and areas where fruitful comparisons rather than contrasts might have been drawn between Japanese behavior on the one hand and European and American behavior on the other (areas such as imperialism, colonialism, racism, and battlefield conduct.)" Many years after the fact Professor Dower prated about cultural differences and that Japanese fanaticism was not inevitable, but on Iwo Jima and Okinawa and elsewhere Americans who were without the benefit of academic efforts to place Japanese behavior in better perspective confronted Japanese soldiers who paid scant attention to "rational appeals to surrender." Attempting to compare the combatants as they were engaged in a terrible war of survival by "seeking fruitful comparisons" between Japanese behavior and those of Americans on the basis of colonialism and racism, etc., was irrelevant at the time and preposterous to suggest as meaningful to understand the war.[2]

Of course Professor Dower was not the only writer to claim that the war against Japan was racist. Stephen Ambrose joined the chorus: "From beginning to end the Japanese-American war in the Pacific was waged with a barbarism and race hatred that was staggering in scope, savage almost beyond belief, and catastrophic in consequence. Each side regarded the other as subhuman vermin. They called each other beasts, roaches, rats, monkeys and worse. Atrocities abounded, committed by individuals, by units, by entire armies, by governments. Quarter was neither asked nor given. It was a descent into hell…. By contrast, the race hatred that characterized the Pacific war was absent in the German-American war."

That is an eye-catching opening to a chapter on the atomic bomb and its consequences. A competent and widely read historian, Ambrose was guilty of more than a little hyperbole in that passage. A review of Nazi and Italian propaganda, or of the counter Soviet and other Allied propaganda, reveals that each adversary depicted the other side in much the same way and called the other side the same names and for the same reasons. It is surprising that Ambrose proposed equivalence between the behavior of the American forces and the Japanese. Individual Americans and small units sometimes did atrocious things, but Ambrose knew full well, Americans conducted no Bataan Death Marches, did not recap the rape of Nanking, practiced no vivisection or poison gas experiments on POWs, and did not work captives to death in coal mines, to mention only a very few of the actions of the Imperial Japanese Army. In a era of political correctness, rhetoric such as Ambrose's is not only popular, it often is expected in order to guarantee an author's credentials as sensitive to the current ethos. Such comparisons trivialize what happened at the hands of the Japanese. No less an authority than Leon Trotsky said that an army is a copy of its society and the military, as a social institution reflects its society. Although American society was far from perfect in the 1940s, it sanctioned none of the atrocious practices that were policies of the Japanese military. That is why it is grossly unprofessional to indict Presidents Roosevelt and Truman, Secretary Stimson, General Douglas MacArthur, General George Marshall and a host of ordinary soldiers, marines and sailors of fighting a racist war.[3]

Although J. Samuel Walker admitted that if the bomb shortened the war and saved lives, the morality of its use was defensible, he was dubious about that and spoke of "the moral desolation of the Pacific war" with the Japanese portrayed as apelike sub humans in American cartoons. He also found that "Hatred of the Japanese, a desire for revenge for Pearl Harbor, and racist attitudes were a part of the mix of motives that led to the atomic attacks." And as Professor Michael Sherry examined the fanaticism of the men conducting the air war, he found that, "… whatever their individual value system, those who waged air war served as the instrument of national passions that were often decidedly racist in character." A more nuanced explanation was given by historian Stanley Falk, who discussed Allied soldiers hatred of the Japanese: "This was not racism or unreasoning prejudice, but simply the understandable action of soldiers toward an enemy who committed atrocious acts."[4]

Edward Linenthal, who was an advisor to the exhibit, wrote what can best be described as a sarcastic comment about what the war produced: "we have come to accept a patriotic orthodoxy that communicates the traditional lessons of the attack, namely, that the events at Pearl Harbor on that quiet Sunday morning were both tragic and fortuitous, for they propelled the nation into a 'good' war against the evil Nazis (in contrast to 'good' Germans) and the treacherous Japanese (the entire culture was so categorized)." A more balanced study of American attitudes toward the Japanese during and after the war by Sheila Johnson pulls no punches about the hostility toward the Japanese during the war, but her nuanced study examined attitudes from the viewpoint of an experienced anthropologist who knew Japan and cast the situation in both countries in cultural terms, without Robert Lifton's psychoanalytical overtones.[5]

Following Professor Dower's theme, Ronald Takaki wrote about "The Racialization of the Pacific War," suggesting that there was a special dimension to war against Japan because of the intense racial hatred by Americans for the Japanese people. Takaki intimated that racism played a role in Truman's decision to bomb Japan because Truman's mother had been a supporter of the Confederacy! Then more directly, "Truman succumbed to the raging hate rooted in a long history of animosity against the Japanese, as well as the fierce memory of Pearl Harbor." Allied to this idea was G. Kurt Piehler's suggestion that racism continued after the war and played a role in the treatment of the war dead. "There is no solid evidence to suggest that the decision not to maintain permanent cemeteries in Asia or other regions of the Third World was motivated by racism.... Nonetheless, government reluctance to place permanent burial grounds in the Third World, particularly in Asia, mirrored the ambivalence many Americans felt toward these regions." The American Battle Monuments Commission had decided against Asian cemetery locations on the grounds of their inaccessibility, certainly understandable in the case of places like Tarawa. Piehler found that rationale suspect. He would be more candid if he eliminated the shallow disclaimer "there is no evidence," and said that in his opinion racism dictated the location of cemeteries, which is the message intended for the reader. Without "solid evidence," or any evidence at all, should the historian leave the reader to assume guilt by innuendo? Another case in which a revisionist indicted a military cemetery for conveying a racist political message is discussed later.

How readers can be manipulated into believing racism was involved in the A-Bomb decision was described by David Robertson. He showed how adroitly the revisionist historian Gabriel Kolko implied that James Byrnes was a racist because he supported a Dixiecrat in 1948, something that was not true. "But this statement, occurring in the chapter entitled 'The War with Japan and the Potsdam Conference,' undeniably and inaccurately imputes to Byrnes a motive of racism in his urging the use of the atomic weapon against the Japanese. Either by scholarly carelessness or by intent, this false statement suggests a spirit of herrenvolk in Jimmy Byrnes as an atomic diplomat."[6]

As he recounted numerous examples of atrocious behavior by individuals and some units in the Pacific, Professor Dower presented an apparently compelling story of American racial hatred of their Japanese adversaries. That such behavior occurred is incontestable, and his explanation for why it happened seems persuasive. It seems persuasive, that is, until one gets past the incidents he mentions to the time and place they occurred. That was done by Eric Bergerud in his excellent study of the men who fought in the South Pacific. Those men were a cross section of American society in the 1940s, who were young and mainly blue collar. Like many Americans they may have shared the conventional prejudices of the day and most had little contact with or knowledge of Asians. They were sent to the Pacific before they were exposed to the cartoons or other propaganda about the Japanese that are so emphasized by historians. In any event, like all GIs they were prone to dismiss such efforts. Their attitudes and behavior in combat were shaped primarily by what they learned from their peers and at first hand from their contact with the Japanese soldier. Americans fought what Steven Ambrose called a barbaric war because of race hatred. However, as Bergerud shows so well, it was the desire to survive in a fight to the death with a brutally effective opponent that led them to fight in the only way they knew how. "The South Pacific was a savage place for the men who fought there. Yet acceptance of the war's necessity and a deep hatred of the enemy were not enough to keep the armies in the field for campaign after campaign ... we must examine the physical and psychological factors that sustained the armies. It is time to look at the complex subject of morale."

That the war encouraged less than chivalrous conduct should be no surprise. Americans did that to the Japanese, and vice versa. Germans did it to the British and Russians and vice versa. Such behavior is not to be condoned, but it has to be understood as happening in the heat of combat and as the price of survival. What the Japanese did in the South Pacific had been honed to an edge by what they learned in China and Manchuria and was a part of their military ethos. British General William Slim, who commanded Allied Forces in Burma, wrote that the Japanese soldier "tortured and starved prisoners of war to death, raped women captives and used civilians for bayonet practice, but there was no braver soldier in the whole history of war." Americans in the South Pacific learned how to behave in the jungles from bitter and costly experience fighting such soldiers. That war was brutal, much as it was in Poland, on the steppes of Russia, in the Ardennes and elsewhere. As the behavior of the troops is assessed many years later, historians might consider that, had they been there, as were William Manchester and Paul Fussell, they might have a more nuanced understanding of why humans behave as they do in life threatening situations regardless of the race of their adversaries.[7]

The virtual equivalence in the war-making of Japan and the United States is a recurring theme in some writing about the Pacific War. It appeared in *The Crossroads'* effort to explain how the United States and Japan changed during the war. Both nations "remained insulated from the harsh reality of total war longer than any other major belligerents of World War II." By 1945, however, both nations underwent profound changes. The Japanese faced daily air raids, severe privation and the threat of invasion, while for many Americans, "combat in the Pacific remained a distant series of events reported through a veil of censorship.... The cost of victory, however, represented a very real concern for all with loved ones in the Pacific."

The carefully crafted narrative of *The Crossroads* may not have intended to suggest that, although Americans with loved ones in the Pacific had real concerns, they obviously were relatively few in number compared to Americans at large who, unlike the Japanese, were not facing privation and the threat of invasion. However, it is not a stretch to see that the script makes that point. It went on to reveal how closely Japan and the United States resembled each other. "The distance separating Japan and the United States underscored the cultural gulf separating the two societies. Ignorance about the other's culture, combined with racism, desire for revenge, and the strain of total war produced virulent hatred on both sides." And a little later, "Like Americans, the Japanese people viewed their enemies in racist terms."[8]

There is nothing unusual in that theme. The introduction to a book devoted mostly to the Asian perspective on World War II, Korea and Vietnam, has a persistent antiphon along the lines of, yes Americans suffered, followed by, but many more Asians suffered. "Certainly, we do not want to denigrate the traumas of Americans who lost loved ones in these wars or who themselves came back from foreign wars crippled in body or spirit. Nor should the sufferings of those who were prisoners of war (POWs) or missing in action (MIA) be forgotten. (Incidentally, the number of Japanese, Korean, Chinese, and Vietnamese MIAs dwarfs that of the American MIAs)." Although claiming not to denigrate the American experience, and it is true that the number of Asian MIAs outnumbered by far the American, that statement showed the author's unsubtle intent to diminish the American experience.

The alleged equivalence in the war-making of Japan and the United States is not unique to American writers. In the 1990s heated debates erupted in Italy about the suffering inflicted by the Americans during the

Italian Campaign, arguing that, like the Germans, the Americans were guilty of wartime atrocities because American bombings were as bad as the many mass killings by the Germans. Like many other debates in Italy, they were ideologically driven and revealed the anti-American bias of the extreme left and the extreme right. What might be inferred from its remarkable similarity to the domestic practitioners of the art?[9]

That there were prejudiced Americans hardly adds up to an indictment of endemic racism unless one is predisposed to find guilt, and that comes easily to those with the mind set of the script's authors. Terrible things happen in war, with Hiroshima and Nagasaki sharing history with Nanking and Dresden, two cities destroyed by armies of their own race. Although the racist hypothesis is a convenient and seemingly plausible rationale for the assault on Japan, it falters because it lacks genuine evidence to support its conclusion, despite what Professor Michael Sherry called his "relatively simple" explanation, "similar consequences can arise out of different motives and impulses." That is a simplistic explanation, based on the untenable racist hypothesis that is fashionable among revisionist historians.

Would President Roosevelt have sanctioned using the bomb against Japan? There can be no definitive answer, although Professor Alperovitz makes a case, based on the interpretations of Professor Bernstein, that he probably would not have done so. That is because in September 1944 Roosevelt asked whether it should be used against Japan in a meeting with Vannevar Bush, Admiral Leahy, and Churchill's science advisor, Lord Cherwell. Professor Alperovitz also found that McGeorge Bundy claimed "There are several tantalizing hints that Franklin Roosevelt was troubled about the basic question of using the weapon against Japan in a way that his successor never was ... twice in less than a week Roosevelt thought about whether and how to use the bomb." Those are slender reeds on which to rest his case. Insofar as President Roosevelt was concerned his fellow whites, the Germans, many of whom had relatives in the United States, would be the first to feel the brunt of the A-Bomb. According to Joseph Marx, in December 1944, during the Battle of the Bulge, Roosevelt asked General Leslie Groves if work on the atomic bomb could be rushed to stop the German counter offensive and the answer was no. General Groves does not mention such a conversation in his book, *Now It Can Be Told*, but Marx tells us that Roosevelt at least toyed with using the bomb in Europe in 1944 and his testimony is at least as credible as Bundy's "tantalizing hints."[10]

Germany was the home of the basic physics of atomic energy and had a scientific infrastructure for conceiving and designing, and the technical expertise to build an A-Bomb. That sparked the concern of Leo Szilard and Albert Einstein and led to Einstein's letter about the bomb to President Roosevelt in August 1939. That led to the Manhattan Project and a race to beat Germany in developing an A-Bomb. One of the ironies of the war is that Axis anti-Semitism drove Jewish scientists, who urged the bomb's development and then managed its creation, out of Europe and to the United States.

The Allies knew that the Germans were actively attempting to develop an A-Bomb. Eventually Germany might have had an A-bomb had it not been for Hitler's losing interest in the project, and the diversion of industrial capacity to other projects; by November 1944, the Allies were confident that Germany could not produce an atomic bomb. Five years earlier, however, knowing what the Germans could do, and were doing, about developing an A-Bomb, there was urgency for Britain and the United States to get there first with a weapon that could be used against Germany. That was clearly in President Roosevelt's mind in December 1944, when he told Alexander Sachs that he was planning to use the bomb against Germany and Japan if it proved necessary.[11] That point also was made by Stephen Budiansky when he compared the importance of ULTRA with the A-Bomb in shortening the war. "Arguments about ULTRA having shortened the war by several years bump up against the one weapon that defies the strictures against unitary explanations of history: the atomic bomb, which, it should never be forgotten, was built from the start with the intention and expectation that it would be used against Germany."

That an atomic bomb was intended for Germany was confirmed by Bill Barney, a radar operator on the B-29 that accompanied "Bockscar," the aircraft that bombed Nagasaki. During his training, "We had a simulated flight, trainer things. You flew two, three thousand miles, bombardier, myself, navigator. You flew these missions. And they was all in Germany. That's what we based our thinkin' [sic] on. Japan was just timing." For those who still have doubts about the memory of a lowly radar operator, there is the statement of a higher ranking person, the man who commanded the B-29 unit created to carry the atomic bomb. According to General Paul Tibbets, in September 1944 he was directed to assemble an organization that was capable of dropping an atomic weapon on both Germany and Japan.[12]

Finally, after yet another allusion to racism as a driving force behind the bomb's use, *The Crossroads* agreed that the bomb would have been used against Germany. General Groves and others had discussed employing the bomb against Japan first, because the Japanese were judged to be less capable of analyzing a bomb that failed to explode. *The Crossroads* suggested that "Racial stereotypes may have had a role in this attitude, but the consensus of most, if not all, historians is that President Roosevelt would have used the bomb on Germany if such an attack would have been useful in the European war." It was generous of the curators to admit that most historians came to the only conclusion warranted by the evidence, but it was consistent with their approach that racism would be insinuated.[13]

In 1943 and 1944 General Leslie Groves, who headed the Manhattan Project, had discussed first employing the atomic bomb in the Pacific. *The Crossroads* said that was because "the Japanese were judged to be less capable of analyzing a bomb that failed to explode. Racial stereotyping may have had a role in this attitude." It also is possible that, based on his colleagues' knowledge of Japanese science, Groves made a reasonable judgment, but to include that idea would not have reinforced the racism theme in the exhibit. To further drive home its point, the script reminded us that it was not only the Japanese, but also Japanese Americans, blacks and Hispanics who faced racism during the war.

There were readily available reasons other than racial ones for questioning whether Japan could develop an atomic bomb. Although Japan attempted to develop one and had the theory in hand, it lacked many of the basic resources in personnel and material to make any real progress in developing a bomb. In his memoirs, Groves seemed positive when explaining why the Japanese could not develop such a bomb, and did so with no racist allusions: "We did not make any appreciable effort during the war to secure information on atomic developments in Japan. First, and most important, there was not even the remotest possibility that Japan had enough uranium or uranium ore to produce the necessary materials for a nuclear weapon. Also the industrial effort that would be required far exceeded what Japan was capable of. Then, too, discussions with our atomic physicists at Berkeley, who knew the leading Japanese atomic physicists personally, led us to the conclusion that their qualified people were altogether too few in number for them to produce an effective weapon in the foreseeable future." Although confident about this, Groves then hedged, saying, "Finally, it would have been extremely difficult for us to secure and to get out of Japan any information of the type we needed. I hoped that if any sizable program was started, we would get wind of it from one of the various intelligence collecting agencies with which we

maintained liaison. In that event, we would have immediately done everything we could to interfere with their operations."[14]

There is an excellent, detailed account of the Japanese atomic effort
by Professor Dower that would have been invaluable to Groves during the
war. It confirmed not what Groves knew at the time but what he reasonably inferred about Japanese ability to create a bomb. Knowing that fact
years later makes an interesting counterfactual, but it is irrelevant to what
people of necessity acted on at the time. After the war it was learned that
the Japanese effort to develop an A-Bomb was frustrated by the lack of uranium and industrial resources, but the intention was to create a weapon
of mass destruction. Deborah Shapley recounted the efforts of the Japanese scientists and the military's interest in an effort that stalled, but one
it was hoped would assure Japanese victory. Their goal may have been a
chimera from the beginning, but those who regret American use of the
bomb might remember that the Japanese intentions and efforts were no
more altruistic than those of Germany. Dower deplored the timing of Shapley's account about something which was known, at least to scholars, soon
after the war but which had received scant public attention. Thus he considered it xenophobic to reopen the story of Japan's "puny and almost
pathetic" effort to build an A-Bomb. While acknowledging that Japan
would have used an A-Bomb if it had one, in effect he dismissed that
"pathetic" effort to develop a bomb, saying that knowledge "may be com-
forting to those Americans who bear, however lightly, a sense of guilt for
Hiroshima and Nagasaki." That dismissal of Japanese intentions might be
expected from someone who considered Hiroshima an act of genocide.[15]

Today it is only of academic interest to know that Lavrenti Beria, the
head of Stalin's secret police, was responsible for the Soviet atom bomb
project. Soviet development of an A-Bomb was substantially facilitated by
information gleaned by Soviet agents in the United States and Britain. The
independent efforts by the Axis powers to develop an A-Bomb, which their
prior actions show they would not have hesitated to use, receives scant
attention from those who denounce America's use of the bomb. Certainly
Stalin, who sacrificed millions of his fellow Russians to create collective
farms, would not have hesitated to use an A-Bomb on Germany or on
Japan. That Stalin would do so should not end the debate about using the
bomb but it establishes a level playing field for considering the A-Bomb
in the real world of 1945.

Professor Martin Sherwin, an advisor to the exhibit who thought
exhibiting the *Enola Gay* was obscene, nonetheless defended the exhibit.
Apparently he favored sharing atomic information with the Soviets, claiming that information about the bomb was withheld from the Soviets

because of a mania for secrecy about the Manhattan Project. In December 1944, several French scientists who worked in the Canadian section of the Manhattan Project demanded to return to France. On the advice of Secretary Stimson, Roosevelt turned them down because on their return they were expected to discuss their work with Frederic Joliot, a prominent French scientist who was a member of the French Communist Party. Before the war Joliot had been involved in a French effort to develop an atomic bomb. Sherwin lamented that by not allowing them to return to France, Roosevelt lost an opportunity "toward formulating a proposal for the international control of atomic energy. Instead it merely confirmed his determination to keep the Manhattan Project isolated from Soviet-American diplomacy."[16] Apparently Sherwin would not have opposed allowing Joliot to serve as conduit to the Soviets for A-Bomb secrets, but it was grandiose of him to suggest that not allowing the scientists to return to France would frustrate the formulation of a proposal for international control of the atom.

A more prosaic reason for the President's refusal might have been the notoriously lax security of the French. General Charles De Gaulle was not told of the pending Armistice with Italy in September 1943 for that reason, and it also was why his headquarters was not told about the Normandy invasion until it was underway. In each instance General De Gaulle was infuriated, but both times General Eisenhower played the game prudently, knowing that the Germans, as well as the Soviets, had an efficient intelligence service. In 1970 Professor Bernstein shared the opinion of *The New York Times* which said on December 16, 1945, that "The insistence by the inventors of mankind's most horrible weapon on withholding the secret from their ally has produced a most evident reaction in Moscow."[17] Despite the concern of Professor Bernstein and *The New York Times*, Soviet nuclear espionage had already insured that the secret had not been kept from Moscow.

When discussing the atom bomb, Strobe Talbot found, "in the back of the mind of some who had a hand in the attacks on Hiroshima and Nagasaki, another, secondary purpose: to intimidate the Soviet Union and establish the United States as the unchallenged guarantor of the postwar order. In that, America was less successful, for the principal effect on Stalin of the American A-bomb program was to stimulate the Soviet A-Bomb program." Stimulation of the Soviet A-bomb's development after Hiroshima may have advanced their bomb by a few years but Russia was well on the way toward developing its own bomb thanks to the talents of its own scientists, and as Talbot must have known, thanks to the assistance of its agents in the United States. And after 1945, of course, it had the assistance of the German talent it "recruited" to work on the A-bomb in the USSR.[18]

Strobe Talbot's contention that a secondary purpose of the A-Bomb was to intimidate the USSR is a recurrent theme in revisionist writing. According to McGeorge Bundy, however, the claim that impressing the Soviets with the bomb was a major factor in deciding to use it "is false, and the evidence to support it rests on inferences so stretched as to be a discredit to the judgment of those who have argued in this fashion and the credulity of those who have accepted such arguments. There is literally no evidence whatsoever that the timetable for the attack was ever affected by anything except technical and military considerations; there is no evidence that anyone in the direct chain of command from Truman to Stimson to Marshall to Groves ever heard or made any suggestion that either the decision itself or the timing of its execution should be governed by any consideration of its effect on the Soviet Union." Professor Gar Alperovitz was called a principal propagator of this "false conclusion."

In his detailed account of the development of the Soviet atom bomb, David Holloway found that "The work of the bomb group was transformed by information from the United States in the early months of 1945." That was made possible because of information Klaus Fuchs received from David Greenglass who told him about Trinity, its probable yield and when the test would occur. Holloway also said there was some evidence that the Soviets learned about Trinity within a day or two of the test at Alamagordo. If there was any doubt about America's unwitting contribution to the Soviet A-Bomb, it vanished after the demise of the Soviet Union, the limited opening of its archives and the revelations of its former intelligence agents. According to Alexander Fekisov, who was the case officer for Ethel and Julius Rosenberg, "It was thanks to Klaus Fuchs, Theodore Hall, the Cohens, and a few other agents who have not been identified to this day, that the USSR was able to create its own atomic bomb." However, someone more authoritative than Fekisov praised the contribution of "some good people who helped us master the production of nuclear energy faster and to produce our first atomic bomb." According to Nikita Khrushchev, "Since I was present at the talks that Stalin had in a limited circle when he mentioned the Rosenbergs with warmth, I feel it is my duty to speak of them now.... I heard from both Stalin and Molotov that the Rosenbergs were very significant help in accelerating the production of our atomic bomb." It is small wonder that Stalin was noncommital when Truman mentioned the A-Bomb at Potsdam.[19]

For many years Americans appreciated the exotic Japan of Madam Butterfly and Lofcadio Hearn but believed they were superior to the Japanese scientifically and technologically. Cheap and poorly made consumer goods were taken as evidence that the Japanese navy and air force also were third rate. Despite Japanese success in the Russo-Japanese war early in the century, the American and British military had little respect for Japanese strategic thinking and tactics. They also had little respect for the fighting qualities of what they considered the poorly trained and poorly armed Japanese soldier. The Japanese reciprocated by denigrating the Allies, who were to pay dearly for their contempt and underestimation of the bravery and ingenuity of their adversary. In one of the few books with an in depth exploration of the Japanese military, Edward J. Drea explained that the 1920s and 1930s were "formative decades that witnessed the creation of the new doctrines, tactics and strategy the imperial forces used to fight World War II. Training, education, and indoctrination of the previous two decades created a well disciplined, professionally led emperor's army whose willingness to fight to the last man became an enduring legacy of the global conflict." When the war began the Allies knew too little about that army, and today the revisionists underestimate or ignore how inevitably that influenced the decisions of Allied leadership.

However, for as long as battles have been recorded, contempt for an enemy has been common. That contempt need not be based on the enemy's race. The British and Americans were contemptuous of the martial spirit of the Italians, considering them good tenors but poor fighters. In the summer of 1943 during a conversation with Prime Minister Churchill, Secretary of War Stimson said, "the American people do not hate the Italians but took them rather as a joke as fighters." Another administration member, Secretary of the Interior Harold Ickes, recalled President Roosevelt saying on June 9, 1940, "so long as Italian soldiers could advance they could keep advancing. Once they were stopped, they were through, and if the line were ever turned, they would run like rabbits." Churchill had a poor impression of the Japanese, referring to them as "the Wops of the East," while Sir Alexander Cadogan of the Foreign Office referred to Italians as "dirty icecreamers." In May 1941 the British Chiefs of Staff considered the Japanese military standards were not comparable even to the Italians while the British Joint Intelligence Committee dismissed the operational value of the Japanese air force as "probably akin to that of the Italians." When the same is said about enemies of different races, which is prejudice and which is racism? That prejudiced attitude was pervasive in the British and

American military and resulted in the failure to make appropriate use of more than a million veteran Italian sailors, soldiers and airmen in Italy between September 1943 and May 1945. Limited to a token combat role, the Italians fought bravely but many more could have replaced Allied troops in the front lines, and taken casualties instead of the Allied troops.[20]

Professor Bernstein argued that it was not hard for decision makers to target the Japanese because, "For Truman, and most of his associates, American lives and purposes were very important, and Japanese lives were not. Such nationalistic thinking did not distinguish policy makers from the bulk of rank-and-file Americans, who also defined US lives as far more important than enemy lives." It is not hard to imagine that the Japanese thought the same way about Japanese lives, but the point of Bernstein's statement is the callousness of a nationalistic America, contemptuous of the lives of its enemies.

Whether he intended it or not, some readers might wonder about Professor Dower's intimating that the striking difference in the number of deaths of Japanese and Americans in island battles was evidence of American desire to wreak vengeance without mercy on their hated enemies. He reported that about 30,000 Japanese died on Saipan, almost ten times the number of American deaths, while on Tinian between 8,000 and 10,000 Japanese died compared to about 400 Americans. Iwo Jima saw 6,000 American deaths compared to between 20,000 to 23,000 Japanese deaths. Dower noted that the Japanese were ordered to fight to the death on Guam where between 8,000 and 10,000 died at a cost of 1,400 Allied lives. He did not mention that what happened at Guam was Imperial Army policy and the context for fighting elsewhere. The comparisons are impressive evidence of how the Japanese military sacrificed the lives of its men in pointless battles to the death. In the European Theater, when the situation demanded, adversaries generally surrendered and often survived. Japanese soldiers were denied that option, which accounts for the disproportionate Japanese losses. The ferocity of Japanese resistance on the islands required fierce counter measures, but when men indoctrinated to fight to the death ignored appeals to surrender, the Allies had no alternative other than to accommodate them.

When portraying attitudes toward racial differences during the war, Dower explained how liberal critics of racism and antiracist academics attempted to provide a more balanced and empirical analysis of Japanese national character, "Always aware that biased perceptions of the Japanese were part of the larger problem of American and English racism in general." Although such an analysis of Japanese culture and society could help to explain the behavior of its military, it had no operational value in 1945. The implication that anthropological and sociological analysis of Japanese culture could have helped the United States to wage a different kind of war in the Pacific makes little sense in serious history.[21]

Debates about using the A-Bomb began soon after the war, centering on what happened to Hiroshima, a seacoast city with a large port. A book by John Hersey painted a vivid and horrible picture of what happened there on August 6, 1945. Hiroshima had a population of about 280,000 to 290,000 persons plus about 40,000 military. In addition to its war industries it housed the naval headquarters of the fleet that attacked Pearl Harbor and the headquarters of the Japanese 2nd Army, which commanded the defense of southern Japan. It also held an army ordnance depot and several other military depots, was an important communication center and had railroad marshaling yards. As an assembly area for troops in 1945, the 145th, 205th, and 230th infantry divisions were activated in Hiroshima. The Japanese Army general staff used Hiroshima as its headquarters to direct the defense of Kyushu against the impending American invasion. According to Richard Rhodes, Hiroshima was not, as Truman said in his Potsdam diary, a "purely military" target, but Rhodes did affirm mildly, "It was not without responsibility, however, in serving the war." Indeed, the unfortunate city was substantially responsible for serving the Japanese war effort beyond the fact that it housed 40,000 military and had industries that were military targets. Despite blockade and the shortage of raw materials, the United States Strategic Bombing Survey found that in July 1945, Hiroshima's production of war materials was at 85 percent of its peak production.

The constant refrain that the A-Bomb was deliberately used against non-combatants, and because of racism, implies that the President's decision ignored the recommendation of his Interim Committee about military targets. But according to David Holloway, "The deliberations of the Interim Committee provide crucial evidence on the thinking behind American policy. By asking how, not whether, the atomic bomb should be used against Japan, the committee proceeded on the assumption that the bomb would be used against Japan when it was ready. This was an assumption that Truman had inherited from Roosevelt and, as Professor Bernstein has argued persuasively, it was an assumption that neither he nor the senior members of his administration questioned. The fact that there was extensive discussion within the administration about the impact of the bomb on relations with the Soviet Union should not obscure the fact that the primary motive for using the bomb against Japan was to bring the war to a speedy end." Another careful student of what happened said the following about James Byrnes, who played such a prominent role in the deliberation of the committee. According to David Robertson, "Byrnes never doubted the willingness of the Japanese soldiers and civilians to fight to their last old man or young boy. His certitude that the Japanese people would be more 'fanatical' in their resistance unless shocked by the use of the atomic bomb was not racist, as a postwar generation of revisionist American historians would claim; contrary to the assumptions of some revisionists, Byrnes could better understand the motivation of the Japanese resistance because he was a southerner." Robertson then gave a credible explanation of why someone from South Carolina born shortly after the Civil War would remember the unremitting resistance of the Confederacy.

The Interim Committee was a high level group appointed by President Truman to advise him on the use of the bomb. It had discussed and rejected a demonstration for the Japanese, although David Robertson believed that it was too briefly considered. The committee recommended that the bomb be used against Japan as soon as possible and only where war plants or military installations were located. Both Hiroshima and Nagasaki met the criteria. The recommendation to use the bomb against military installations and war plants would not exclude civilian areas because all the primary targets were surrounded by the homes of workers and other civilian facilities, which by that time, in both theaters, had been bombed by the Axis partners, including Japan, and the Allies. Although Professor Alperovitz asked "why urban populations had to be attacked and why a second city destroyed," his researchers easily would have found that war materials were manufactured in dispersed, often small shops and plants inevitably located, and some might say hidden, in residential areas for their workers and often near transportation facilities.[22]

Then he might have compared the situation of Japanese cities during the war with that of Chicago. During World War II Chicago was home to a large army headquarters and naval pilots were trained at a suburban airport and practiced carrier landings on Lake Michigan. A large war plant producing torpedoes was located in a residential suburb of Chicago, while an important factory producing instruments for the Air Force was in a residential area in the city. So were a major aircraft engine factory and the Hawthorne Plant of Western Electric, at the time perhaps the largest producer of communications equipment in the country, while the largest army supply and procurement facility was in a residential neighborhood. That says nothing about the host of small factories and machine shops committed to war production that were in residential areas of the city. The city's major airport was in a residential area, and so were the nation's largest rail marshaling yards, and some of the nation's largest steel mills were close to a residential area. Only two large munitions plants had been located in farmland at a distance from cities in the region. All would be considered important and legitimate military targets by all the combatants, and if attacked, except for the munitions plants, inevitably there would have been "collateral damage." Unfortunately, Japanese cities shared the same combination of military facilities that made significant contributions to their nation's war effort and, as in Chicago and other cities, were located near civilian homes.

Although not directly alleging racism as a reason for targeting Japan, Professor Bernstein sought to persuade his readers that the bomb was to be targeted on Japan, not Germany. "American leaders assumed that the bomb would be a legitimate weapon in the war ... they slowly came to define the target as Japan, not Germany, and to plan to use the weapon on a city, not a purely military installation." The words "slowly came to define" insinuate that Japan became the preferred target when Germany was defeated, not because of timing (with the bomb untested), but because of racism. He also did this when asserting that JCS estimates were that "only between about 20,000 and 46,000" deaths would have happened during an invasion of Japan. "Such pre-Hiroshima estimates could not deter the use of the A-bomb, because it was deemed a legitimate weapon in a just war against a hated enemy, who was also yellow." After thus affirming the importance of racism in the decision, he continued, "Race did not however, shape the decision. No policymaker wanted to risk even a few thousand American lives to save many more Japanese lives.." Professor Bernstein conceded that "Indeed it is difficult to believe that any major World War II nation that had the bomb would have chosen not to use it in 1945 against an enemy." In addition, "it undoubtedly would have been used against Germany had the bomb been ready much sooner."[23] The disclaimers hardly overcome the repetition of his pervasive theme of racism. Finally, after leaving the impression that racism drove the decision to use the A-bomb against Japan, along with most revisionists *The Crossroads* acknowledged that the A-Bomb would have been used against Germany. Because Germany surrendered before a bomb was ready, the matter became moot.

However, the insinuation that racism motivated the decision to make Japan the A-Bomb target lingered to poison the historical record.

America's "war of vengeance" was supposed to be driven by racism, according to Ronald Takaki, who imputed racism to President Truman, although he presented no evidence to support that claim. Surely after diligent searching in the archives, if there was evidence that major policy makers in Washington were racists it would be well documented by historians and widely publicized. But there is no evidence that Secretaries Stimson and Hull, General Marshall and Admiral King, who played significant roles in directing the conduct of the war were racists. President Roosevelt and Harry Hopkins, often considered his "eminence grise," were not racists, and many of their strident critics hated them for not sharing such ideas. One should not ignore the influence of Mrs. Eleanor Roosevelt, who many considered the conscience of the administration on such matters. She was known for her advocacy for minorities and the poor long before her husband became president and spoke for them during FDR's administration. That the nation and the military harbored racists is incontrovertible, but that is far from justifying calling the war itself a race war.

VI

The Question of Casualties

One of the most contentious issues in the debate over dropping the A-bomb is whether it prevented an invasion of Japan, and if so, how many American lives may have been saved because of the decision to drop the bomb. Its importance in the *Enola Gay* controversy is shown by the fact that a dispute over casualty figures was the straw that broke the camel's back for Director Harwit. That is why this chapter, and the one following, spend considerable time sorting out casualty estimates. An invasion of Japan was planned under the overall code name DOWNFALL, which was to begin with the invasion of the island of Kyushu on November 1, 1945, under the code name OLYMPIC. That would be followed, if necessary, by the invasion of the island of Honshu on March 1, 1946, under the code name CORONET. The final assault on Imperial Japan would involve as many as five million men in the Allied forces.

The idea of an invasion was not pulled out of thin air in 1945. After lengthy study, in July 1944, the U. S. Joint Chiefs of Staff had agreed that an invasion would be necessary to defeat Japan; then in the following September the British-American Combined Joint Chiefs of Staff approved the concept. Unaware of the A-Bomb and familiar with what the Navy and Air Force proposed, and also their limitations, the chiefs considered an invasion the best way to end the war. It should be remembered that before Trinity Admiral William Leahy, President Truman's close advisor, remarked about the A-Bomb in the presence of Truman and Vannevar Bush, "That is the biggest fool thing that we have ever done. The bomb will never go off, and I speak as an expert in explosives." The Admiral was not the only one to have doubts about the A-Bomb. That is part of the context in which to examine estimates of casualties as high as 500,000 to a million that supposedly served as a justification for using the bomb. On the other hand casualty estimates of about 40,000 to 65,000, and even less by some revisionists, argue that the bomb was unnecessary.

It is unfortunate that too many of the discussions of Pacific war casualties ignore how ending the war saved the lives of countless other soldiers, sailors and airmen in the Allied forces, as well as civilians in China, Korea, Burma, Indonesia and elsewhere who were at risk from the Japanese military, as well as Japanese civilians also at risk because of their military. It should not be forgotten that the United Nations estimated that the number of Indonesians who were killed or died because of the Japanese occupation of Java was three million, while another million died on the outer islands.[1] Nor should it be discounted that Japanese occupation there and elsewhere ended because of Hiroshima and Nagasaki. Any debate over potential casualties if there was an invasion should keep in mind that the Japanese still had more than 2,000,000 troops on the home islands at the surrender.

More or less plausible sources can be found for high and low estimates but there is no way to be absolutely certain about the estimated invasion casualty figures because they are based on figures prepared for different purposes at different times by different people. That should not be surprising because in the normal course of planning, information from various sources would be integrated, or perhaps discarded as new facts appeared. Therefore, when considering how many American casualties might have occurred had Japan been invaded, one is confronted by several possible scenarios and has to try to reach a reasonable, probable estimate. Ideally, this should be done not as an apologia for either side of the argument, but to get the facts as straight as possible long after 1945. A capable treatment of this matter is found in Richard Frank's chapter on casualties.

The Crossroads accepted the conclusions of those who believed that the casualty estimates for an invasion were overstated. "Many analysts continue to argue that the bomb ended the war quickly and saved lives— even if the American deaths in an invasion of Japan would have been significantly lower than the postwar estimates." It should be noted that by referring only to "postwar estimates" *The Crossroads* ignored the fact that those estimates also were known in the spring and summer of 1945.[2] Richard Kohn, who was an advisor to the NASM, said that the *Enola Gay* controversy became "mired in a senseless contest over the number of casualties expected in the planned invasion of Japan — a symbol of whether the bombing was necessary." In June 1994 Kohn had explained to Harwit that the casualty argument was lacking in context; the real issue was the campaign, not the invasion. "With Japan prepared to fight all-out indefinitely

... the casualties would have been just tremendous on both sides, and everybody at the time knew it." Whether the differences about casualties were senseless remains to be seen, but the energy with which exhibit defenders attacked the allegedly fabricated high casualty figures suggests that they, at least, did not consider casualty estimates an unimportant issue.

The alleged duplicity of the government when using casualty estimates was outlined in stark terms by Laura Hein and Mark Selden. "One way in which history has been silenced is through the official manipulation of the story of the decision to drop the bombs. We now know that bomb memories have been officially constructed in a remarkably consistent way within each country for fifty years. The research of Monica Braw, Barton Bernstein, and James Hershberg has revealed U.S. officials' preoccupation in the late 1940s with combating negative Japanese and American reactions to the use of atomic bombs. Not only did they suppress unfavorable publicity and maintain a U.S. monopoly on nuclear research, they also deliberately published false information and disinformation as a means to defend the moral legitimacy of the U.S. decision to use the bomb. The calculated inflation of the projected American death toll in a land invasion of Japan is the best-documented, but not the only, example of deception. It is no coincidence that the final collapse of negotiations over the *Enola Gay* exhibit occurred when the curators were forced to deal with the discrepancy between official casualty projections, published following the surrender, and the far lower unpublished ones that military planners used before the surrender. Critics of the exhibit, fearful that lower U.S. casualty figures would undermine the official case for using the bombs, cried 'revisionism' to undermine the authority of those who returned to primary sources to challenge official mythologies. The exposure of the history of the invention of 'better' numbers undercuts the credibility of government, making official spokespersons seem deceitful, politically motivated, and deeply cynical in their treatment of Americans as well as other people."[3] Such statements help to set the stage for this essay's discussion of the casualty controversy. However, before examining the question of possible invasion casualties, one might note that Professor Gar Alperovitz would have neatly removed casualties from the table by arguing that in April 1945, Washington knew that "an initial November invasion landing on the island of Kyushu (was) only a remote possibility."[4] Although admitting that contingency planning was necessary, Alperovitz believed that Soviet entry into the war and allowing the retention of the Emperor would have induced Japanese surrender. Ergo, neither an invasion nor the A-Bomb was necessary and the matter of casualties was irrelevant.

It is unclear whether Professor Alperovitz was aware that, until July 16, there was no certainty that the A-Bomb would work. Among the military who knew about it, there were doubts that it would work, and that was a reason why a demonstration for the Japanese was rejected. Before the Trinity test at Alamagordo the expected power of the explosion, if it worked, was estimated to be between 500 to 1500 tons of TNT. The actual power was a surprise to almost everyone involved in the Manhattan Project. That awesome power was, of course, unknown during the spring and early summer of 1945. It would be obvious to scholars who examined the massive military build-up in the Pacific that the invasion of Okinawa and the increased B-29 raids on Japanese cities were more than mere contingency planning. If an invasion was an alternative, how many ships, tanks, aircraft, supplies, munitions and men would be needed to bring it off? There were precedents for answering those questions, as well as how many replacements would be needed for casualties. As a result the "contingency" buildup was enormous. Exactly how "remote" was the possibility of an invasion may be deduced from the contingency planning mentioned by Professor Alperovitz. The June 16 Joint Staff Planners report that was prepared for the president tells about the overwhelming number of naval ships allocated to the invasion of Kyushu. The list referring to naval forces alone included 107 aircraft carriers of various sizes. The scale of that commitment of resources to the invasion has long been known, which leads to the question, why was it ignored by scholars familiar with the archival and other sources of information about events in the summer of 1945?

Commenting on the role of signals intelligence in U.S. military planning, Douglas MacEachin said, "Obviously the importance of the bomb in concluding the war was of such magnitude that it is not plausible to examine intelligence related to invasion planning without addressing the question of whether and to what extent that same intelligence might have influenced the decision to drop the bomb. It also is not plausible to argue that the military calculus concerning an invasion of Japan does not bear directly on evaluations of the bomb decision."

At a meeting with the President on April 23, 1945, General Marshall was keenly aware, according to Ed Cray, of the "increasing fury of Japanese resistance as they drew closer to the home islands. He also was aware of the planners' estimates that the invasion of Japan would cost as many as 250,000 American casualties." So the Joint Chiefs were provided with an educated guess as to the human cost of an invasion. At the time there were different estimates about the number of casualties, some believing the estimates too high; other certain they were too low. After the A-Bomb the matter became academic, both literally and figuratively, until revisionists began arguing that Truman exaggerated the number for his own purposes.

A notable example of this would be in Truman's memoirs a decade after the war: "General Marshall told me that it might cost half a million American lives to force the enemy's surrender on his home grounds."[4] That contrasts with his earlier statement in 1953, in a letter to Professor James Cate, that at Potsdam just after Trinity, General Marshall told him that in his opinion "an invasion would cost at a minimum one quarter of a million casualties, and might cost as much as a million, on the American side alone, with an equal number of the enemy." In the hand written draft of the letter to Cate dated December 31, 1952, Truman had written "¼ million casualties would be the minimum cost as well as an equal number of the enemy."[5]

Professor Bernstein described how the President's four page hand-written draft was reviewed by members of his staff, who suggested certain changes to conform to Secretary Stimson's version of larger casualty figures, resulting in what Bernstein called "the president's very dubious claim." Bernstein considered the hand written draft authentic, and because of the changes, that the letter sent to Cate was a construct. Further, Professor Bernstein claimed that General Marshall never suggested that the invasion would cost more than "about a quarter of a million casualties and, therefore, under fifty thousand American dead."[6]

Maceachin found that an enormous naval force was committed to the invasion. "By March 1, 1946 the following number of major combat ships are scheduled to be fully operational in the Pacific Fleet: 10 (Battleships); 13 (Old Battleships); 26 CA (Heavey Cruisers); 33 CL (Light Cruisers); 2 CB (Large Cruisers); 8 CL (AA) (Light Cruisers) (Antiaircraft); 2 CVB (Aircraft Carriers (Large); 22 CV (Aircraft Carriers); 9 CVL (Aircraft Carriers (Small); 74 CVE (43 combat) (Aircraft Carriers Escort); 364 DD (Destroyers); 326 DE (Destroyer Escort Vessels); 189 SS (Submarines). The above figures make no allowance for attrition. Three months after the Kyushu operation it is estimated that approximately 10 percent will either have been lost or still undergoing repairs to damage received in this operation. Of the operational ships in service 75 percent will normally be constantly available for any single operation. Others will be either undergoing operational repairs or be otherwise employed. It is estimated that approximately 3,600 carrier-based aircraft wl01 be available on 1 March 1946" (MacEachin, op. cit., Document 5, *Tab E*).

Relying on staff members or others to check facts is not unusual. Professors have graduate assistants do it routinely. That someone as busy as Truman would forget who attended a meeting months earlier, or an exact number, should surprise nobody. Even a professor might not remember everyone who attended a faculty meeting months earlier. In an article in *Diplomatic History,* Professor Bernstein thanked nine individuals for discussions of issues, as well as an unspecified number of persons in two seminars at Stanford University. Undoubtedly those discussions helped Bernstein clarify his thoughts and led to the kind of revision, if not revisionism, of which he accuses Truman.

That Truman's recollection about casualties was "dubious" is a plausible interpretation of the fact he erred, although a less paranoiac one is just as plausible, that he remembered being told something about numbers on different occasions, or by different aides. Without definitive evidence one way or another, Professor Bernstein overreaches when he attaches the worst possible interpretation to events. He might remember what General Eisenhower told the historian Douglas Freeman, who suggested the desirability of documenting his decisions. Tactfully, the general replied, "I am unable to say whether or not the records of my office are sufficiently explicit to establish, in every case, reasons for decision taken ... since some are made under circumstances where no secretaries are present, preliminary discussions do not find their way to paper."

Insistence on a neat archival paper trail may seem to add to the historian's pretension to accuracy and authenticity but it ignores the reality that not everything in life is or can be documented, whether on a clay tablet or somewhere in the National Archives. Mark Stoler reported that Roosevelt "blew up" when General John Deane, the Joint Chiefs of Staff secretary, attempted to keep a written record of proceedings. No notes were taken at meetings with the President and thus the precious paper trail does not exist, to the dismay of many historians who trust no other source. In December 1945, when he was questioned about Pearl Harbor by a Congressional Committee, even General George Marshall had to admit that he could not recall all the events of December 1941. "I think it is not unduly remarkable that I would not remember the detailed conversations and the frequency of conferences [or] at which one we discussed this, and at which one we discussed that." Revisionists might have conceded as much to Truman if they were not certain from the start about his mendacity.

As the European war ended, the Pentagon was aware of the limited manpower it had to deal with Japan. According to the Biennial Report of the Chief of Staff, "In May 1945 we had only two divisions that had never been committed to action — the 13th Airborne Division in Europe and the 98th Infantry Division in Hawaii." When that fact is coupled with the politically unpopular transferring of divisions from Europe to the Pacific and the increased drafting of 18-year-olds, the limited number of experienced troops to serve in the Pacific should be obvious. It also should be obvious that knowledge about these facts would condition Pentagon and White House thinking about how to deal with Japan.

What also should be kept in mind as the matter of casualties is considered is that, unlike Hitler and Stalin, casualties were of constant concern to Truman and General Marshall. Both remembered the hideous number of casualties in World War I. As 1945 proceeded, according to Ed Cray, "The shortage of replacements would vex them until VE Day, for even as his army grew, what General Marshall later called 'the terrible measure of casualties' also increased. The chief of staff took to sending graphic casualty charts in color to the president as a reminder of the human cost of implementing geopolitical policies. 'I tried to keep before him all the time the casualty results because you get hardened to these things and you have to be very careful to keep them always in the forefront of your mind.' Theirs was a concern, if not a preoccupation, about casualties at a time when the army was inducting 18-year-old draftees and giving them eight weeks for training before sending them into combat. General Eisenhower complained about this practice but Congress had left the military no alternative. Having lost his own stepson in Italy, General Marshall was no stranger to the meaning of casualties." Admiral Leahy noted that the president wanted to know the number of men and ships needed for an invasion: "He wants an estimate of the time required and an estimate of the loses in killed and wounded that will result from an invasion of Japan proper.... It is his intention to make his decision on the campaign with the purpose of economizing to the maximum extent possible in the loss of American lives. Economy in the use of time and in money cost is comparatively unimportant."[7]

J. Samuel Walker was a friend of the exhibit who claimed, "Scholars have not provided a single explanation for why former policymakers felt compelled to exaggerate by several orders of magnitude the estimated casualties of an invasion of Japan. Presumably they believed that citing a huge number made the decision to use the bomb appear unassailable, or at a minimum, less vulnerable to ambiguities that smaller (and more accurate) estimates might have created." But either the "scholars" did not search, or they ignored evidence that the large estimates existed in the spring of 1945, making Walker's argument meaningless. It raises the question why scholars continue to drag such red herrings across the archival trail when they could and should know that the estimates existed. With regard to the presumed smaller number, Geoffrey S. Smith found that "a mere forty-six thousand Americans would have died or been injured in an invasion of Japan." Statistics are abstract and antiseptic in the aftermath of war, which is why Geoffrey Smith could refer to a "mere forty-six thousand" casualties. Professor Bernstein joined him, saying that he and Professor Martin Sherwin had not "dwelled on the small but painful American losses that might have occurred if the war had lingered on a few more weeks or even a month or so after mid August in 1945." How small and painful those losses might be was not worth dwelling on in view of their anticipated, but risky, gain had the A-Bomb not been used and the war drifted to an end.

That dispassionate attitude toward casualties can be compared to what happened near the end of the war in the European Theater after Operation Sunrise. Aware the war was lost, on March 8, 1945, SS General Karl Wolff, who commanded Waffen SS forces in Italy, approached Allen Dulles, the head of the office of Strategic Services (OSS) in Switzerland, to negotiate the surrender of German forces in Italy. Stalin was furious when he learned of Wolff's approach, suspecting that an easing of pressure in Italy would strengthen German resistance in the east, and accused Roosevelt of bad faith. Roosevelt ordered contact with Wolff ended but he made another approach on April 25th that led to the surrender of the German forces on May 2, 1945. Critics of "Sunrise" contend that it fed Soviet suspicion of American motives while Gabriel Kolko, a prominent revisionist, saw it as politically inspired and having contributed to the Cold War.

Others argue that "Sunrise" had a minimal humanitarian impact, but William Casey, who had been in the OSS during the war, thought that the war might have ended weeks or days earlier and saved many lives. When Wolff first approached Dulles the Allies were assaulting the formidable Gothic Line and intense fighting continued for another six weeks. The troops who fought and died in the Apennines during those weeks ought not be discounted by those who are comfortable when dealing authoritatively with statistics and high policy from a distance. The same is true of discussions about ending the Pacific war.[8]

Writing about what he considered the strange myth of half a million American lives saved, Rufus Miles argued that the two bombs saved no more than 20,000 lives, and perhaps none. There were, in his opinion, viable alternatives to the bombs that could have ended the war with few casualties. One was a negotiated peace, and Miles noted that the Joint Staff Planners had suggested a definition of unconditional surrender that the

Japanese could understand, that would have brought surrender, but for some reason Miles did not add that the Joint Chiefs had considered and rejected that idea, a fact that the reader should be aware of whether or not one agrees with the rejection. Another alternative was intensified conventional bombing and blockade, based upon knowledge that the Japanese situation was desperate, or seemed so to the Allies, and seemed to be confirmed after the war by the Strategic Bombing Survey.

The Navy and the Air Force each knew that their unimpeded efforts could end the war without an invasion and did not want to be diverted from their favored strategy. The inherent rivalry between them appeared, for example, in late 1944 when the Air Force was asked to assign B-29s to lay mines to aid the blockade of Japan. Craven and Cate reported that after much foot dragging the Air Force "embarked on a B-29 mining program, grudgingly, because the Navy lacked suitable aircraft the situation was not wholly unlike that which had taken the AAF into antisubmarine work in 1941. Evidently the air planners did not envisage the extraordinary success that was to follow, but it is questionable whether they could have acted differently if they had. Like the Navy advocates of a blockade, they hoped to win the war without an invasion; their weapons and their doctrine had been conceived in terms of an attack on industrial targets, however, and in their view any air operations over Japan, bombing or mining. demanded first the destruction of the sources of Japan's air power. This had been the experience in Germany, and the opposition to Nimitz came, it must be realized, when the overworked 73rd Bombardment Wing was taking heavy losses. To begin laying mines in January would have disrupted the bombardment program, as yet unsuccessful but going through a necessary period of adjustment, and in objecting to this Hansel and Arnold's officers were not unreasonable. Yet in light of the spectacular results of B-29 mining operations later, it is ironical that the decision to cooperate with Nimitz came from the logic that often colored inter-service comity during the war: the fear that otherwise the AAF might allow a possible major usage of long-range aircraft to develop, by default, into a matter of special interest to the Navy." Somehow the services had to rise above such understandable but essentially dysfunctional efforts to maintain control of turf, and that they did was the genius of General Marshall.

Despite attempts by revisionists to obfuscate this matter of alternatives to an invasion, the record is clear that continued bombing and blockade had been considered and rejected for substantial military reasons. Although General Marshall, whose strategic sense guided most of America's participation in the war, was aware of an invasion's potential cost, he was convinced that ultimately an invasion was necessary. That conviction was not a ukase but a reasoned decision after the other services had their say. With perfect hindsight, however, Miles believed that, had that option been selected, American casualties would not have exceeded 5,000. He did not say where that number came from. The third alternative Miles discussed was the invasion of Kyushu, which was presented to the President on July 18, 1945. During the meeting, he said, "all projections of losses were in terms of casualties. No figures on expected deaths were presented or discussed." That was a strange comment because the participants knew, if Miles did not, that the word casualties included those killed, as well as those wounded and missing.

Miles went on to say that the War Department plan suggested strongly that, by the time southern Kyushu was in Allied hands, Japan would surrender. He did not mention, however, that invading southern Kyushu was not viewed optimistically by the planners, who said, "it would be a pure gamble that the Japanese would admit defeat under such conditions." Miles also claimed that the cost of Kyushu would be 31,000 casualties and seven or eight thousand deaths. Although he noted that the casualties for the first thirty days would be 31,000, a moment later he said that the Army ground forces had persuaded the air corps and navy to think that the conquest of Kyushu could be accomplished at a tolerable cost — 31,000 casualties, and 7,000–8,000 deaths. However, the JCS plan did not imply that the "conquest of Kyushu" could be accomplished in a month. The 31,000 figure was for the first 30 days of an invasion expected to last several months.

The upshot for Miles was that *if* Japan held out beyond November 1, 1945, *if* Kyushu was invaded successfully, *if* Russia entered the war in August and engaged the Japanese in Korea and Manchuria, and *if* at that point Japan surrendered, American deaths "almost surely would have been not more than 20,000 and probably less than 15,000." There would be 5,000 for air and naval losses before the invasion, not more than 10,000 during the invasion of Kyushu, and 5,000 for unforeseen losses. No source was given for these small casualty figures.

Having proved to his own satisfaction that the numbers Truman and others used were mythical, Miles said they found them necessary because of a "subconscious compulsion to persuade themselves and the American public that horrible as the atomic bombs were, their use was actually humane, inasmuch as it saved a huge number of lives." After that psychic assessment, Miles said that his analysis pointed strongly to the conclusion that dropping the two bombs saved "with a high degree of probability, not more than 20,000 and quite probably considerably less." And further, "The question for the military and civilian officials was not whether the bomb should be used, but how. The legitimacy to gain a quick end of the war was taken for granted. That this was the most powerful single influence in the decision to use the bomb seems highly probable."

Miles ended by saying that to fault Truman for his decision would be to ignore the circumstances and atmosphere that surrounded the decision. Instead one should ask why the circumstances and atmosphere allowed the use of nuclear weapons, and he concluded that the premise that the bombs would save a large number of American lives was false. The case Miles built for that conclusion would seem persuasive only if one glides over all the speculation that is the foundation of his counterfactual argument. Putting the most optimistic gloss upon some statistics and ignoring others, minimizing the importance of the Japanese buildup on Kyushu and taking a month's casualties as representative of a campaign expected to last several months are only a few of the missteps that led to his conclusion.[9] In what can best be characterized as an extended counterfactual, Miles wove together possibilities and so-called probabilities, numbers drawn from who knows where and conclusions based upon psychologizing that the editors of *International Security* found plausible.

The path Miles explored was followed by Peter Maslowski who also considered that Truman played a numbers game. Former President Herbert Hoover's estimate of high casualties in an invasion in a memo prepared in late May 1945 for President Truman, was noted as having been rebuffed as excessive by the Pentagon, but strangely, the significance of having his estimates brought to Marshall's and Truman's attention was ignored. Also, there was the assumption that the first scenario mentioned in the June 15, JWPC report to the Joint Chiefs, the invasion of southern Kyushu followed by the Tokyo Plain, would have ended the war with "a total of only 193,000" casualties. As did others, Maslowski overlooked the JWPC caveat that it would be a gamble that the Japanese would surrender before the Tokyo Plain was reached. If there was no surrender the third scenario, which was an advance on the Tokyo Plain, would have led to higher casualties.[10]

Did the exhibit's critics play a "numbers game," using Truman's allegedly inflated figures to discredit the exhibit? Were those numbers another of the myths treasured by the exhibit's critics? If that was the case one must ask why historians Barton Bernstein, Ronald Takaki, Martin Sherwin, Rufus Miles and others made President Truman's allegedly exaggerated numbers a major issue when indicting the United States for its use of the

A-Bomb? Obviously it was because, in their mind, Truman used the public's fear of heavy casualties to justify the A-Bomb's use. If Truman had "grossly exaggerated" the number of casualties as Martin Sherwin claimed, then more sinister reasons such as intimidating the Soviets or justifying the billions spent on the Manhattan project were behind Truman's decision to drop the bomb.

Questioning the relevance of the number of estimated casualties gets one off a serious stumbling block. If one assumes that Truman dissembled, and used the bomb for diplomatic or political reasons and concocted a plausible rationale after the fact, then the reasons for the number of potential casualties can be ignored. Essentially that was the approach taken by Professor Alperovitz, who found Truman's aides as much concerned with containing the Soviets as they were with ending the war. Roland Takaki also discounted the numbers argument, finding that estimates submitted to the Joint Chiefs of Staff belied Truman's numbers.

The stumbling block, of course, is whether the number had genuine meaning at some point in the decision making process and either did, or could have, influenced the thinking of Truman and his advisors. Therefore, the numbers cannot be casually dismissed as irrelevant, whether or not they were solely determinative in the final decision made after the A-Bomb was tested and found to be operational. Honest scholarship requires ascertaining whether the numbers Truman mentioned existed and whether they could have influenced the thinking of the Joint Chiefs of Staff and played a role in the President's decision to proceed with invasion planning and the use of the bomb.

Sherwin, Bernstein, Takaki and others relied on the numbers found in the Joint War Plans Committee (JWPC) report of June 15, 1945, to contradict Truman.[11] But they misconstrued those numbers. They also ignored later estimates that the number of Japanese defenders on Kyushu had increased so quickly and significantly that the June 15 figures were obsolete before the A-Bomb was tested. Had Trinity been a fiasco the invasion of Kyushu would have reaped many more casualties than estimated on June 15, 1945.

Thus because the number of estimated casualties has been hotly disputed it merits careful consideration. Before proceeding, however, it will be useful to examine what is meant by "casualties." The word includes those killed in action, those wounded in action, and the missing. Projected casualty figures will not include the deaths from severe wounds that occur some time after a battle. There often is confusion between the terms deaths and casualties. Thus, if the figure of 500,000 casualties was mentioned by President Truman it may have been understood by some people as the number of anticipated deaths, and not the overall number of persons taken out of action because they were dead, wounded or missing.[12] Because military operations produce casualties, planners must be realistic in estimates that are based on experience, so there will be enough supplies and replacements, and sufficient medical services, etc., during a battle. The assault on Japan was a massive undertaking that was estimated to require as many as three million Americans plus other Allied military. When the war with Germany ended in May, troops began to be transferred from Europe to the Pacific and large numbers of draftees were inducted. Both of these moves posed serious domestic political problems for an administration facing a Congress and public tired of the war. The same was true in Britain, which had been at war for six years. Under the circumstances of the summer of 1945, that had to be factored into any decision made by Allied leaders. The A-Bomb met the requirement to end the war before the Allies lost the will to persevere and pushed to end war by compromising the almost hard won goal of ending Japanese power and domination of Asia.

When writing about the Pacific war it is important to remember that the United States was not alone in this endeavor. The attack on Japan was to involve coordination with the British and other Allied naval and land forces in order to prevent the enemy moving forces into the home islands. Although the United States played a primary role in the Pacific, as the war was ending the British, French, Dutch, Australians and Canadians sought roles in the attack on Japan. There were post-war political as well as military issues involved, and John Skates has a good account of the negotiations that went on between the Allies. It may seem strange that the United States was hesitant to have the involvement of Allied forces unless one considers the serious logistical, communications and other problems involved in any joint operation, let alone one as massive as the planned invasion. As Skates said, although the American public hardly could be expected to forgo Allied aid, "there were rational military reasons for restricting the use of Allied forces." The French were asked to participate in the invasion despite knowing how the temperamental General Charles De Gaulle's demands had antagonized General Eisenhower when Free French divisions were preparing to fight in Italy. However, for diplomatic and resource reasons and because it was assumed that an invasion would be necessary, "Early in July," General De Gaulle said, "the Pentagon even asked us if we would be disposed to send two divisions to the Pacific. 'It is not out of the question,' I replied." Thus two French colonial divisions were made available. Had the A-Bomb not intervened one can only imagine what might have been the interplay of the massive egos of General De Gaulle and General MacArthur, who would have commanded the invasion forces.[13]

Precious little attention is given to the fighting in the China-Burma Theater, nor are the losses of the Chinese, Indians, Australians, and Dutch often mentioned or factored into the cost of the war in the South Pacific. After the defeat of Germany, significant Japanese forces remained outside of Japan in China, Manchuria, and places little known to Americans such as Indonesia, Burma and Malaya. To dislodge the Japanese in Malaya a major operation almost the size of Normandy was planned by the Allies. This was OPERATION ZIPPER, scheduled for early September, a British operation led by Admiral Louis Mountbatten to retake Singapore. The Japanese commander in Singapore initially refused to follow the Emperor's order to surrender his 77,000 troops, so Japanese intentions were uncertain. In Steven Harper's description of the planning and problems that faced ZIPPER one finds that the political considerations that afflicted an ally paralleled and may have exceeded those that hampered American operations.

When Churchill's coalition government was replaced by Clement Atlee's Labor Government, it came under intense pressure to demobilize troops that had been in service for as much as five years. In the Far East this meant that the most experienced officers and troops were withdrawn from operational units, and few replacements were available. Although the military, which had continuing responsibility for planned operations, protested these losses, the decisions made in London were inflexible, and the planned operations proceeded under severe constraints. Fortunately, before OPERATION ZIPPER was fully implemented, the Japanese surrendered on September 4th and the invading force took up occupation duties. Had there been resistance, the well-prepared Japanese might have decimated the invaders.

What happened when the landing took place was described by Stephen Harper: "The first waves of assault troops were quickly clear of the beaches, and into the cover of the plantations beyond. Trouble began when the first waves of landing craft with vehicles hit the beach. Lorries and jeeps and other motorized equipment sank deep in the mud that underlay the deceptive surface sand, and many were swamped by the incoming tide. Only the first wave of LSTs (Landing Ship Tanks) managed to get armor ashore before nightfall, twelve hours after the assault began. Had the Japanese still been fighting, men who were on the beach that day believed the landings would have been the bloodiest of the war.

"The blunder was lost in the general jubilation over the end of the war and hardly even noticed in the history books. The authors of the British Official War History let it pass with telling understatement: 'Had the Japanese offered any resistance to the landings ... the invasion force would have been roughly handled, and at least pinned down to the beaches for some time. ..in view of the chaos the troops landed at Morib might have had to be withdrawn. Although it was realized the information about the beaches might not be accurate, a risk was accepted that might have proved unjustifiable had the Japanese opposed the D-Day landings with even a few battalions." The ships, aircraft and troops assigned to this invasion were spared casualties because of the Emperor's decision to surrender, but their escape from the consequences of what Harper described finds no place in the accounts of the revisionists. After seeing what happened during ZIP-PER's unopposed landing one can imagine how the larger Operation OLYMPIC might have fared under Japanese resistance.[14]

Italy declared war on Japan on July 14, 1945, and offered to send warships and troops to the Pacific. The value of Italy's participation was discounted by the Pentagon planners and the matter became moot after August 6th. Whether because of pride or prejudice, although there were Italian naval vessels in the Pacific, the American Navy believed that Italian ships were not suitable in the Pacific. We need to be reminded that British, Indian, Australian, New Zealand, Dutch and Chinese forces were involved in the war in Southeast Asia in the summer of 1945, and were as eager as the Americans to see the war end. When we think of American lives saved by the A-Bomb remember that the Allied lives that were saved were as precious as any other.

Much of the fighting in the Pacific involved Japanese troops who received few if any reinforcements and could not easily be supplied. Eventually, after brutal fighting, and at a high cost, they were overwhelmed by American forces but the ferocity of combat in the Pacific can be seen at Iwo Jima where 75,000 Marines fought 22,000 Japanese. There were 5,931 Marines killed and 17,372 were wounded for a total of 23,303 American casualties while almost all of the isolated Japanese died. According to William Manchester, "The price of the little island had been 25,851 Marines, including 19 battalion commanders. Battle casualties in the rifle regiments had come to 60 percent in the Third Marine Division and 75 percent in the Fourth and Fifth divisions."

Invading Japan's home islands in November 1945 would mean facing larger Japanese units that could be reinforced and receive supplies. Based on what happened at Iwo Jima and Okinawa, American planners had to assume heavy casualties when the home islands were the target.[15] And for William Manchester, who was wounded on Okinawa, "It was depressing; the closer we came to Japan, the more tenacious the defenders were. No one wanted to talk about, or even think about, what would happen when we invaded their home islands."[16] Casualties were high not only in the Pacific but in Europe, and they could come as a surprise both to Washington and to generals in the field. The Battle of the Ardennes, known as the Battle of the Bulge, began on December 16, 1944, and lasted one month. Earlier the pundits said the exhausted Germans would be surrendering by Christmas, but they surprised everyone and in thirty days cost the Americans 78,000 casualties, 8,000 of whom became POWs.

The Japanese home island of Kyushu was to be invaded on November 1, 1945 and, if necessary, followed by the invasion of Honshu on March 1, 1946. Before examining the Kyushu invasion it may be instructive to think of it against the background of the invasion of Leyte in the Philippines. Admiral Halsey received intelligence that Leyte contained no Japanese forces. It also was assumed that Japanese air forces were near collapse and that American carrier forces could provide adequate air cover. That led to a decision to advance General MacArthur's forces from the planned invasion of Moratai, where he would have air cover, to Leyte, which was beyond land based air cover. "The gamble seemed to be one worth taking And so it was, as events proved. Yet the risk was also proved to have been even greater than that anticipated." That was because the Japanese veteran 16th division was stationed on Leyte, and other intelligence about Leyte proved misleading. The Japanese had strengthened their defenses and concentrated their remaining air assets on Leyte. Although ultimately successful, the invasion of Leyte hardly went according to plan, because of the activities of the Japanese navy and the tactics of the Japanese army.[17] The invasion of Kyushu would be more massive than Leyte, and American intelligence was unable to probe Japanese resources and plans any better than it had at Leyte. That was not a reflection on intelligence gatherers but a reality associated with the fog of war. Revisionists seldom if ever mention what Clausewitz called the fog, friction and chance or fortune of war, the imponderables that often defeat the best laid plans. "Everything," Clausewitz said, "is very simple in war, but the very simplest thing is difficult." He went on, "Friction is the only conception which in a general way corresponds to that which distinguishes real War from War on paper." The war in 1945 was a "real War," not a war fought in professional journals.

Southern Kyushu was determined to be the best and least costly place to invade the home islands, and would involve some 766,700 Americans ground troops. In May 1945 the Japanese had four million men overseas and an estimated 2.5 million on the home islands. On May 16, 1945, planners estimated that there were 390,000 Japanese troops on Kyushu. A rule of thumb used by the Americans when attacking was to have a three to one advantage over the enemy. In planning the Japanese defense of Okinawa, Colonel Hiromichi Yahara said the same: "In order to gain their objective, invaders must have at least three times the troop strength of the defenders."[18] On the other hand, Soviet doctrine in World War II preferred a five to one advantage for infantry attacks. Assuming no additional Japanese reinforcements before November 1, the American advantage would be only about two to one. By July 24, however, the Japanese were able to reinforce Kyushu to an estimated 455,000 troops and a week later the estimate was upped to 525,000 troops on the island, creating an even less acceptable ratio in the attack.

In a mid August 1945 report, the U. S. Army identified the order of battle of the Japanese ground forces on the home islands and elsewhere. Issued as the war ended, it had been in preparation before the Japanese capitulated, and it revealed the manpower then available for defense against invasion. Army ground units were supplemented by navy and air force ground units that served as infantry as well as other troops for the purpose of defense. On Honshu, which was to be the ultimate goal of the invasion, there were 1,375,000 men for the island's defense while there were 560,000 on Kyushu, the initial point of invasion. The Japanese had activated at least 42 new divisions in Japan in 1945, and were in the process of activating several more new divisions. A surprisingly large pool of available manpower remained that could be formed into ground combat units.

Another element that invasion critics emphasize is the lack of food in Japan because of the naval blockade and bombing. Although by the summer of 1945 Japan was experiencing a severe shortage of food, as yet the situation was not desperate. A report on the Japanese order of battle in mid August 1945 found that "Japan's food situation, although more seri-ous than at any previous time in the war, is not believed so critical as to preclude the activation of additional troops if the 1945 harvest is normal and imports from the continent continued."

On August 4, the JCS reported that Kyushu's defenses had been strengthened by laying mines to impede landing craft and the construc-tion of bases for small suicide boats. Because the number of soldiers to defend Kyushu had increased dramatically beyond the number originally anticipated, using the June 15 estimates grossly underestimated the price that would have had to be paid had Japan not surrendered. General MacArthur had assumed that casualties on Kyushu would be less than the planners originally estimated and favored the figure of 31,000 casualties in the first 30 days of the invasion. Admiral Chester Nimitz, however, believed that casualties in the first thirty days would be similar to those in Okinawa and he projected 49,000 casualties in the ground forces and 7,700 in the Navy, or a total of 56,700 in the first month of the invasion. Japanese recalled discharged soldiers who needed little if any training, and other young men could be drafted. Although there was a shortage of heavy weapons such as large artillery, there were plenty of rifles, mortars and machine guns to arm newly formed units and to replace losses. Far from fielding weak, poorly armed forces as some have claimed, the Japanese could have resisted an invasion with adequately armed and trained troops. They would be supported by hastily mobilized civilians who were willing to die for their country. Their defensive posture may not have been ideal, but echoing Churchill, they were willing to meet the enemy on the beaches. The Allies would have faced what is known today as asymmetric warfare as the Japanese put up ferocious resistance under adverse conditions.

Japanese Ground Strength, August 15, 1945

	Army ground	Other ground	Total
N. Honshu	140,000	40,000	180,000
NC Honshu	380,000	200,000	580,000
C Honshu	190,000	50,000	240,000
SC Honshu	150,000	75,000	225,000
W. Honshu	120,000	30,000	150,000
Kyushu	370,000	190,000	560,000

Another estimate of the strength of Japanese forces in August 1945 by Steven Ross reported that there were "over 2,000,000 men under arms in the home islands—fifty-six infantry divisions, two tank divisions, seven tank brigades, three garrison brigades and four anti-aircraft divisions.

Japan also had some 10,000 aircraft of all types, thirty-eight submarines, and 3,300 suicide boats." Unlike Germany, Japan capitulated with significant well-armed forces intact, not only on the home islands but in the Philippines, in China and Korea, in Malaysia and on bypassed islands. Absent a surrender those forces would have to be eliminated, something that would pose major problems and added losses for the Allies. Those would be in addition to the losses that would have to be faced in Operations OLYMPIC and CORONET.[19] Lest there be carping about the differences in estimated numbers, it should be understood that estimates were made for different purposes by different planning bodies at different times. That means that data often came from updated intelligence with inevitable changes in numbers. Those differences are inconsequential when one considers the magnitude of the numbers found in any report of the period.

Return for a moment to the Japanese forces on bypassed islands. Operation ZIPPER, which is mentioned elsewhere, can serve as an example of the dimensions of forces needed to defeat about 77,000 well equipped troops in Malaya. ZIPPER was to involve almost 200,000 men, a large fleet and air force units. The initial assault would be by seven divisions and three brigades, or by as many as 90,000 men. Assuming strong Japanese resistance, there could be an estimated 36,000 land combat casualties plus other losses from kamikazes. Fortunately, ZIPPER encountered no resistance, but had there been a hostile reception the consensus of participants was that there would have been a disaster. Dozens if not scores of similar large and small operations would have been necessary had there not been a surrender, and all would have resulted in unavoidable casualties. The human cost of reducing the Japanese forces has not been factored into the simplistic estimates of the revisionists.

Professor Bernstein contended that because the full-scale invasion was not until the spring, "there was no reason to fear losses of 500,000 or 1,000,000 in the autumn, as later statements by officials charged. Indeed the estimates were about 31,000 for the first thirty days on Kyushu." But Professor Bernstein reported only the 31,000 figure and overlooked or ignored Nimitz' estimated 56,700 casualties in the first thirty days. More important, however, Truman and others spoke of estimates for an invasion expected to last for months, and not only its first thirty days that would account for only some of the casualties. By giving an estimate for the first thirty days of an operation that was to last for months, Professor Bernstein, like Professor Miles, neatly sidestepped the potential eventual cost of the operation. How an experienced researcher could do that is hard to fathom, unless the documents were not fully examined or were ignored. The problem with such misleading information is that it gets repeated as authoritative. Robert Lifton, for example, repeated Professor Bernstein's assertion that American lives lost in an all-out invasion of Japan would range from twenty-five to forty-six thousand, "grim enough but a fraction of the number asserted by Truman, Stimson, and others."[20]

Another who questioned the purported large number of casualties was Ronald Takaki, who said that the Joint War Plans Committee gave different estimates of casualties than Truman for the invasion of Kyushu. "The estimate for the total number of soldiers who would die was not 'half million,' but forty thousand." Along with Bernstein, Takaki was selective and misleading in his choice of information. He reproduced only a part of the Joint War Plans Committee's report to the Joint Chiefs of Staff on June 15, 1945, that gave estimates of casualties for the invasion of Kyushu.

Estimated Casualties, S. Kyushu

	KIA	WIA	MIA	TOTAL
S. Kyushu*	40,000	150,000	3,500	193,500

followed by Toyko Plain to mid–1946

Martin Sherwin made essentially the same point as Takaki, calling Truman's figure "grossly exaggerated," saying that casualties for both southern Kyushu and the Tokyo Plain would be 193,000.[21] On page 7 of the JCS document, which was reproduced by Sherwin, additional estimates immediately follow those Takaki mentioned. It is necessary to examine the complete JCS document in order to understand these casualty figures. As does any technical or professional document, the language of a military document can pose a problem for a lay person. The plan presented by the JWPC to the JCS was seen by persons who had a common professional background that enabled them to understand the document and its caveats. The plan presented three possible scenarios. The first was for the invasion of southern Kyushu, which, it was hoped, could be followed four months later on March 1, 1946, by action on the Tokyo Plain. The planners were pessimistic about that outcome. "Should it be decided to follow the southern Kyushu operation by another operation such as against northern Kyushu in order to exploit bombardment and blockade, and should this bring about capitulation of the Japanese, the casualties should be less than for the presently planned campaign. We consider at this time it would be a pure gamble that the Japanese would admit defeat under such conditions. If they do not, invasion of the Tokyo Plain might still be required with resultant increased total casualties."[22] Although casualties for the northern invasion should be less than those for southern Kyushu, they would be substantial and added to the earlier ones. If after taking southern Kyushu the Japanese did not surrender, the third scenario would include an attack on the Tokyo plain. It is strange but obvious that Takaki and Sherwin missed the import of a discussion that made clear that there could be a sequence of invasions with increasing casualties. The table below shows the anticipated casualties for each of the three scenarios with the third scenario, which was the most probable, resulting in 220, 000 casualties.

Casualties by Phases of Invasion

Phases	KIA	WIA	MIA	TOTAL
I. Sou Kyushu	40,000	150,000	3,500	193,500
II. Nor. West Kyushu	25,000	105,000	2,500	132,500
III. I + II + Tokyo Plain	46,000	170,000	4,000	220,000

It is clear that the worst case scenario presented by the planners was an estimate of the casualties to be expected if the fighting on the home islands did not end in southern Kyushu but continued from November 1945 until mid 1946. The report to the Joint Chiefs of Staff may have referred only to the Army and Marines ground troops who would be in the invasion. There also would have been Navy and Air Force casualties that were not factored into these figures. According to early planning documents, the estimated casualty rate for Kyushu would be 24.8 percent. If one realizes that from the beginning of the battle of Iwo Jima to the end of the operation, 7.9 percent of the 75,000 troops involved were killed while overall 31 percent of the men became casualties, then casualties are placed in perspective. At Okinawa 170,000 men made up the assault force and the casualty rate was 26 percent. Later intelligence showed much larger Japanese troop concentrations on Kyushu than initially anticipated, and stronger beach defenses. An intelligence estimate of July 26 noted that the Japanese had 3,162 fighters, 1,212 bombers and 6,203 training planes remaining in their inventory.[23] All of them could be used in suicide kamikaze attacks on the invasion fleet. Thanks to the experience the Japanese gained at Okinawa, it is not unreasonable to assume that the percentage of casualties from kamikaze attacks could easily have reached the level of Okinawa or higher.

Casualties, June 15, 1945, report

Sou Kyushu	No. West Kyushu	Toyko Plain	Total
106,000	87,500		193,500
106,000	26,500		132,500
106,000	26,500	87,500	220,000

More documentation on JCS planning came from *The Entry of the Soviet Union into the War Against Japan: Military Plans, 1941–1945*. Prepared in September 1945, its section of the planned invasion is a useful overview of that process. When overall Pacific strategy was reviewed by the JCS on April 24, 1945, it was pointed out, "the early invasion of the Japanese home islands represented the most suitable strategy to bring about unconditional surrender." As early as July 10, 1944, the Combined Chiefs of Staff had concluded that "our concept of operations against Japan ... should envisage an invasion into the industrial heart of Japan. While it may be possible to defeat Japan by aerial bombardment and the destruction of her sea and air forces, this would probably involve an unacceptable delay." That conclusion was reinforced in the April JCS planning document, which said that bombardment and blockade strategy did not "provide assurance that it will lead to unconditional surrender or defeat. It is a strategy of limited aim and may bring about a negotiated peace falling short of complete fulfillment of our war aims." There was concern that the Japanese forces on the mainland would continue to resist unless it was clear that the homeland had capitulated. "Therefore, the invasion of Japan is considered the most suitable strategy to accomplish unconditional surrender or ultimate defeat."

Among the options presented, it was estimated that more than a million men would be needed to encircle the home islands. These troops would invade Korea (507,000 men), the Kuriles (200,000 men) and other places (398,000 men) over a period of months after VE day. If these forces were committed, however, there was no allowance for their possible extrication and re-use as part of the forces needed to invade the home islands. That led to the conclusion that "there is no assurance that the execution of this sequence of blockade and bombardment operations and, in fact, even the seizure of still other positions would obviate ultimate invasions."

Jointly OLYMPIC and CORONET would involve 36 divisions and 1,523,000 men. Estimated casualties for these operations were compared to prior invasions and found that the expected average casualties for land forces per day per thousand, for operations in Guadalcanal, Attu, Leyte, New Georgia, Marshalls, Marianas and Palau, were: KIA, 1.78; WIA, 5.50; MIA, .17 or a total of 7.45 per day, per thousand. In the European theater for protracted land warfare the average casualty rates were: KIA, .36; WIA, 1.74; MIA .06; for a total average of 2.16 per thousand, per day. These were only for ground forces, excluding naval and air force casualties.

The June 15 plan presented to the JCS called for a Kyushu invasion force of 766,700. Using the average daily casualty figures mentioned above, casualties for the first 30 days would be (766,700 X 7.45) or 5,710 daily and 171,330 in the first 30 days, of whom 42,832 would be fatalities. Again, these figures were only for ground forces. Operations on the home islands were to continue for perhaps five or six months, perhaps with somewhat decreasing casualty rates, but perhaps with constant or even higher rates affecting the million and a half men to be committed to the invasion and its follow up. If the 7.45 average per thousand figure is used with the 190,00 men in the invasion that was mentioned by Marshall, the daily casualties would be 1,415, or 43,750 casualties in the first 30 days of Kyushu and 13,462 would be fatalities.

According to Professor Dower, the number of kamikaze pilots who gave their lives was about 5,000. He continued: "It is often observed, in passing, that during the early stages of the war Allied fighting men who faced hopeless situations often sacrificed themselves in what amounted to a suicide attacks, including crashing their planes into enemy warships." Professor Dower also mentioned that "the number of United Kingdom airmen who gave their lives in World War Two was ten times greater than the Japanese who died as kamikaze pilots. The acceptance of certain death by the latter did indeed set them apart, but the difference can be exaggerated." William Manchester made a similar point. "Home-front America was shocked by Jap kamikazes, but its own sons were capable of similar sacrifices, and not just Marines. The Devastator torpedo bombers who crashed Nip warships at Midway knew they were diving to certain death, and so did the Air Corps pilots over Ploesti."

Although Japanese and Allied airmen perished in such attacks, there was a significant and not subtle distinction between the kamikazes who either volunteered or were ordered to go on what was known as a suicide mission; and the Allied pilot who may have volunteered or been ordered to go on a mission with little chance of survival, but was not ordered to commit suicide. Unlike the Japanese, there was no American policy to deliberately train and order individuals to perform suicide missions. A Japanese naval officer on the Battleship Yamato who knew about kamikazes said about one such episode of sacrifice: "Now and then a hostile plane was shot down and plunged flaming into the sea, but its mission of dropping torpedoes or bombs had already been accomplished. Not a single enemy plane was rash enough to carry out a crash-dive attack on us." Professor Dower also tried to make the point that the many British airmen who died (in five years of combat) could be compared with kamikazes. He did so to support his theory of the equivalence of racist conduct on both sides. However, as noted above, the differences between them need no exaggeration in order to be understood by fair minded readers. Perhaps the essential distinction was best described by George Feifer: "The American infantrymen who threw themselves on Japanese hand grenades in order to save their buddies were expressing an impulsive, unthinking surge of camaraderie, not an intentional desire to kill themselves.... An uneducated American footslogger on Okinawa summed up the difference as tellingly as any historian or sociologist, revisionist or otherwise: 'Our infantrymen landed on Pacific islands knowing they might die but hoping they wouldn't. Kamikaze men knew the outcome in advance.'"[24]

To strengthen their defenses the Japanese deployed motor boats for suicide missions. These craft were similar to those used in both the British and the Italian navies which also had frogmen, piloted torpedoes and motor torpedo boats that were directed at targets. The British and Italians did not have suicide craft; in all cases the pilots were expected to escape. Using explosives laid by frogmen, in December 1941, Italy's "Decima MAS" (Motoscafi Armato Siluranti/motor boats armed with torpedoes) heavily damaged two British battleships in Alexandria, Egypt. Earlier, in March 1941, six MAS boats attacked ships in Suda Bay in Crete with partial success. All the Italians survived and became POWs. The MAS, like the British, engaged in brave and risky business that often was fatal but not deliberately so.[25]

Contrary to J. Samuel Walker's opinion, the human cost of OPERATION OLYMPIC could have been far in excess of the June projections, a fact well known to JCS staff. Walker contended that, although the unexpected reinforcements to Kyushu would have caused the Joint Chiefs to revise their estimates upward from the earlier estimate, there is no evidence they were asked to examine their earlier projections. Walker should understand that such updating was done routinely by staff without waiting for requests.

When Denis and Peggy Warner made a detailed analysis of the Japanese defenses, they included the terrain and the units to be employed in the defense of Kyushu, as well as of the Allied units to be in the invasion. Their study showed that the land battle would have been as difficult as the one in Northern Italy, while the Navy would face more kamikazes than there were at Saipan, Tinian or Okinawa. The Japanese could not have stopped the Americans but they would have delayed them, perhaps for months with mounting casualties on both sides. As will be seen later, the Warner's information was overlooked by many of the writers, who argued that the situation on Kyushu would not be critical for the invading troops. Another account of the potential for disastrous casualties in the event of an invasion is found in an article by Jack Bauer and Alan Coox in *The Marine Corps Gazette* in August 1965. They explained in detail the massive American preparations for the invasion of Kyushu as well as well as the state of morale and the preparations the Japanese made to defend their homeland. It is unfortunate that such information, countering claims that an invasion would not be costly, was not discovered by revisionists, although it has long been available.[26]

The kamikazes had taken a heavy toll and were a source of great concern to the Navy. After the landing at Leyte the Japanese strategy became clear when high ranking Vice Admiral Masabumi Arima flew his plane at an American aircraft carrier. According to Robert Sherrod, "Only at war's end did we learn how effective the kamikaze had been: 26.8 percent of them found their shipping targets during the Philippines campaign (174 hits or damaging near misses out of 650 attempts); at Okinawa the percentage was slightly lower, 14.7 percent, but the number of ships hit was higher (27.9 in 1,900 attempts). In ten months the suicide planes accounted for 48.1 percent of all U.S. warships damaged and 21.3 percent of the ships sunk during the 44-month war." Sherrod went on, "The kamikaze was the single most effective air weapon developed by the Japanese in World War II."

After Okinawa, and in preparation for an invasion of the home islands, the Japanese had saved about one million gallons of gasoline, according to the USSBS. Although there was a limited amount for training, a kamikaze needed only about 70 hours of training to dive on a target, thus there was ample gasoline for thousands of suicide attacks by the kamikazes defending Kyushu. There were 10,700 aircraft hidden on small fields, half of them converted for suicide purposes, and the rest could have been so used by the remaining 18,000 Japanese pilots. When the invasion came, the Japanese planned to fly a wave of 300 to 400 kamikazes every hour the short distance to the ships off shore. If they maintained their attacks at the Okinawa rate they would have sunk about 90 ships in the Kyushu landing and damaged about 900 of the more than 3,000 ships slated to be involved in the invasion. Although a few revisionists like Professor Alperovitz have disparaged the potential damage by kamikazes during an invasion (he referred to "sporadic Kamikaze attacks" in the summer of 1945), that may have been because they did not see the available American literature about kamikaze attacks, or a Japanese account by Toshiyuki Yoki. Those should have given them pause if they were interested in what kamikazes achieved at Okinawa. The lessons the Japanese learned from their use there, adapted to the situation on Kyushu, would have been implemented on a large scale and at a heavy cost to an invasion force.[27]

More support for the fact that high casualty rates were expected comes from other evidence that moved in tandem with the estimates of the JWPC planners. Obscure indicators can provide a "bottoms-up" approach that gives a good idea of what planners were thinking about long before the A-Bomb. A seemingly small matter they had to address was the number of Purple Heart medals to be awarded to men wounded or killed during the invasion. On the basis of the casualties experienced in landing on hostile shores in the Pacific, in the spring of 1945, the Navy ordered 50,000 Purple Hearts for the anticipated casualties in the invasion. Okinawa alone required the Navy to award 20,000 Purple Hearts to sailors and Marines involved in that operation, and the invasion of Japan's home islands was expected to be more costly. The 50,000 medals were ordered after experienced planners who had no knowledge of the A-Bomb, but were aware of the ferocity of past Japanese resistance, estimated the price the Navy could pay to defeat the Japanese on their home ground.[28]

What that price might be can also be derived from the fact that, although the Southwest Pacific area had 44,000 hospital beds in December 1944, more were needed as the war moved closer to Japan. On the island of Tinian, for example, the Navy constructed a 600 bed hospital for the men on the island and it was expanded by another 400 beds in March 1945. A larger one thousand bed hospital was almost completed by the time Japan surrendered.[29] Additional hospital facilities on Okinawa included Special Augmentation hospitals 3, 4, and 6 and Fleet Hospital 106. In anticipation of the invasion, the Seabees built 338,000 square feet of hospitals on Okinawa in the months before the war ended. In preparation for OPERATION OLYMPIC, by the end of October 1945, the Army alone intended to have 14 evacuation hospitals, ten field hospitals, 22 station hospitals and 51 general hospitals in the Southwest Pacific area. Obviously such large hospital facilities would not have been constructed unless the military expected a large number of wounded. In Professor Bernstein's opinion the invasion planners probably exaggerated the need for blood and other supplies for fear of being caught short. A July 31, 1945 medical plan estimated 394,859 casualties in the first four months of the invasion and estimated the need for 149,000 pints of whole blood. Had Professor Bernstein consulted the Army's report on the problems of obtaining enough blood to treat casualties, he might have not been so cavalier. Accusing the planners of deception without the archival evidence that Bernstein touts as indispensable is a base reflection on men responsible for planning to save the lives of their comrades.

By the war's end, between Army engineers and Navy Seabees, there were 80,000 construction troops on Okinawa. That large number of support troops indicates the magnitude of the overall preparations for the invasion. "To build so many airfields in so short a time required the largest aviation engineering project ever attempted. There were to be some twenty-five miles of paved airstrips, while the hardstands, taxiways, and service aprons would require a paved area equal to 400 miles of a two-lane highway. Some five and one half million truckloads of coral and earth would have to be moved.... By 6 August, six of the new airfields were operational and most projects were due to be completed by mid-October." Whatever was happening at Potsdam and elsewhere, the military was not engaged in contingency planning in the Pacific.[30]

VII

Where Did the 500,000 Come From?

Where did the often quoted figure of 500,000 casualties used by President Truman come from? It was disparaged by Professor Bernstein in his article, "A Postwar Myth: 500,000 U. S. Lives Saved," which was called a strong but fair comment by McGeorge Bundy. That lends credibility to Professor Bernstein's charge that casualty figures were exaggerated. Did the figure come from Truman's faulty memory or was it concocted to justify dropping the bomb? Contrary to allegations that there is no evidence that Truman and his advisors were aware of large casualty estimates if Japan was invaded, such evidence did and does exist. The estimates were based upon the experience at Iwo Jima and Okinawa, and intelligence in late July and early August. Revisionists have dismissed that evidence as anecdotal and lacking in documentary confirmation. The pros and cons of the argument are the focus of this essay. Documents that refer to the large numbers are dismissed by revisionists as low level and lacking proof that they were brought to the attention of high ranking officials, with no credence given to even its possibility. Any defense of what revisionists persist in calling the "myth" of large numbers of casualties faces the difficult problem of rebutting the clamor that Truman dissembled, used dubious numbers or just plain lied about using the A-Bomb. The inevitable result of persistent repetition has been the disinformation that clouds any discussion of the number of casualties to be anticipated if there was an invasion.

The most recent extensive effort to set the record straight about casualty estimates was made by D. M. Giangreco in 1997. His explanation of the history of casualty estimates by the United States Army describes how they were produced at different levels in the army and the problems faced in their development. This provides an excellent background to the con-

sideration of the estimates in 1945. Although called confused and intellectually sloppy by Professor Bernstein, Giangreco's treatment of the various estimates produced during the spring and summer of 1945 really needs
no defense. His work will be convincing to anyone with knowledge of military operations and processes, or to anyone who is open minded about
the subject.

The most cited casualty estimates are from mid June 1945, and at the
most show "only" 220,000 casualties. That was before intelligence about
the Japanese build-up of men, small suicide boats, kamikaze planes and
strengthened shore defenses became available to the invasion planners.
Such information would lead to an upward revision of the June estimates.
We do not have a document that integrates the newer intelligence and
revised the estimates, but JWPC documents show that it was aware of
those facts, and that would have made it aware that higher casualties were
possible. That there was recognition and concern about the evolving situation on Kyushu is clear because on August 4, 1945, after receiving reports
about the increased presence of Japanese troops and defensive measures
on Kyushu, the Joint War Plans Committee recommended "that commanders in the field should review their estimates of the situation, reexamine objectives in Japan as possible alternatives to OLYMPIC, and
prepare plans for operations against such alternate objectives." General
Marshall knew of the revised estimates of Japanese forces on Kyushu but,
according to Professor Bernstein, "there is no evidence ... that he thought
that American casualties would be astronomical."[1]

On May 31, 1945, at a meeting of the President's Interim Committee
that was to recommend the use of the A-Bomb, the question of a demonstration for the Japanese was discussed and rejected. According to Secretary of State James Byrnes, on July 1 the committee recommended that the
bomb be used against Japan as soon as possible and only where war plants
or military installations were located. "With the exception of Mr. Bard,
the committee recommended that it be used without warning. This last
question we had carefully considered." When Byrnes gave the Committee
report to the president he said, "The military experts informed us that,
from the facts at their disposal, they believed our invasion would cost us
a million casualties, to say nothing of those of our Allies and of the
enemy."[2]

According to Professor Bernstein, "Nowhere in Stimson's diaries and
official Secretary of War Papers, in the files of the Joint Chiefs and the
President and in related military archives, did any high-ranking American official in the summer of 1945 forecast any number like a million American casualties, or even half a million." That made it possible to ignore what

Byrnes told the President when reporting the conclusions of the Interim Committee. As evidence of the Japanese build up increased, Professor Bernstein also said that specific battle-casualty figures were increased in Washington's thinking. "But there is no pre-Hiroshima archival record of specific higher estimates in the summer of 1945 of likely future U.S. casualties in the invasion." Professor Bernstein may be correct that no "high-ranking American official" (depending on whatever his self definition of "high ranking" means) placed those numbers on a document, thus leaving an archival record that Professor Bernstein would accept as the only valid evidence. He did agree, however, that undoubtedly casualty figures were increased in Washington. In addition to intelligence about Japanese reinforcements that would complicate an invasion, and therefore increase casualties, there were sources for the large numbers that curiously have been ignored or dismissed as irrelevant. Even without a "smoking gun" and despite artful wording by Professor Bernstein, one can find support for the large numbers in earlier documents that are available. Contrary to Professor Bernstein's claim there is a record. General George Marshall, certainly a high-ranking American official, once mentioned the 500,000 number, although he thought it was too high.[3]

On June 1, 1945, the Chief of Staff, General Marshall, asked General Hull for staff reaction to a paper received from the Secretary of War, who got it from the President. On May 28, 1945, former president Herbert Hoover had been asked to visit Truman to discuss the food situation in Europe as the war ended. Hoover quickly prepared a paper on the subject in which he stated that by making peace with Japan "America will save 500,00 to 1,000,000 lives and an enormous loss of resources." General Marshall sent Secretary Stimson a reply that said, "It is obvious that peace would save lives and resources, but the estimated loss of 500,000 lives due to carrying the war to conclusion under our present plan of campaign, is considered to be entirely too high." General Marshall and Secretary Stimson saw Hoover's numbers and Marshall disagreed with them. Thus the numbers had floated around the Pentagon and the White House. Persons in both places, like Samuel Halpern, whom Bernstein ignored, presumably because he was not a "high ranking official," also knew about a 500,000 figure. Truman's memoirs do not reveal former president Hoover as the source of those disputed, "exaggerated" numbers. The internal evidence is strong, however, that at some time in the spring of 1945, Truman saw those numbers in writing from former president Herbert Hoover, a person he respected. There was a source for the "exaggerated" numbers; a Republican, who can be added to the others who allegedly conspired with the president to provide cover for dropping the A-Bomb, and did so before Hiroshima.

Mike Wallace made a tortuous effort to contradict the idea of large casualty estimates before the bomb was dropped. Like Richard Minear, he found that David McCullough referred to a June 4, 1945, memo that dismissed Hoover's figures as too high. According to McCullough, the memo "shows that figures of such magnitude were then in use at the highest level." Wallace and Minear pointed out, as did Bernstein, that the memo did not say that. The basis of their claim hinged on his words "in use." Questioned by a reporter, McCullough said he made a mistake. It is remarkable that anyone would question McCullough's statement that the high numbers were in use at the highest level, simply because the memo did not say that, although it obviously was used, whether agreed with or not, by high level individuals. Critics failed to understand the implications of Hoover's memo that showed, whether accepted as realistic or not, that the high estimate was *known* at a very high level in the Truman administration. Wallace, Minear (who elsewhere identified himself as an "historian of conscience") and Bernstein carefully parsed their comments about the memo, avoiding what should have been obvious to diligent scholars: that the memo was evidence that among others, Marshall, Stimson and Truman had seen Hoover's estimate of high casualties.[4]

Professor Bernstein and his fellow revisionists take the easy road of personalizing their accounts of decision makers instead of relying on substantive analysis of events in the context of the times. An egregious example of this practice appears in Professor Bernstein's exploration of Truman's psyche. He reported that "Some analysts have speculated that the use of large numbers in his memoirs was probably designed by Truman out of a need to stifle whatever uneasiness he felt about the mass killings at Hiroshima and Nagasaki." Further, "Before Hiroshima, in what might be termed an act of self-deception, Truman had managed not to admit to himself that the bomb would mostly kill civilians." He also thought that Admiral Leahy's harsh words about the bomb should have been regarded as a betrayal by Truman who also should have been troubled if not offended by the anti-Hiroshima claims of Arnold, King, MacArthur and Eisenhower. "Strangely," he said, "there is no record of Truman's responses." Professor Bernstein seemed unaware that Truman had more than yes men as advisors, and listened to strong opinions by advisors until he made a final decision.

To disparage any possible evidence of the existence of high casualty estimates, Professor Bernstein cavalierly dismissed references to William Shockley's report predicting high casualties during an invasion because he was not a "high-level official," and occupied a "minor position" in the Pentagon. Professor Bernstein also called Shockley "a well intentioned amateur who knew little about the history of war ... (he) lacked the sensitivity to investigate historical and cultural matters." Prepared for Secretary Stimson's office, Shockley's report assessed training and manpower needs for the rest of the war and used all available relevant Pentagon information in its preparation. In Professor Bernstein's opinion, it was questionable that Stimson ever saw Shockley's report, which may be the case because the war ended. However, because he worked for Stimson's office it is entirely possible that his report's findings were shared with Stimson's aides and informed opinion in that office. Shockley had a far from minor position; he was director of research for the navy's Anti-Submarine Warfare Operations Research Group. As to his competence, he won the Nobel prize in Physics in 1956. (As did Joseph Rothblat, whose opinions about the A-Bomb should not be disparaged because he was not an historian and his opinions mirror Professor Bernstein's). Although a scientist and not an historian, Shockley was a keen analyst who had made major contributions to wartime projects and had been around the Pentagon long enough to be familiar with military matters. The Shockley report exists, and it is a better resource than the many speculations about Truman that sprinkle Professor Bernstein's writings. The snobbish disdain showed for Shockley because he was not a "high official," or an historian, as if that tainted his ability to analyze statistical data, is unworthy of Professor Bernstein. Incidentally, like Professor Bernstein, Shockley was a member of the Stanford University faculty.

In Professor Michael Sherry's judgment, "the armed services never arrived at a firm figure of their own — nor does it appear they were asked to — and the challenge to Hoover's figure apparently never got passed along to Truman." He sought to undermine the credibility of Stimson's number of casualties by noting that Stimson did not disclose who "informed" him that American casualties might exceed one million, and placed informed in quotes as if there was a mystery involved. He ought to have known that one source was obvious. There is no secret that Stimson had been "informed" by Hoover's memo, which the president had given to Stimson for comment. Professor Sherry went on to fault planners for the "loose calculations" prevalent in June. He found how "loosely they framed their alternatives and how easily they convinced themselves of the bomb's legitimacy as a benign alternative to ground warfare." Perhaps there was the same undefined "looseness" on his own part when he overlooked or ignored the cautions expressed in the JWPC document mentioned earlier that deliberately avoided giving firm estimates of casualties at the June 18 meeting with Truman. He also did not tell the reader that alternatives to the invasion had been discussed before Trinity and the knowledge that the bomb would work. Professor Sherry also overlooked the fact that the planners preparing the estimates were not aware of the bomb and could not have factored it into their planning.[5]

Another source for the 500,000 figure can be found in the JWPC report of June 15, 1945. That report said 1,026,000 men would be needed to invade the Tokyo Plain and used a casualty rate of 25.2 percent to arrive at its estimated casualties. The rate was not pulled out of thin air but was the product of harsh experience, not only in the Pacific but in the invasions in Europe. It was conservative considering what happened during other Pacific invasions. The casualty rate on Okinawa had been 26 percent while on Iwo Jima it had been 31 percent, something that could happen on the home islands, although, thanks to air interdiction and the attrition of Japanese forces and resources, it was considered unlikely. Using an earlier and more conservative JWPC casualty rate of 24.2 percent showed the number of estimated casualties among the soldiers and marines committed to each scenario. Had the third phase been necessary, and given the number of men involved in that scenario, the estimated casualties could have been well over the 500,000 so often referred to.

The JWPC documents reveal that the JCS sought to avoid estimating casualties in its report to Truman. The paper prepared for the president did not contain the casualty figures shown in the report dated June 15. Far from exaggerating casualties, every effort was made to avoid using numbers so as not to dismay Truman, who was concerned about possibly heavy casualties. An internal memo to General Marshall read: "Our experience in the Pacific war is so diverse as to casualties that it is considered wrong to give any estimates of numbers." That probably was because when planning OVERLORD, the fear of heavy casualties was a "basic difficulty with the Prime Minister which clouded and hampered all our preparations for the cross-channel operation now demonstrated as having been essential to victory in Europe." Evidently the planners hoped to avoid a repetition of Eisenhower's problem with Churchill in the presentation to the president.

Estimating the number of casualties was a sensitive matter both within the military and between the military and their political masters. As seen in the case of Churchill's concerns about casualties for D-Day in Normandy, the military, although wanting to be frank, did not want to scare the politicians who made the ultimate decisions. Within the military there were eternal optimists who predicted light casualties and the doom sayers who predicted horrendous losses. Finding a balance was not easy. An example of the difference between estimated and actual casualties can be found in what happened in OPERATION TORCH, the invasion of North Africa. Planners anticipated 16,000 casualties for the landings, which involved some 170,000 men. Fortunately, there were only 1,800, thanks to the agreement with Admiral Darlan.[6]

General MacArthur was an optimist who tended to form opinions that supported the course of action he favored. That was nowhere more evident than when he commanded in Korea. When asked about anticipated casualties for OLYMPIC he sent General Marshall the figure of 50,800 for the first 30 days, and 27,150 in each of the following thirty days for a total of 105,050 casualties.[33] MacArthur also estimated that each thirty days there would be 4,200 non battle casualties, for a total of 12,600 in the first 90 days of the invasion.[7]

Although Professor Bernstein is dismissive of non-battle casualties, they were far from incidental for planning purposes, eventual medical care and the logistics of evacuation of those seriously ill of malaria and other tropical diseases and serious accidents. MacArthur deducted from battle casualties an unspecified number of men, the lightly wounded, for example, who were returned to duty. That number was not as inconsequential as MacArthur intimated by omitting their number. Thus the total number of battle casualties would have been some number larger than the 105,050 reported for the first three months in Kyushu. If fighting was prolonged, casualties could have continued at the rate of another 27,150 a month. Kyushu was to be followed in March by CORONET. Whatever casualties occurred there would have to be added to those from Kyushu. MacArthur also compared Kyushu to the invasion of Leyte, where there were 31,000 casualties in the first 30 days. That figure could be misleading because Japanese tactics on Leyte avoided naval gunfire by not defending the beaches, hoping to draw the attackers inland and fight them from prepared positions inland. To gauge the situation facing the invasion, one should be aware that the terrain of Kyushu was rugged and not unlike Okinawa's. In similar terrain in Italy the American units of the Fifth Army, with 180,000 men, had 80,000 casualties in the first four months of the campaign, only 24 percent of which were men killed or wounded. Most of the casualties were from accidents or other injuries and sickness. A significant number of replacements were needed to cope with such losses, and the same would be true in Kyushu.[8]

When General Marshall asked MacArthur to clarify his original estimate, MacArthur explained that the estimate was routine and academic and said that he did not expect such high losses. The original figures, he said, were made for medical and replacement planning alone. He did not specify what the lower estimate might be or why the original figures that planners used in order to anticipate the number of men needed to replace the dead and wounded, and the medical services needed to treat the wounded, were only routine and academic. Given his imaginative use of statistics and depreciation of the efforts of his own staff, it would be easy to say that the general was less than candid and was deceptive in his response to General Marshall, but that would be too easy. He wanted the war to end and was confident that he knew how to end it, without worrying about bean counters. Admiral Leahy did not believe MacArthur's optimistic casualty figures. Based upon what happened at Okinawa, during the first phase of the invasion Admiral Leahy's estimate was 268,465 casualties. Edward Drea found that "MacArthur's determination to lead the greatest amphibious operation in history blinded him to ULTRA's disclosure of the growing risks of invasion. Indeed throughout the war, MacArthur had paid scant attention to intelligence forecasts urging caution or delay." Stanley Weintraub, an OSS geographer, recalled estimates at the time of a quarter of a million casualties. Such anecdotal material can be questioned but ought not be ignored as irrelevant.[9] In another artful effort to downplay the problem posed by possibly high casualty numbers, J. Samuel Walker first agreed that the high numbers of Japanese that U. S. intelligence reported in Kyushu after June caused the Joint Chiefs to revise their estimates upward from those in mid June. However, he said, "there is no evidence that they were ever asked to reexamine their earlier projections. Nor is there any conclusive evidence that Truman was given new casualty estimates ... before he authorized the dropping of atomic bombs. Even if military officials had calculated higher casualty estimates and delivered them to the president in late July, it is inconceivable that the numbers would have totaled in the range of 500,000 to 1 million casualties and/ or deaths, given the estimates that were circulating among knowledgeable officials in mid-June. Furthermore, the number of Japanese troops disclosed nothing about their combat experience, morale, or the quality of their training, equipment, and leadership. Indications are that they were less formidable than the Japanese forces that had defended Okinawa and other islands."

The claim that the Japanese troops on Kyushu were second-rate and poorly armed argues that invading Japan would not have posed the same problems as at Okinawa. That argument is flatly wrong. Even if such questionable information surfaced after the war it would be irrelevant for invasion planning because planners were not privy to it in the summer of 1945 and had to plan accordingly. Thanks to Herbert Bix we now know on the night of August 9–10, Hirohito met with the Supreme War Leadership Council and told them the Army Minister reported that the materials needed to complete the armament of the divisions that were to fight on the Kanto plain would not be ready until September. If the armament for more than half a million troops would be ready by September, it surely would have been ready before the invasion of Kyushu that was scheduled to begin on November 1st. That report revealed that as late as August the Japanese had not exhausted their ability to arm their divisions.[10]

According to Walker, "Scholars have also cited the estimates of the medical department of MacArthur's command, which came to 394,859 for the first 120 days of the Kyushu operation…. The medical department's figures included non combat as well as combat casualties." Then Walker quoted Bernstein, who stated that the medical department "undoubtedly chose to err on the safe side, and thus probably exaggerated the number of casualties…." He added that whatever the accuracy of the medical department's figures, "there is no evidence that they ever were conveyed to Truman." This is a classic example of piling a Pelion of irrelevancy on an Ossa of non sequiturs. Casualties are casualties, whether combat or non-combat, and they need care. The obvious implication of Walker's statement is that by including the non-combat casualties in their estimates the planners inflated their estimates with less important non-combat casualties. In the real world it made little difference whether a badly injured man was shot or hit by a truck; he needed treatment, planners were aware of that fact, and Walker should have been aware of it. There is none of the archival evidence that Professor Bernstein demands elsewhere to show that planners "undoubtedly chose to err on the safe side." That cheap shot has no place in a supposedly serious historical study. Furthermore, why would Truman be expected to be informed of the medical department's estimates, as if this would somehow have sanctified their credibility? It might help Walker and others to understand the importance of preparing for even non-combat casualties if they became aware of the fact that, "In hospitals on Guadalcanal, only three percent of the patients were battle casualties while 97 percent had malaria, dengue or dysentery. This ratio should be considered as normal in base hospital planning for the tropics."[11]

Another instance of avoiding the implications of evidence that casualties could be high was Walker's response to Allen and Polmar's finding that 370,000 Purple Heart medals had been ordered for those killed or wounded in the invasion of Japan. He did not deny that the medals were ordered, but said, "This is doubtless another case in which those submitting the orders were inclined to err on the side of caution to make certain they did not run short. Further the authors do not show that Truman or any of his top advisors were involved in ordering Purple Hearts nor do they show that officials at the depot were privy to the deliberations at the highest level of the American government. Therefore the number of medals ordered has no relevance to the question of casualty projections and their impact on policy." That is a fatuous argument. Anyone with the slightest appreciation of the scale of preparation for war and the operation of government would know that Truman, et al., would have nothing to do with ordering extra Purple Hearts, more supplies of blood, or bed pans for the hospitals being built on Tinian and Okinawa. The extraordinary idea that the office ordering the medals should be aware of deliberations "at the highest level" reveals a distressing ignorance of the operations of large organizations. Finally, to impugn the motives of whoever ordered the medals for "doubtless" erring on the side of caution, is another cheap shot, unworthy of someone presumably writing serious history.[12]

That approach was typical of the "undoubtedly" and "probably" straw men set up by revisionists. Admit that the Japanese had strongly reinforced Kyushu, then contend that there were "indications" the reinforcements were "less formidable" than those encountered before, as if there was any evidence that the new arrivals were less formidable and presumably would pose less of a threat to an invasion force. Admit that medical department estimates were very high, then dismiss them as "probably were exaggerated," a safe allegation since dead men cannot contradict you. Add that there was no evidence that those medical department figures were seen by Truman, as if unless seen by Truman they could be discounted. Walker admitted that the Joint Chiefs revised their casualty estimates after June but suggests that evidence was lacking that they were asked to do so. That is a red herring. If they revised the estimates it is irrelevant whether Stimson or Truman asked them to do so; planners had the new estimates whether or not Truman had them before he ordered the dropping of the bomb. There is no evidence Marshall told Truman about new estimates and nothing to prove that "undoubtedly" and "probably" Marshall did not. Unhappily for history, careful readers of Walker or Bernstein will find that too often they have relied on innuendo for their claims.

The dismissive manner of referring to the lightly wounded exemplifies the ignorance of the commentators. Anyone out of the line of battle reduces the effectiveness of a unit. Suppose a platoon loses five men who were lightly wounded by shrapnel and they have to be sent out of the line and hospitalized for several days before returning to duty. In the meantime the platoon may not get replacements, and the loss of five men leaves the unit weaker if attacked. The temporary loss of the five men could mean the loss of more men or the rest of the platoon in a firefight. Relying on statistics is easy, arm chair, ex post facto history that cannot come to grips with the gut wrenching reality of seemingly small matters that can make the difference between life and death for men in combat. Also referred to dismissively are the non combat casualties, as if they did not count. A truck driver hospitalized because of an accident means one less truck carrying supplies, perhaps to the front, perhaps with shells for a battery that needs them to support infantry in the attack. That missing driver might play a more critical role in a combat action than the men at the front, yet he and his fellows are depreciated as somehow unimportant in the grand scheme of battle.

How conveniently the Hoover estimates can be slighted appeared in an article in *Defense Week* by its editor, Tony Capaccio. He called the casualty estimates of President Truman and Secretary of War Stimson "the most discredited official reasons for the U.S. decision to use the atomic bombs against Japan." Referring to comments by McGeorge Bundy, Peter Maslowski, John Skates and Barton Bernstein, each of whom believed the estimates were exaggerated, Capaccio concluded that an invasion of Japan would have cost 193,000 casualties "if a two-phase invasion was executed," noting that *Defense Week* retrieved this figure from the National Archives (which also could have been done from several other easily available sources). As mentioned earlier, the 193,000 estimate was an early one by the Joint War Plans Committee which, in addition to that estimate, stated it was less than optimistic that the Japanese would surrender in the initial two phases of the invasion, and that a third phase could become necessary. That caveat was overlooked or ignored by others citing those JWPC figures, including Capaccio.

At the very end of his article, Capaccio referred to the estimate of half a million casualties "floated" by former President Hoover, which was "debunked" by a member of General Marshall's staff as entirely too high. Whether Marshall agreed or disagreed with the estimate, he saw Hoover's memo, and so did Truman. That could be the source of the "discredited" estimate that Truman mentioned. It is strange that the revisionists, and Capaccio, make so much of the lack of a paper trail for the half million figure in General Marshall's papers when we know that there is a paper trail showing that in May 1945 Marshall saw a memo with an estimate of casualties, and so did President Truman.[13]

Suppose everyone agreed that the million casualties figure was too large, and that the half a million figure was unlikely but that the planners saw a real possibility that if the third phase was needed the cost could rise to 220,000 casualties, a figure that was used before it was learned about the Japanese build-up on Kyushu during late June and July. It is doubtful that would help to exculpate Truman and his fellow myth makers because the revisionists would move to the high moral plane or insist on the Miles figure which was not large enough to justify the bomb.

Peter Maslowski downplayed the risk of attacking Kyushu, arguing that Japan's military situation had deteriorated to such an extent that the invasion would face ill fed, poorly trained and demoralized troops. If true and known at the time, that would have been useful intelligence, but ex post facto it is a highly questionable and speculative assessment of the Japanese forces on Kyushu in the summer of 1945. Furthermore, he said, only training planes remained to challenge the invasion, but he neglected to tell the reader that training planes made effective kamikazes and that several thousand of the remaining 10,000 planes in the Japanese inventory that were dispersed on Kyushu were there to attack the invasion fleet. Writing in 1995, Maslowski would have benefited from reading about the elaborate defenses found by the Warners in their 1982 on-site study of the defenses of Kyushu. Their study was available before Maslowski and others wrote about Truman's alleged numbers game. And even if one assumed that the speculative assumptions made long after the fact by Maslowski were correct, they could not have been factored into a decision in the summer of 1945.[14]

No matter how extensively and intensively a subject is researched, inevitably one can miss, or discard, a bit of important evidence. That happened in the case of an elaborately and expensively researched book in 1995 about the A-Bomb by Professor Alperovitz in which he downplayed the idea that there could be heavy casualties during an invasion. Unfortunately, he or one of his many research assistants missed the Warner's 1982 book, which has an excellent account of the defenses the Japanese prepared on Kyushu while waiting for an invasion. Alperovitz was not alone in overlooking what Denis and Peggy Warner reported in *The Sacred Warriors*. The table below shows the year of publication of several writers who discuss casualty estimates attributable to an invasion and whether they mentioned the Warners' book in a bibliography and/or the index in a book published after 1985.

References to Warners' Book

Author	Bibli		Index	
	Yes	No	Yes	No
Walker '97	—	X		X
Sherwin '87	—	X		X
Sigal '88	—	X		
Allen/Polmar '95		X		X
Feifer '92	X	—	X	
Alperovitz '95	—	X		
Hogan '95	—	X		X

At the time of the *Enola Gay* controversy we do not know how many libraries owned a copy of the Warner book. In July 2001, however, it was listed in 721 libraries and thus is available for anyone interested in comparing the Warner evidence with that of other writers on a topic that critics and defenders of the exhibit have considered important. Of course, there is no firm rule that says every possible resource must be used, or even examined, but in a work compiled with the ample resources available to Alperovitz, for example, it is surprising that the Warner book was overlooked, as well as some others, including Ronald Spector's *Listening to the Enemy*, which has valuable information on the Japanese order of battle in the late summer of 1945. When such information is so readily available, it is reasonable to ask why it is not found in purportedly serious studies of the events of 1945.

Because so much attention has been given to the "numbers game" by the revisionists, what can be said about the so-called game? The large numbers mentioned by Stimson, Truman and Marshall at various times have been disparaged by almost every revisionist writer on the subject. We believe that it is important to stress that an estimate of a large number of casualties had been seen by Stimson, Truman and Marshall before the bombs were dropped, and while planning for an invasion was in progress. That some called the estimate too high testifies to the fact that it was seen by high-ranking persons in the administration. The later memories of Truman and others may not have been perfect, but to accuse them of deliberate deception in order to justify using the bomb is akin to the conspiracy theories that surround the Lincoln and Kennedy assassinations, and go marching on despite all the contrary evidence. The passion with which revisionists pursue their agenda of American guilt based on the numbers game is uncannily similar to the way our home grown ultra right militias pursue their fight against the government. Hard core militia groups decry a government conspiracy to take away their guns and collect the income tax, others claim a cover up of visiting space ships and more sophisticated conspiracy addicts claim that Truman and others conspired to falsify the account of why the A-Bomb was used. In each case, nothing will disabuse them of their beliefs.

Whatever numbers Truman might have used, he could not satisfy the revisionists. But the question of casualties can be answered reasonably by those who care to explore Truman's explanation about casualties, regardless of the clarity and accuracy of his recollection of exact numbers. When the revisionists play the numbers game it is a convenient tool that has nothing to do with facts or morality. It seeks to advance an ideological/political agenda that sees the post war world corrupted by American imperialism. That apocalyptic vision may be sincerely held by it advocates, but it has nothing to do with history and the messy reality of 1945.[15]

All history is to some extent selective because there simply is too much information to encompass. Some facts, however, are too important to select out, instead of into, the narrative. Writing about the Holocaust, Michael Grobman and Alex Grobman distinguished between "revision" and "denial." They pointed out that history often revises our understanding of the past because of new discoveries and that this differs from the denial of events like the Holocaust. Thus they preferred to write about "deniers" instead of revisionists. The distinction is important and can be used to help us understand what is written about the Holocaust and other events in the past.[16]

Such denial is found in Professor Bernstein's refusal to credit, even in passing, Samuel Halpern's account of the estimated 500,000 casualties expected if Japan was invaded. In the *Bulletin of the Atomic Scientists* (July of 1986), Professor Bernstein argued that the figure of 500,000 American casualties was a post war creation. As told by Bruce Lee, in July 1990, Halpern told Professor Bernstein that while working in the Pentagon on the planning staff, he first heard of the 500,000 figure in early May 1945. After some archival research Halpern found that the 500,000 figure had been used by military planners months before the decision to drop the first atomic bomb. Although some planners took exception to those casualty figures as too high, in view of the high casualties experienced elsewhere in the Pacific, and based on the projected number of men needed for the invasion, the 500,000 estimated casualties was not unreasonable. More important, that number had been used by planners who were unaware of the atomic bomb and needed to prepare for the logistics of caring for a large number of casualties during a "conventional" invasion of the Japanese islands. In his subsequent writing Professor Bernstein made no reference to Halpern's information, effectively denying testimony about a crucial fact that ought to be made available to readers in a footnote, even if he disagreed with it.

Before the war ended in Europe, General LeMay had been told by General Lauris Norstad, "You go ahead and get results with the B-29. If you don't get results you'll be fired.... If you don't get results it will mean eventually a mass amphibious invasion of Japan, to cost probably half a million more American lives." This was LeMay's recollection of a conversation held twenty years earlier, long before the A-Bomb test, and it is without a paper trail. As memory it need not be taken as gospel but there is little reason to believe that it was concocted by LeMay. General Andrew Goodpaster also recalled that when he was a lieutenant colonel serving in the Strategy Section of the Joint War Planning Committee in the Pentagon, the 500,000 figure had been used by Secretary Stimson. That shows the half million figure was *known* at a high level in the military long before the A-Bomb was available. One can still object to such testimony, but to completely ignore it and deny others the opportunity to consider it verges on malpractice.[17]

That there was awareness that those estimated casualty figures were known is important because of the continuing argument that there were no objective military reasons for using the bomb. If the casualty estimates were a cynical ex post facto creation to justify the bomb's use, then one can argue Truman's moral culpability, and some will do so even in the face of what Halpern said and the fact that planners anticipated the need for much more hospital space for casualties. The ineluctable fact was that the military was prepared to handle massive numbers of casualties long before the A-bomb was tested. The facts are clear. Reasonable people believed, based on extensive prior evidence about contested landings in Europe and the Pacific, that the level of anticipated American casualties during an invasion would be very high; plans were made to cope with them, but the projected casualty rate was militarily unacceptable. That says nothing about the inevitable death and destruction to be visited upon Japan if there was an invasion. Troops fresh from defeating Germany were already en route to the Pacific and large draft calls continued. After serving in Europe some troops were virtually on the edge of mutiny when told they were slated for the Pacific. There was popular and Congressional pressure to end the Pacific war, and that had to be considered by decision makers. Thus, after years of war and heavy casualties, neither Truman, the military or the public were willing to trade more casualties for the bomb.

Unfortunately, accounts such as Halpern's have made no impression on those dedicated to indicting America for its use of the bomb. As individuals the deniers are free to argue against using the bomb. Historians are not free to refuse to acknowledge available facts that help us understand why decision makers may have been influenced to act as they did, even if eventually history may consider they were mistaken to do so.

The dispute about the estimated number of casualties led to a final confrontation between the NASM director and the American Legion that ended the exhibit. How did it happen? Director Harwit had approached the American Legion, a large veterans organization, to seek its input and support for the exhibit. After some meetings the American Legion seemed to sign off on the exhibit. Suddenly the situation changed radically. What put the fat in the fire, insofar as the American Legion was concerned, was the NASM's reducing the number of estimated casualties for an invasion of Kyushu. In a January 9, 1995, letter to the American Legion, Martin Harwit said that Professor Bernstein showed Harwit numbers from Admiral Leahy's diary entry for the June 18, 1945, meeting at which the invasion was discussed with President Truman. Leahy reported that General Marshall said that "such an effort will not cost us more than 63,000 of the 190,000 combatant troops estimated as necessary for the operation." In his letter Director Harwit said "As Bernstein pointed out to us, 63,000 represents 30 percent of 190,000, and that evidently is the figure that Leahy had in mind at the meeting that afternoon." Harwit said that the number came from a 1986 Bernstein article in the *Bulletin of the Atomic Scientists* and that led to reducing the number of estimated casualties in the exhibit from 250,000. The American Legion reacted vigorously to the change.

The 63,000 casualties mentioned by Admiral Leahy is 33.1 percent of 190,000, but Professor Bernstein's rounding off can be tolerated despite his passion for exactness. Bernstein and Harwit did not say where Marshall obtained the 190,000 figure that the admiral noted on page 384 of his memoirs: "General Marshall was of the opinion that such an effort would not cost us in *casualties* [*sic*] more than 63,000 of the 190,00 combat troops estimated as necessary for the operation." It is important to note that the admiral referred to casualties and not to fatalities. If there were 63,000 casualties, about one in four, or 15,750, could be deaths. The June 15 Joint Planning Committee estimate of scenario one casualties was 193,000, of which 40,000 would be deaths. From what is known of the information presented to the president, there was Army reluctance to present casualty figures for reasons explained elsewhere. The June 15 report had the number of men in the land invasion force as 766,700 with estimated casualties of 193,000, or 25.2 percent. If the casualties were the 30 percent referred to by Bernstein, the number of casualties would be 230,000, and if at 33.1 percent the number would be 253, 777. Perhaps Marshall used the 190,000 figure for the initial landing and estimated heavy casualties in the first days of fighting. Certainly, there could be no suggestion in the planning for the invasion that only 190,000 troops would be needed to take Kyushu. The basis for the 190,000 figure is not explained and the resulting lower casualty figure coming at the last minute angered the American Legion.

Greg Mitchell, a member of the Historians' Committee for the Free Discussion of Hiroshima, and coauthor with Robert Jay Lifton of *Hiroshima in America: Fifty Years of Denial*, said that he found himself near the center of the struggle over the exhibit. He referred to the 63,000 figure as "deaths allegedly averted only by use of the bomb." However, Leahy had referred to 63,000 *casualties* and knew the difference between casualties and deaths. Mitchell did not have the facts straight.

It has been suggested that the American Legion wanted to kill the exhibit and used the changed casualty figures as an excuse to do so. If so, Harwit supplied the weapon. The NASM did not look into Bernstein's "new discovery" from a book published in 1950 to determine if it substantiated his claim. Harwit must have known that, for different reasons, the casualty estimates were a sticking point with both the critics and the curators, and although the latter would be pleased with the lower figure, it would be a red flag for the critics. It is not a matter of disputing Leahy's diary entry, but the importance of understanding where the casualty figures came from and what they meant. In any event the ensuing furor over this latest change meant the end of the much revised exhibit and led to Harwit's resignation.[18]

With the fervor of true believers, those who contest the possibility of high casualties during an invasion continue to juggle quotations and numbers to prove that Truman was a liar. Their strongest argument is that nowhere is there an archival copy written by a "high official" that contains what Professor Bernstein called an "astronomically high" figure. A similar argument is made by Holocaust deniers who claim that the absence of a signed order by Hitler to execute Jews indicates that he did not know about their fate. In both cases context requires reasonable persons to believe otherwise. After more than half a century it is fair to say that, if by casualties in an invasion of Japan anyone meant American lives lost, then a figure of one million would be too high. If the military definition of casualties is intended, then the most probable estimate under optimum conditions would be about 250,000 for a campaign that went from the beaches of Kyushu to Tokyo, with the real possibility of reaching 500,000 or even more under adverse circumstances. Using the military's rule of thumb of one death for each four casualties, American deaths in Japan could range from 62,500 to 125,000. Certainly casualty figures would be much higher than the mistaken 31,000 mentioned by some writers and the figure Director Harwit was given by Professor Bernstein. Revisionists were on strong ground, according to McGeorge Bundy, when they questioned assertions that the bomb saved a million lives. "What the best of them do not question, however, is the reality of the conviction in the Pentagon that without the bomb there must be readiness for repeated invasions of the home islands against resistance that could be fierce and sustained."

What might have happened if the A-Bomb was not used and the war continued, depending on blockade and conventional bombing, leading ultimately to an invasion of Japan? Other outposts were still held by the Japanese, including a large force on Luzon and large forces in Korea and Formosa. Eliminating those forces as well as those in Indonesia and China would not have been easy, and Allied sailors, airmen, marines and soldiers would have died to accomplish those tasks. It should be remembered that the Japanese held all of Korea since early in the century, knew the country and terrain, and that it was held by several hundred thousand experienced combat troops. The American experience later in the Korean war suggests what would have been required to deal with the Japanese forces in Korea had there not been a surrender. There is no way to estimate those potential casualties except to refer to the death before dishonor defenses at Iwo Jima and Okinawa where the garrisons fought to the last man, or committed suicide, often taking Allied soldiers with them.

The cavalier manner in which revisionists have handled the casualty issue was well expressed by Geoffrey Smith who maintained that a "mere forty-six thousand" Americans would be killed or injured during an invasion of Japan. That figure is contradicted by too many others to be taken seriously but it reveals how, at a long distance from the summer of 1945, a revisionist could refer to "mere" deaths. The thought of low casualties may have comforted Smith and others who argued that invasion losses would be low, but even that figure, dismissive as it was, would not have comforted the families back home entitled to exchange their blue star for a gold star in their window.

In a very real sense Richard Kohn was correct when he told Director Harwit that the casualty argument was lacking in context; the real issue was the campaign, not the invasion. "With Japan prepared to fight all-out indefinitely ... the casualties would have been just tremendous on both sides, and everybody at the time knew it." That should be coupled with Admiral Leahy's recollection that President Truman was "completely favorable toward defeating our Far Eastern enemy with the smallest possible loss of American lives. It wasn't a matter of dollars. It might require more time — and more dollars — if we did not invade Japan. But it would cost fewer lives." And Robert Newman was right to fault Secretary Stimson for his account of why the A-Bomb was used. It would have been best to say it was to end the war quickly and everyone would have understood that that would have saved many lives. How many lives would have been lost can be debated and never accurately known, but the magnitude of the American losses, whether 60,000 or 126,000, or even more, would have been intolerable. Instead of nit-picking about the number of casualties when they knew that more deaths in the Pacific were intolerable, they might have devoted their considerable talents to fostering genuine understanding of the war and its tragic ending.[19]

This essay began by mentioning that McGeorge Bundy was impressed by Professor Bernstein's critique of the administration's casualty figures. As someone close to Secretary Stimson and with a distinguished career in government, such testimony lends credibility to Professor Bernstein's contention that the figures were exaggerated. Professor Bernstein's contention that Truman's statement that the bomb saved half a million lives was a myth may seem plausible, until his sources are examined. Professor Bernstein's optimistic view of losses during the planned invasion ignores the intelligence obtained after mid July 1945 as well as the planners pessimism about the possibility of Japanese surrender after Kyushu, explaining that it would be a "pure gamble that the Japanese would admit defeat under such conditions," and thus it would probably be necessary to move onto the Tokyo Plain. It is unfortunate that McGeorge Bundy, when a professor of history at New York University, and someone who tried for balance in his assessment of persons and policies, did not have one of his assistants dig into the background of the debate about casualties instead of relying on Professor Bernstein's rosy assessment of potential casualties.[20]

VIII

Defending the Exhibit

When considering the educational role of the museum, Spencer Crew, the director of the Smithsonian's National Museum of American History, was of the opinion that "Visitors also can bring experiences and information to museum presentation which might generate interpretations at odds with the findings of the curator. Their perspective deserves the same consideration which scholars give to colleagues." That injunction was not heeded by the curators or by those vigorously and often acerbically defending the exhibit. Many of the defenders were known for their ideological positions vis-a-vis American policy past and present. That is why the focus of this essay is on the positions taken by a representative group of them, in order to show the background and tenor of the defense of the exhibit.

When Steven Dubin defended the exhibit, he attempted to place the controversy in a broad socio-historical context. The role of the museum in contemporary America was described as educational, confronting the dark side of the nation's past, unlike the old-fashioned commemorative style that served little or no authentic educational purpose. Dubin overlooked the fact that when the NASM framed the debate between critics and curators in that manner, they carefully avoided grappling with the veracity of the script, which was assumed to be substantively above reproach. That tactic avoided the core of the controversy, which was that the curators designed an exhibit that seriously misrepresented the history of the summer of 1945.

Rufus Miles, another friend of the exhibit, found that Truman grossly exaggerated the estimated casualties if there was an invasion, and that there would have been very few casualties had alternatives to the bomb been used. In hindsight, however, he said that to fault Truman for his decision "would be to ignore the circumstances and atmosphere that surrounded the decision. The more appropriate question is: Why were the circumstances and atmosphere not conducive to terminating the war without the onus being placed on the United States for the legitimization of nuclear weapons in the arsenals of the world?" After convicting Truman of gross exaggeration and worse, Miles seemed to ease Truman's culpability a bit by suggesting that he was a victim of circumstances, but implied that the war could have been terminated without the bomb. However, just how that might have been done was not specified.[1]

Miles did, however, raise an important question about the context in which decisions were made during wartime, something rarely considered by the revisionists. Wartime meant constant crisis with decision makers buffeted with many more problems than the decision about the atom bomb. That may be difficult to understand when reading files in the archives, but it was the daily menu of people like Dean Acheson who served as an assistant secretary of state, and later became Secretary of State. In his memoir he wrote: "The period covered by this book—1941 through 1952—was one of great obscurity to those who lived through it. Not only was the future clouded, a common enough situation, but the present was equally clouded. The significance of events was shrouded in ambiguity. We groped after interpretations of them, sometimes reversed lines of action based on earlier views, and hesitated long before grasping what now seems obvious."[2]

Another version of the same problem confronting policy makers came from a conversation on the evening of June 30, 1945, when Navy Secretary James Forrestal had a dinner conversation with presidential aide Harry Hopkins and they discussed England's future. The two men disagreed about England's increasingly socialistic turn but did not pursue the subject at length. Walter Millis noted that "opportunities for this kind of broad and philosophical review of the world history they were making were comparatively rare. The immediate issues of high policy were urgent."[3] In times of crisis, thinking about alternative courses of action for an unknowable future in a manner that would satisfy revisionists, competed with the pressure of dealing with immediate problems like saving lives and ending a war that need urgent attention. The impossibility of thinking about matters that surfaced long after the fact and in the light of what might have happened long after the fact comes best to academics with an unworldly mind set.

"Historical Controversies: Was the Decision to Drop the Bomb Justified?" was how *The Crossroads* introduced a subject to which it returned several times in different contexts. The script set the stage for its view of how and why the A-Bomb was used by introducing President Truman's role in the decision to use the A-Bomb as follows: "President Truman was like a little boy on a toboggan. He never had the opportunity to say 'we *will* drop the bomb.' All he could do was say 'no.'" That quotation came from General Leslie Groves, a man not known for modesty in portraying his role in the development and use of the A-Bomb, and it fits neatly into the revisionist portrayal of Truman as a passive captive of events. It surprises Truman scholars that *The Crossroads* found that "Truman's role in the 'decision to drop the bomb' was largely confined to verbally confirming proposals by his advisers."[4]

The Crossroads concluded that the current scholarly consensus is that, while the Soviets played a role in the thinking of Truman and his advisors, "saving American lives and shortening the war were more important. Most historians also agree that there was scarcely any 'decision to drop the bomb.' Truman merely approved the preparations already underway; the Manhattan Project had a great deal of momentum and the strategic bombing of German and Japanese cities made atomic bombing easier to accept." According to Professor Sherry, General Groves said that the burden of decision fell on Truman but that as far as Groves was concerned "his decision was one of noninterference — basically a decision not to upset the existing plans." That would have been as affirmative a decision as could be made, because Truman could have said no, and was explicit in stating that he alone would issue the order for its use. However, Stanley Goldberg, a member of the NASM's advisory committee for the exhibit, suggested that the bombing of Nagasaki came as a surprise to Truman.[5]

That was akin to what some historians have suggested, that once Truman gave the order to use the A-Bomb, the process would have continued inexorably. Actually, the situation was quite different, as anyone acquainted with military operations knows. In a January 2, 1953, memo Robert Ferrell found that, "According to Dr. Rudolph Winnacker, Historian of the Office of Secretary of Defense, it is clear that the Gen. Handy order could have been countermanded in the event Japan had responded to the Potsdam ultimatum — just as any military order can be countermanded. The fundamental decision to use the bomb preceded the Gen. Handy letter, and the decision to 'trigger' its use and define the targets was made by the President as indicated in his memorandum."

Further evidence that the bombing was under control, and not handled in a Dr. Strangelove scenario, came from the official history of the Air Force. After the Japanese note of August 10, bombing strikes against the home islands continued. Because he feared that area bombing might complicate negotiations, General Carl Spaatz limited operations to precision bombing. A scheduled strike was canceled because of bad weather, but the American press interpreted this as a cease-fire order. "Believing that the resumption of B-29 attacks would in turn be played up as an indication that negotiations had failed, the President on 10 August ordered that all strategic bombing stop, even to the extent of recalling planes which might be in the air." That contradicts the allegations that the bombing was on autopilot and beyond presidential control. With negotiations hanging fire on the 14th, the bombing was resumed until the Japanese surrendered, or, as they argued, they accepted the Proclamation.

Assuming that there were no written orders to use the bomb, Professor Sherry said "countless other cities had been destroyed without the signed orders of prime minister or president. It was fitting that they were also not required for Hiroshima or Nagasaki." In Professor Sherry's mind that showed Truman's passive role in the bombing. In fact it reveals Professor Sherry's lamentable lack of knowledge about how military operations are carried out in modern times. Once upon a time kings and emperors were present to give orders as Napoleon did at Waterloo. But that time was long past by World War II. When the broad parameters of an operation are decided, subordinate levels in the chain of command issue specific orders, not the president.

When slighting President Truman's role in the decision to drop the bomb, Professor Sherry said that Truman waited until May 16 to even attempt to learn what the military's plans were for securing victory and only in June did he and Stimson begin thinking seriously about how to speed victory. That implies that after he became president he did not meet with General Marshall, among others, for the briefings that were routine in the White House. As warrant for the claim that Truman failed to plan for victory, Professor Sherry referred to page 235 in President Truman's memoirs published in 1955. A review of that page and the following pages show that Truman and Stimson discussed war plans, as well as the Morgenthau plan, which Truman opposed. There was no indication that the war had not been discussed earlier.

But Professor Sherry was wrong to claim that Truman delayed learning about the war. That process began as soon as Truman became president. President Roosevelt died on Thursday, April 12, 1945, and according to Ed Cray, on Saturday, April 14, "At 10:00 a. m. that day, the new president met for the first time with his Joint Chiefs and the secretaries of war and navy.... For the next hour the military leaders briefed the president." Further evidence that the president was kept current with military affairs comes from the fact that, when there was a question about Eisenhower pushing on to Berlin, as a matter of policy the Joint Chiefs continued what had been sustained by President Roosevelt, who left such matters to be decided based on military priorities. That policy was reaffirmed by Truman little more than a week after he came into office. The president would not have done that without the input of his military advisors.

It was not enough to be mistaken about Truman learning about the war. Professor Sherry went on to say, "As for the bomb in the context of the war with Japan, Truman, as he knew, had inherited such a weighty legacy assuming its use that for him to question it would have required exceptional intellectual and political courage." Professor Sherry's opinion of Truman's intellectual ability was based on Truman's self knowledge, which somehow had been communicated to Sherry. If more historians had Sherry's ability to intuit what a dead president was thinking, the writing of history would be much easier and dramatic.

It should not be necessary to rebut the tendentious references about Truman's supposed intellectual and political limitations. Although without the graduate education enjoyed by his revisionist critics, Truman's life experiences admirably prepared him for his responsibilities. *The Crossroads* repeated portrayal of Truman as a captive of an inevitable process and a virtual puppet is at odds with the astute, politically savvy (and far from saintly) historical person known for independent judgment and decisiveness.[6]

In the section "Alternatives to an Invasion and Dropping the Bomb" *The Crossroads* concluded, "It is also clear that there were alternatives to both an invasion and dropping atomic bombs without warning." Professor Dower had confidently claimed that "there were indeed 'roads not taken' available to Pres. Harry S. Truman and his top advisors at the time." Much earlier Professor Bernstein had asserted as much in regard to the Emperor: "a guarantee of the Emperor's government might have removed the chief impediment to peace." Similarly Alan Cranston said, "It will never be known whether an alternative policy could have ended the war, for none was ever considered." However, "Since these alternatives are clearer in hindsight ... the debate over the 'decision to drop the bomb' will remain forever controversial." That was a singularly uninformed comment in the face of evidence that the alternatives had been considered and rejected by Washington. Those alternatives were: demonstrating the bomb, depending on the blockade and conventional bombing and awaiting a Soviet declaration of war.

Cranston's opinion was echoed by Kai Bird and Lawrence Lifschultz who said "Nor was there evidence at the presidential or cabinet level of thoughtful deliberation or serious consideration of alternatives to the bomb." What Bird and Lifschultz might consider thoughtful and serious deliberation is not made clear. Obviously the meetings of the Interim Committee did not reach the high standards they set. In an effort to persuade the reader that there were viable alternatives to using the A-Bomb, Professor Alperovitz used an excerpt from an Army report prepared for the Chief of the Strategic Planning Section in April 1946, which replays the report of the Strategic Bombing Survey: "The war would almost certainly have terminated when Russia entered the war against Japan." The excerpt is not in quotation marks in the book but presumably is complete as reproduced. It reviews the Japanese efforts to induce the Soviets to "serve as a medium for arranging the peace." Then, without mentioning the bombing of Hiroshima, the report went on to say, "While the Japanese were awaiting an answer from Russia, there occurred the disastrous event which the Japanese leaders regarded a utter catastrophe and which they had energetically sought to prevent at any cost — Russia declared war upon Japan." The report continued, "Investigation shows that there was little mention of the use of the atomic bomb by the United States in the discussions leading up to the 9 August decision. The dropping of the bomb was the pretext seized upon by all leaders as the reason for ending the war, but made it almost a certainty that the Japanese would have capitulated upon the entry of Russia into the war."

By 1994, when Professor Alperovitz published the revised edition of *Atomic Diplomacy*, much more was known about what happened in Tokyo during the summer of 1945. There was a Japanese decision to end the war on terms at least minimally acceptable to Japan by appealing to Moscow, and there was tension between the so-called peace party and the military hard liners until the very end when Hirohito intervened. Even then matters teetered in the balance until the final meeting with the Emperor. As did Paul Nitze's Strategic Bombing Survey, this 1946 report not only downplayed the effect of the bomb on Japanese policy, it made it an unnecessary sideshow.

The Soviet declaration certainly played a role in Japan's surrender. One can argue about how significant it was, but for the report to downplay the impact of the A-Bomb and conclude that Soviet entry in the war was the decisive factor causing surrender is excessive. In view of Nitze's report, what was written in 1946 might have made that case, but for it to be cited in the 1990s in support of the author's hypothesis is disturbing. Extensive contrary evidence was available that should be mentioned, for example, Ronald Spector's *Eagle Against the Sun* that appeared in 1985, and his *Listening to the Enemy*, that appeared in 1988. Failing to do so seems like an effort to cook the books.[7]

The alternatives listed by *The Crossroads*, and then admitted to be such in hindsight, appear in other places in the script along with reasons why they were rejected. Although finally called "speculative," the manner in which the alternatives are presented leaves the reader with a clear impression that they were genuine alternatives in 1945. If they were speculative, and in hindsight, then there was no way NASM could validly make the definitive statement that those alternatives were "clear," implying that they actually had existed as such at the time. The seeming reservations expressed in the script would have been of little weight in a heavily visual presentation.

Under the heading "Military Opposition to the Bombing," *The Crossroads* revealed that some top military figures, including Admiral Leahy and General Eisenhower, expressed opposition to dropping the atomic bomb without warning, although *The Crossroads* expressed some skepticism about Eisenhower's opposition. The "Interim Committee" appointed to consider the use of the bomb was concerned that a warning about the bomb could endanger Allied POWs and that a demonstration might be ineffective or a failure. *The Crossroads* believed that "the proposed alternatives were examined so briefly, however, that many scholars have argued they did not get the attention they deserved." A following sentence reported that other scholars defended the decision against a demonstration or warning, but the tilt in the script's presentation is evident in the assertion as fact that the proposed alternatives were discussed so briefly that many scholars have argued they did not get due attention. In fact, however, discussions about use of the A-Bomb do not reveal there was the undue brevity that *The Crossroads* stated so emphatically. In his lengthy discussion of the pros and cons of a demonstration, McGeorge Bundy, who favored a warning and or demonstration, nonetheless presented cogent reasons why each was rejected. His account would have helped the curators understand the issues involved had they bothered to check his 1988 book.

Professor Bernstein is perhaps the most prolific and seemingly authoritative writer about the war's end and the use of the atom bomb. When criticizing the decision to close the exhibit he cited political pressure from

Congress and veterans, accusing them of "misconceived patriotism," of wanting to preserve the idea of the "good war" and ignoring contested issues such as the use of the A-Bomb. Claiming the critics successfully blocked free inquiry, dialogue, questioning, and dissent, he mentioned that "After World War II some of America's most respected military leaders, including Gen. Dwight D. Eisenhower, Gen. Douglas MacArthur, Adm. William Leahy, and Adm. Ernest King, questioned whether use of the A-Bomb had been necessary. In their view, Japan was near collapse and surrender. Some — like Eisenhower and Leahy — went further, asking also whether the bombings had been moral." At Potsdam, Eisenhower had told President Truman that he did not believe it was necessary to use "this terrible thing" to force the already defeated Japanese to surrender. His opposition is often mentioned, but unmentioned by Professor Bernstein is that Eisenhower later candidly admitted that "My views were merely personal and an immediate reaction; they were not based upon any analysis of the subject."

In his memoirs Admiral Leahy referred to the bomb as "this barbarous weapon," and believed that it was of no material assistance in the war with Japan. The opinions of those men deserve very serious consideration and are often quoted, and Professor Bernstein accused the exhibit's critics of seeking to bar the words of Leahy. He failed to add, however, that Leahy also said, "I am forced to a reluctant conclusion that for the security of my own country which has been the guiding principle in my approach to all problems faced during my career, there is but one course open to us: until the United Nations, or some world organization, can guarantee — and have the power to enforce that guarantee — that the world will be spared the terrors of atomic warfare, the United States must have more and better atom bombs than any potential enemy."

General Marshall is invariably mentioned as another high-ranking officer who opposed the A-Bomb. He masterminded the United States military strategy during the war, so his opinion was of utmost importance. Marshall's attitude toward using the A-Bomb can be gauged from an account by Arthur Holly Compton, who was a member of the scientific advisory panel that assisted the President's Interim Committee on the use of the A-Bomb. When there was a discussion of a demonstration to warn Japan, Compton said, "Though General Marshall was thus noting a real military objection to any demonstration of the bomb, he seemed to accept the fact that its use was nevertheless important. This I verified in subsequent discussions. He was fully convinced at this time that the bomb should be used. This was primarily to bring the war quickly to a close and thereby save lives." It is clear from Compton's account that a great deal of thought went into the effort to decide whether there could be an effective demonstration of the bomb before it was used militarily. The final virtual consensus was that a demonstration was not feasible. Although Marshall had reservations about the A-Bomb, after the war he had no doubt about the use of the two bombs. "I think it was quite necessary to drop the bombs in order to shorten the war. There were hundreds and hundreds of thousands of American lives involved in this thing.... We had notified them of the bomb. They didn't choose to believe that. And what they needed was shock action and they got it. I think it was very wise to use it." It was clear, according to McGeorge Bundy, "that Marshall always assumed the bomb would be used when ready, that he truly anticipated the need for invasion."

Constant repetition that some high ranking officers "questioned" the use of the bomb conveys the idea that they opposed its use, which was not the case. Questions were raised about its use and about countless other matters of strategy and tactics, but the "questioning" about the A-Bomb had none of the implications suggested by Bernstein. As for Leahy asking about the morality of the bomb, like many others he had such questions, but Bernstein failed to mention, as revisionists commonly fail to mention, that at the time Leahy took no principled stand against its use and after the war reluctantly approved the A-Bomb. In the interest of intellectual transparency Professor Bernstein might have added that fact to his discussion of patriotism.[8]

In "An Ultimatum to Japan" *The Crossroads* implied that at Potsdam, Secretary of State James Byrnes was responsible for preventing Japan's surrender. The Potsdam Proclamation of July 26, 1945, called on Japan to surrender or face utter destruction. *The Crossroads* said, "Because of political opposition in America to concessions or modifications of 'unconditional surrender,' Secretary of States [*sic*] Byrnes eliminated any reference to the retention of Emperor Hirohito on the throne. Also eliminated were any direct references to the atomic bomb or Soviet entry into the war. As a result of these changes, the Proclamation was not effective in changing the position of the Japanese government." That the Proclamation should have threatened Soviet entry into the war, a decision reserved to Stalin who was not a party to it, revealed how little the curators understood Potsdam. In addition, because Japan's military discounted the significance of Hiroshima, what impression would have been made by an announcement that

America had an atom bomb? If the intention was to leave the reader with the impression that Byrnes alone was ultimately responsible for drafting the Proclamation and thus for its failure to force Japan's surrender, it was successful. Byrnes is the revisionist's Rasputin who guided a puppet Truman.

That becomes clear in a chapter Professor Dower wrote later which mentioned several reasons why Truman, on the advice of James Byrnes, had deleted a reference to the monarchy at Potsdam. One was that it was considered domestically risky, a fact well known from other historians; another was an unwillingness to compromise United States control over Japan in the way it happened in Germany. Yet another reason, according to Professor Dower, was that "It also is possible — and this is the most cynical reading of the decision — that he wished to make the bomb known to the world in the most dramatic fashion and thus deliberately chose to render the warning statement unacceptable to the Japanese leadership." His reference to Truman's hypothetical cynical reason for using the bomb is exceeded only by his cynical attribution of that reasoning to Truman, without a shred of evidence in a bald statement that was slyly covered with "It also is possible."

Professor Dower also made much of the fact that the Soviet Union was not consulted about the Proclamation or invited to join in issuing it. He did this knowing that the Soviets were not as yet a party to the war with Japan. The Soviets played their cards close to their chest and even at that late date denied American bombers landing rights on territory they controlled in order to keep up the facade of neutrality in the war with Japan. That also is why Stalin did not sign the Potsdam Declaration. However, some historians will use any stick to beat such a dead horse. Perhaps because of space limitations Professor Dower did not mention that at Potsdam Stalin had approved continuing the unconditional surrender policy. What is paradoxical about Dower's account of the final days of the war is that his editors said they hoped that the stories in *Days of Destiny* in which his chapter appeared "will suggest to you something of the diversity of historical experience and the variety of historians' approach to the past." No diversity or variety appeared in Dower's account of the war's end. The repetition of the standard revisionist arguments ended with his recommendation of the work of Martin Sherwin and Gar Alperovitz for further reading. Not one dissenting voice was mentioned.[9]

It could be anticipated that as an advisor to the exhibit, and also because he was known for his extensive study of the Truman administration, and especially of the decision to use the A-Bomb, Professor Bernstein would defend the exhibit. Never reluctant to ascribe base motives to those he criticized, in a 1983 article Bernstein had noted that 23 American POWs were killed at Hiroshima, and that the information was suppressed for fear of a public backlash. "Probably officials did not want to risk unleashing a dialogue that might challenge government decisions, threaten careers, and make future combat use of the A-bomb more difficult." He failed to mention that one reason a demonstration of the A-Bomb was rejected was concern that POWs might be moved to the site. In any event, it was not known for certain that POWs were in Hiroshima. Bernstein was off base when imputing unseemly self-interest to unnamed officials, who could only be the top men in the administration, if a "dialogue" was unleashed.

It helps to understand Professor Bernstein's approach to such matters by reviewing what he said some years earlier about post war American policy: "My own essay on American foreign policy emphasizes that American leaders sought to reshape much of the world according to American needs and standards, and thereby contributed significantly to the origins of the Cold War.... Failures to reach agreement on international control of atomic energy, efforts to use economic aid to coerce the Soviet Union, and disagreements on Germany contributed to the antagonisms even before Truman, in seeking aid for Greece and Turkey, declared a war of ideology in his 'Truman Doctrine' speech of March 1947. Blinded by their own ideology to evidence of indigenous revolution in Greece, American policymakers wrongly interpreted it as a Soviet plot."

If nothing else Professor Bernstein has been consistent in his basically sympathetic treatment of Soviet policy. His account of what happened after the war resembles that of Melvyn Leffler, who saw Stalin as an insecure person without any consistent strategic program, but driven by self-interest. Leffler's portrayal of Eastern European nations immediately after the war saw them almost as emerging democracies, until American policies forced Stalin to create a *cordon sanitaire*, called the Iron Curtain, to maintain Soviet security. Such authors seem never to have encountered Alex De Jonge's study of Stalin or Robert Conquest's studies of the Soviet system, just two among the many that have a more nuanced view of the Soviet system, and one confirmed by material from the Russian archives; and Russian authors who no longer hew to a party line, unlike many Western authors who voluntarily toed that line. In the final analysis, according to Vojtech Mastny, despite Western missteps "The unbridgeable chasm between Stalinist and Western values was also the ultimate reason why the post-Stalin leadership could not be brought to entertaining the idea of genuine accommodation with the West even if the West had tried."[10]

When the NASM made even slight changes to the original script the defenders believed that the museum was abdicating its responsibility to defend revisionist orthodoxy. In Michael Hogan's opinion the historical record shows that the controversy was between veterans' memories, or "personal narratives" that validated their identity, versus the historical documents and consensus of the experts. Along with other *Crossroads* defenders he made scant reference to the criticism leveled against the script. It was not until much later and reluctantly that the curators made some changes, not in terms of substance but in an ultimate act of condescension, to acknowledge the "feelings" of the veterans. Without referring to specifics, except in the case of the number of possible casualties, the exhibit's defenders made much of what they called professional consensus, freedom of speech and academic freedom. However, none of the critics wanted to limit the free speech of the curators, they merely wanted them to be honest. The pretense that the critics denied curatorial freedom of speech was both a clever and specious argument. NASM staff are government employees and free to say whatever they want, and so were those who criticized the exhibit. The freedom of speech guaranteed by the First Amendment protects citizens against government efforts to close debate, it does not insulate the government against citizens expressing their discontent with governmental actions. When Michael Hogan and the curators cried freedom of speech they enlisted the visceral reaction of much of the media to free speech claims, as illustrated by Peter Jennings' diatribe against the veterans. It was a clever public relations ploy but had no relevance to the issues raised by *The Crossroads*. Indeed, by crying wolf, NASM sought to deny critics the right to complain about the aberrations contained in the exhibit. Likewise, the claim for academic freedom for the museum staff was ludicrous, a deliberate red herring that had no relevance in the debate. As a former professor Martin Harwit had been accustomed to the idea of academic freedom but was confused when he applied the concept to a museum. The professional staff deserved respect for their expertise and a fair hearing of their ideas. They no more enjoyed academic freedom than the professionals at the Department of Agriculture or the Department of State.

It would be asking too much to expect the NASM staff and its advisors, after investing themselves so heavily in their proposal, to take a detached view of *The Crossroads* and the critics' comments. Their agenda was under attack and they responded defensively, as might be expected. Their later reaction to sometimes shrill and politically charged criticism also was understandable, but as professionals they should have expected no less, given their stated purpose, which waved a red flag before the public. With that agenda it was impossible for them to react to a challenge by a careful examination of the specifics of the criticism instead of retiring behind appeals to the authority of "historical consensus," and decrying traditionalists who promoted the myths of yesteryear. By using non-responsive and provocative language that, in its own way, was as shrill as the language of some of the more opinionated critics of the exhibit, they helped to create a battleground ruled by invective. The debate did not begin in that fashion, and had there been a more transparent, collegial response to the men "who were there," it would have cost the NASM nothing and might have avoided the debacle that followed.

Sometimes snide and understandably weighted in favor of the exhibit, Michael Hogan gave the controversy a blow by blow description that ought to be read if one wants the flavor of a well-written defense of the exhibit. Characterizing the battle as one between conservatives and the forces of reason who believed that the "Smithsonian should have an independent voice in shaping historical consciousness," as much as anyone Hogan and his colleagues politicized the debate by using "conservative" to demonize the exhibit's critics.

The president of the Organization of American Historians (OAH) joined the fray, cautioning that "outside interference by special interest groups, ideological partisans, and politicians" would compromise the exhibit and imperil academic freedom. Evidently the OAH did not consider itself a special interest group or an ideological partisan of the exhibit. By referring to academic freedom the OAH, an organization of academics, surely knew better than to agree with the irrelevant claim advanced by Director Harwit that the curators enjoyed academic freedom. The OAH was joined by Roy K. Flint, president of the Society for Military History, who noted that while historians might disagree about Truman's decision, they supported freedom of speech. That was an irrelevant comment because freedom of speech was never a genuine issue in the controversy but a convenient distraction waved like the bloody shirt to rally support for the exhibit. Both sides spoke freely and sometimes heatedly about their opponents. Flint also wanted the Smithsonian to take a stand against the politicizing of scholarship in public discourse. That was ironic considering what Smithsonian insider Otto Mayr later said about the exhibit having no problem had Democratic majorities continued in Congress. Critics of the exhibit heartily agreed, because that is exactly why they began their struggle with the NASM. One can wonder whether the representatives of the historical journals had studied the original script for *The Crossroads* before coming to its defense. Had they done so they would have seen that it could be legitimately criticized.[10]

Although exhibit supporters made much of the fact that they represented the consensus of scholars, they might more accurately have claimed to represent the interests and consensus of some scholars who were influential in their field. Too much can be attributed to the fact that professional associations rushed to the exhibit's defense. Professional associations issue such statements to defend their turf because, like any interest group, they react instinctively to what seems an attack on even the fringes of their interests. They defended what they saw as an intrusion on the professionalism of a relatively small number of committed scholars. Adept at public relations, the exhibit's defenders skillfully inflated the issues involved in the controversy. However, apart from pro forma statements by the associations, it is important to note that there was no massive outpouring of support from other historians.

As the number of revisions in the script mounted to five, 48 "historians and scholars" wrote to the NASM asking for the restoration of the exhibit to its earlier format. They objected to "a transparent attempt at historical cleansing" and wanted the exhibit to reflect "the broad range of debate over our nation's history — and not just what is perceived at the moment as patriotically correct history." One of the signers was Professor Noam Chomsky, of the department of linguistics and philosophy at the Massachusetts Institute of Technology, a scholar (although not an historian) and a long time fierce critic of American foreign policy. After W. Burr Bennett, who was an early critic of the exhibit, wrote to him, Chomsky replied on December 12, 1994, telling Bennett he was unaware that the veneration of the *Enola Gay* had reached the stage of idolatry. He agreed that "Japan did commit a crime on Dec. 7–8 1941, bombing air bases in two US colonies that had been stolen from their inhabitants ... and slaughtered hundreds of thousands of defenseless people in the traditional style. But these Japanese crimes, though real enough, rank so low in the scale of those we have regularly committed, before and since, that no honest person would take them very seriously as a justification for invasion."

With arrogant condescension he told Bennett that his examples of alleged removal of context from the exhibit, even if taken seriously, were trivial and hardly worth discussion. "If you think otherwise, you should contact the authors of the statement, not the signers, most of whom, like me, probably only agreed with the general drift, not necessarily the details." For a "scholar" to admit to such unprincipled (in academic terms) behavior that would imperil the future of a graduate student, reveals Chomsky's contempt for the standards expected of the professorate. Chomsky probably would argue that he was speaking not as a "scholar" but as a political advocate. In either role he was pretending to be knowledgeable about an issue when he was not. Fierce polemics against the United States and attracting public attention are Chomsky's forte. That surfaced again in a hastily prepared book published a month after the September 11, 2001, World Trade Center attack in which he echoed his remarks to Bennet, claiming, for example, that the United States is a leading terrorist state, and doubting that there was credible evidence that Osama bin Laden was involved in the attack. However, according to *The New York Times*, the book and his others have received little mainstream press attention because they are regarded by editors "as too extreme to merit comment."[12] However, his ranting receives attention abroad as a fierce critic of American policy and has a following on many a university campus.

Paying attention only to the cries of outraged innocence by the curators and their advisors, and in all probability along with Professor Chomsky, without seeing the script that caused the controversy, the knee jerk reaction by the historical associations was strikingly similar to the blue code found in some police departments when one of their members is accused of some fault. It is not surprising that academics, like other in-groups, have a culture of self-protection that leads to overlooking the importance of evaluating sources before jumping to the defense of supposedly embattled colleagues. That culture also discouraged reasonable discussion of the issues involved in the controversy. According to Richard Posner, who discussed the open letters and large advertisements by scholars in newspapers like *The New York Times* (that may cost $100,000), a salutary norm would be "disclosure in open letters and full-page advertisements of the relevant expertise of each signer and a certification by the signer that he had acquainted himself with the facts pertinent to the position taken in the letter or advertisement." Although possibly salutary in terms of requir-

ing some accountability from the signers, there is little chance that anything similar could keep Chomsky and others from exploiting their celebrity
status.

Martin Sherwin said that the revised exhibit had nothing to do with
the history of the end of the war as it is known to serious historians. And
Michael Hogan, with not uncommon condescension, found that when the
critics needed expert support "they pointed invariably to the authors of
popular histories, such as David McCullough, or to military historians,
who were seen as somehow uncorrupted by the 'revisionist' disease. But
mostly the critics were their own experts or found among American veterans, whose collective memory constituted a more authentic past than the
archival accounts of professional scholars."

Those memories, in Hogan's opinion, "became weapons not only in
a vigorous anti-intellectual assault on the practice of professional history
but also on the principle of free speech and the tradition of academic freedom." He considered criticism of the exhibit a political statement that
encouraged censorship and a false consciousness of the past. Finally, as a
last word, and leaving aside academic courtesy, Hogan made the ridicu-
lous comment that John Correll, the editor of *Air Force* magazine, was like
Henry Ford who believed history was "bunk." They both "sought to build
a romanticized version of the past as an alternative to the one offered by
historians."[13] According to Philip Nobile, also a vigorous defender of the
exhibit, John Correll "borked (sic) the Smithsonian's exhibit as 'politically
correct curating'" and he was upbraided for a lack of journalistic ethics
and accused of foul play because he elided or omitted part of a statement
that did not change its meaning. Objecting to a common practice in academia and journalism was a strange and pointless accusation by Nobile.[14]

Michael Hogan's 1998 book, *A Cross of Iron*, deplored the influence of
interested parties in the battles between Congress, the Pentagon and the
White House in the development of national security policy after World War
II. He has a finely detailed account of those debates which were orders of
magnitude more significant than the *Enola Gay* debate. His attitude toward
American policy comes through clearly in comments such as the following:
"The United States had emerged from World War II as the leader of a 'free
world' coalition, with global obligations and responsibilities it had not shoul-
dered before. The merits of its postwar foreign policies and the degree to
which they advanced the cause of freedom are still subjects of historical
debate." Obviously, American policy failed to advance the cause of post-war
freedom to Poland and the Baltic states, but would Hogan argue that an effort
to do so should not have been tried? He leaves one stranded by that assertion when he fails to reveal how debatable is the claim that Japan and South

Korea became freer, thanks to American policy, than would have been the case had they become subjects of Stalin.

Summarizing Walter Lippman's critique of American foreign policy in the late 1940s, Professor Hogan also was critical of Truman, George Kennan and others who saw "foreign policy in broad ideological rather than specific historical and geographical terms, who saw Soviet policy, in other words, as driven by the goal of world domination rather than the search for security along the Russian frontier." After spending time in Moscow during the war and having to deal with the Soviets, George Kennan saw Russia quite pragmatically. Writing about the European situation just after the war, he said, "The entire vision of the future rested on assumptions concerning the nature of the Stalin regime which I knew to be unrealistic and misconceived.... For the long run no hopeful solution was visible. It was all a bad show. But it was idle, as everyone with any depth of diplomatic experience knew, to try to look too far into any political future." He went on to say that it would be necessary to allow for gradual change and both sides needed to give up unrealistic hopes. "The Russians, of their hopes for some sort of political conquest over the remainder of Europe in the wake of what they supposed would be unilateral withdrawal of American armed forces from the continent; the Americans, of their fatuous dreams of a happy and chummy collaboration with Moscow in the restoration of prosperity and stability throughout Europe, along liberal lines." Kennan described a situation based not on ideology but on power relations that formed the context within which American policy developed.

Professor Hogan's much later assessment of the confrontation between the two powers shares the limitations of all long distance analysis. It is unclear the degree, if any, to which he saw America's not unselfish contribution through the Marshall Plan and NATO, for example, contributed to a "free world." It would be interesting to have him expand on the implications of that comment and whether events such as the fall of the Berlin Wall, the regained independence of the Baltic states and the demise of the USSR, were related to America's post-war policies. American policies were not always enlightened and wise, but on balance was the outcome desirable for America and other nations? After more than fifty years it is perplexing to find Hogan picking up Henry Wallace's torch, pleading for understanding of Stalin's need for security. At least Wallace had not been aware of Soviet achievements in Czechoslovakia and North Korea, or observed what happened in Poland and East Germany when he expressed his sympathy for Stalin's need to secure the borders of the USSR from an aggressive United States.[15] With such ideas in his intellectual background, the position Professor Hogan took in the controversy should be no surprise.

Of course, Professor Hogan was not alone in questioning American aggressiveness. Years earlier Professor Bernstein found that "By overextending policy and power and refusing to accept Soviet interests, American policy makers contributed to the Cold War…. Though it cannot be proved that the United States could have achieved a modus vivendi with the Soviet Union in those years, there is evidence that Russian policies were reasonably cautious and conservative, and that there was a least a basis for accommodation." Professor Bernstein also was critical of Allied failure to open an early second front. "In the early years (of the war) when Russia was bearing the major burden of the Nazi onslaught, her allies postponed for two years a promised second front which would have diverted German armies." Ever empathetic when it came to the Soviets, presumably Bernstein meant that in June 1942, two years before Normandy, Britain and the United States should have opened a second front, presumably in Europe, only six months after American entry in the war.

Although his endnotes show Professor Bernstein as a scrupulous collector of quotations, his understanding of the European war leaves much to be desired. When General Marshall broached the idea of an invasion of France for 1942, it was soon acknowledged as an impossibility due to German submarine warfare, the slow military buildup in England and the obvious strength of German air and ground forces on the Atlantic coast. Although not as early as he desired, it is perplexing that Professor Bernstein did not mentioned the Allied invasion of North Africa on November 8, 1942, and later, of Sicily and Italy in 1943, each of which eased pressure on the Soviet Army on the Eastern Front. As Sicily was invaded, Hitler withdrew two corps from Russia to reinforce the Italian front. That contributed to the Soviet victory at Kursk, a critical turning point on the Eastern Front.[16]

The Crossroads had a favorite resource for the original script in Professor Alperovitz. His was the only book mentioned for possible inclusion in the exhibit. Had the script writers read him carefully, however, they would have found that his speculations about events often transcended the bounds of reliability. One example is his reference to "a troubling explanation suggested by former Undersecretary of State William R. Castle. This was that Truman and Byrnes in fact wished to use the atomic bomb — preferred to demonstrate its power — and therefore explicitly chose not to end the war by offering assurances to the Emperor.... Castle's basic question was put this way by a Japanese investigator in a recent interview: 'Might they simply have been trying to delay the surrender for two weeks until the bomb could be shown?' Castle does not specify exactly why a decision might have been made along these lines, but his theory is compatible with an implicit or explicit argument that Truman and Byrnes felt it was important to demonstrate the bomb to the Russians." Despite the footnotes, the crystal ball used to intuit Castle's intent, and the use of words such as "like," "might," and "not specify exactly," a theory compatible with an implicit or explicit argument, reveal Alperovitz' skill at stretching "evidence" to make a case.[17]

The invariable positive gloss that Professor Alperovitz placed upon Soviet actions is exemplified in his assertions in 1965 and again in 1994. "At this late date in the Cold War it is extremely difficult to recapture the assumptions and conceptions of American diplomacy in 1945. It must be emphasized that at the time the optimistic American appraisal was not simply wishful thinking. Stalin's December 1944 abandonment of the Greek Communists seemed very real evidence of his willingness to cooperate. In France, Italy, and Belgium, the Communist parties, at the height of their influence because of their predominance in the resistance movements, meekly yielded much authority to Western-oriented governments."[18]

The idea that the Communist parties of Western Europe "meekly yielded" to anyone reveals Alperovitz's unfamiliarity with the actual post war situation in Western Europe. The threat of a Communist take over in Italy was not the product of fevered imaginations. In the summer of 1948, the Christian Democrats won at the polls but on July 14, the attempted assassination of Palmiro Togliatti, the leader of the Italian Communist Party, threw the nation into turmoil. Large spontaneous strikes erupted, government buildings were seized by mobs, and for several days the Communist leadership was caught off balance. When Togliatti's second in command, Pietro Secchia, sent his brother Matteo to the Russian Embassy, he returned with news that the Russians would not support any illegal action. The Party then proceeded to actively discourage violence and the crisis ended. The Italian Communist Party realized that the objective condition for a coup, as in Czechoslovakia, was the presence of the Red Army, and that was missing while the Allies were still present. That meant the PCI arms caches as well as those of the Christian Democrats remained hidden, and the time never came for their use.

That dimension of the Alperovitz approach to the immediate post-war situation in Europe helps us understand his tunnel vision when he attempted to explain what happened in the summer of 1945. It is difficult to understand how he and others could fail to acknowledge the succession of incidents that led to the cooling of Soviet-American relations. By 1944, although the praise for the USSR that marked the public comments of Washington and London continued, it was heard less in top government circles as the reality of Soviet behavior in Poland became more evident. Although Poland was clearly within an agreed upon Russian zone of influence, the brutal inaction of the Soviet army during the Warsaw uprising in the summer of 1944, and Stalin's refusal to allow Allied supplies for the Polish Home Army, added to Allied disillusion with their ally. John Colville, who was one of Prime Minister Churchill's private secretaries said, "We and the Americans want to help in every way possible; in sending supplies we have been losing up to thirty percent of our aircraft. The Russians are deaf to all pleas and determined to wash their hands of it all. They have even refused to let American bombers land and refuel on Russian air fields if their purpose is to help Warsaw." But keeping the USSR in the war was the paramount concern so criticism was muted, although George Kennan was not alone in voicing concern about the Kremlin's future behavior. For the Allies the chances of implementing the provisions of the Atlantic Charter in Eastern Europe became increasingly dim as the Soviet army pushed into Hungary and Romania.[19]

It was against that background that concerns mounted about the future of American and British relations with the Soviet Union. Washington would have been naive and irresponsible not to wonder about postwar relations with the Kremlin. Revisionists are skeptical about those concerns and implicit in their writings is Henry Wallace's vision of continued Soviet-American friendship. They believe that America missed an opportunity to maintain friendly relations with the Soviet Union after the war and for failing, it bears a heavy if not major responsibility for the Cold War and the nuclear arms race. However, after examining Soviet atomic policy in its formative period during and after the war, David Holloway came to the conclusion that "One of the recurrent questions in the historiography of the period is whether things could have taken a different course, whether there were missed opportunities to avoid or end the nuclear arms race. I have been skeptical in this book about the possibility that changes in American policy would have elicited significant shifts in Soviet policy.... I have argued also that there was no plausible missed opportunity to avoid the development of thermonuclear weapons, because Stalin would not have reciprocated American restraint." Holloway went on to say, "All attempts to imagine an alternative course of postwar international relations run up against Stalin himself. It is difficult to think counterfactually about this period without assuming Stalin away. His malevolent and suspicious personality pervades the history of these years."[20] For at least fifty years scholars have known that Stalin's drive for total power led to the famines of the 1920s and the purges of the 1930s. Few of his Bolshevik colleagues survived after helping him to power, and the Gulag was a known quantity, yet revisionists could advocate trusting the western world to his cooperation.

That some historians continue to see criticism of the exhibit as a serious infringement on their turf is evident in comments such as those of Richard Minear in 2001. "In the United States in 1994 the Republican landslide in the off-year elections led to the fiasco at the Smithsonian Institution, when congressional and other pressures forced the gutting of an exhibit on the Enola Gay, the plane that dropped the atomic bomb on Hiroshima, and the purge of the Smithsonian's executives. American intellectuals experienced then the threat that Japanese intellectuals like Ienaga have lived with for decades— that politicians and their bureaucratic allies impose on the nation's cultural institutions a party line that flies in the face of scholarly consensus. The debacle at the Smithsonian may give Americans a new appreciation for the context in which Ienaga has operated since the late 1940s."

When Minear wrote a book that was critical of the Tokyo War Crimes Trials he did so "under the heavy impact of my own opposition to the American war in Vietnam," adding that his modest goal was "alerting American readers to American myopia and prejudice against Japan and of attacking American imperialism." He went on to say that Japanese historian Saburo Ienaga faced many of the issues that "historians of conscience in the United States and other industrialized states face today: how to resist the master narrative of the state, battle censorship and the conservative push for national standards and achievement testing to enforce those standards, and fight off restrictions on the academic freedoms that many in the academy — at least in the United States— have taken for granted."

Others who entered the controversy in 2001 were T. Fujitani, Geoffrey White and Lisa Yoneyama. Earlier the latter had explained the irony of the exhibit's vengeance statement. Their attitude can be gauged from comments about a mural in the "Punch Bowl" military cemetery in Honolulu that identified the battles between the Japanese and Americans. "This visual representation crystallizes dominant U.S. narratives of the war that construct the Pacific War as a military clash in which a uniform United States and a unified Japan were the only significant historical subjects. All other lands and peoples are simply background or, more precisely, battlefields for the clashes of the great powers ... their differential experiences of waves of imperialism and colonialism, are completely effaced by the simple, celebratory, and teleological narrative that moves from the 'sneak attack' on Pearl Harbor to V-J Day." Obviously the critique of the war goes beyond the mural, which merely provides an opportunity to preach about imperialism and colonialism. Evidently it was not enough that visitors to a cemetery see a map showing where its residents fell in battle.

Continuing the defense of the exhibit in 2002, Professor Eric Foner, a former president of the American Historical Association (AHA), recalled that in the 1990s "One series of acrimonious disputes centered on whether the 'new history' was producing an insufficiently uplifting version of the nation's development.... A planned exhibit at the Smithsonian Institution to mark the fiftieth anniversary of the dropping of the first atomic bomb was denounced by veteran's groups for alleged pro-Japanese bias and for suggesting that the use of the weapon may not have been necessary. In the end, the museum was forced to remove virtually all historical material that was to have accompanied the display of the Enola Gay, the plane that bombed Hiroshima." He went on to speak of the "evisceration" of the exhibit and said that although "vigorous debate about how history should be studied and taught is healthy and inevitable in a democratic society ... too often critics of innovative exhibitions ... reveal a desire for a history that eliminates complexity from our national experience." Director Harwit sent the OAH a copy of the third script in September 1994 and Professor Foner's comments may have referred to that revised script. Had he studied the original script, Professor Foner would have found that the curators eliminated the complexity of the war's ending, relying instead of a simplistic portrait of Truman, his allegedly insufficient consideration of alternatives and other misrepresentation of elements of the complexity he endorses. Neither Professor Foner or any of these other commentators addressed any of the issues of substance that were raised by critics of the exhibit.[21]

In a book dedicated to the art of historical detection and aimed at apprentice historians, James West Davidson and Mark Hamilton Lytle provided a not atypical, imaginative account of why Nagasaki was bombed. They replayed the idea that Truman was a captive of the momentum of events as the Washington bureaucracy pushed to use the bomb despite evidence that the Japanese were on the brink of surrender. As Japan discussed ending the war, American routines of organization and the weather, not diplomacy or military strategy, dictated the bombing of Nagasaki. Following the military's standard operating procedure, control over the bomb shifted from Truman to the commander of the bomber group on Tinian. However, "Had the original plan been followed, Japan might well have surrendered before the weather cleared. Nagasaki would have been spared. But the officer who ordered the attack had little appreciation of the larger military picture that made Nagasaki a target or that made the Soviet Union a diplomatic problem connected with the atom bomb. He weighed factors important to a bomb squadron commander, not to diplomats or political leaders. The bombing of Nagasaki slipped from the hands of policy makers not because of some rogue computer or any power-mad, maniacal general, but simply because of military SOPs. And so two bombs were dropped and the world entered the atomic age." The resulting nuclear arms race "turned the United States into an armed camp."

Davidson and Lyle would benefit from some knowledge of how the military functions as well as less exaggeration about armed camps. The authors acknowledged that they "naturally gravitated toward the work of those historians we most respect." With regard to the specifics of using the bomb, they gravitated to what was written by Rufus Miles, Gar Alperovitz, Barton Bernstein, J. Samuel Walker, John Dower, Michael Sherry, and Philip Nobile. One can only hope that apprentice historians will look for advice to other historians, whether respected or not, because that might lead to some balance and the importance of accuracy when learning their trade.

Questioning whether Truman controlled the bomb seeks to confuse the reader by imagining that once Truman approved use of the bomb, and General Handy on July 25 sent a letter to General Spaatz authorizing the A-Bomb's use after about August 3, 1945, a *deus ex machina* moved the bomb inexorably beyond the president's control. Craven and Cate deal with the apparent issue the different dates seemed to create. "The document is dated 25 July, one day before the Potsdam Declaration and two days before Suzuki's rejection thereof on the 28th, Tokyo time. There is no reference to the ultimatum and no instruction as to procedures to be followed should the Japanese offer to surrender before 3 August. Under such circumstances, of course, responsible authorities might have countermanded the order by a radio message to Guam, but without further elaboration the directive to Spaatz could be interpreted to mean that the decision to use the atomic bomb had been made before, and without real regard for, the ultimatum issued at Potsdam."

The apparent discrepancy in evidence seemed important enough to warrant a request for information from President Truman, and he responded, "The directive was given to Spaatz on 25 July, the President said, because 'it was necessary to set the military wheels in motion, as these orders did, but the final decision was in my hands, and was not made until we were returning from Potsdam.'" And again, in the same context: "I ordered atomic bombs dropped on the two cities named on the way back from Potsdam, when we were in the middle of the Atlantic Ocean." The President sailed from Plymouth on the cruiser Augusta on 2 August; Spaatz's directive authorized an attack as early as the 3rd, so the final decision would seem to have been made on one of those days. In the meantime, Spaatz had reached Guam on 29 July and final preparations for the attack had been completed rapidly. At any time before August 6 the attack on Hiroshima could have been stopped, a fact revisionists ought to know but continue to misrepresent.[22]

Civilization is a magazine of the nation's premier library, the Library of Congress, which is a neighbor of the Smithsonian Institution's National Air and Space Museum. An article by William Lanouette gave its imprimatur to *The Crossroads* script, defending the neighborhood against the veterans' assault. The defense was a repetition of what Barton Bernstein, Michael Hogan, Martin Sherwin, J. Samuel Walker and others claimed was the authentic historical consensus on why the bomb was dropped. Lanouette touched on the claims of high losses, asserting they actually would be quite low if there had been an invasion. In passing he noted that the American death toll on Okinawa was extremely high, "But the number of Japanese killed on Okinawa was far higher." Every death on both sides was a tragedy, but what were decision makers to do about a ratio of about 10 Japanese deaths for every American? Was the ratio somehow unfair to the Japanese?

The standard argument that the Japanese were preparing to surrender led Lanouette to ask why the United States rushed to use the bombs. Following the lead of Martin Sherwin and Gar Alperovitz, he knew that Secretary of State James Byrne's main motive was to prepare for the Cold War, and not simply ending the war. He repeated Professor Dower's claim that using the bomb to end the war was the dominant myth and that actually the bomb was dropped "to make a political point to the Russians." He recycled the canard that the momentum to use the bomb included justifying the enormous cost of its production. "One of the reasons some in the Truman administration feared postwar investigation of the bomb effort was old-fashioned politics." Using the bomb would mute criticism that pork barrel politics had been involved.

Whether the bomb was needed to end the war will be disputed, according to Lanouette, but "it is beyond dispute that the decision to do so was messy and more haphazard than we might expect." Secure in his high expectations of the presidency, he portrayed Truman as a weak captive of events. Although he needed advisors with various points of view, "The problem with the bomb decision was that these points of view were not isolated, weighed and examined for ulterior motives." Certainly not Truman but "Perhaps Roosevelt alone had the political stature not to use the weapon he had helped create." Lanouette's concluding judgment on Truman was that his decision was not made after "mature consideration" and "that failure may be the most important legacy of the Pacific war." That judgment echoed one by Professor Bernstein who thought that Truman never sought "carefully to consider the use of the A-Bomb."

Lanouette's insight that the decision to use the bomb lacked "mature consideration" clashes with the fact that Robert Newman found that the president discussed the atomic bomb with Secretary Stimson on 14 days between April 15 and the Hiroshima bombing. Stimson had discussed the atomic bomb with many other persons including General Marshall, Secretary of State James Byrnes and Winston Churchill, in addition to many discussions with his aides. What happened in those conversations would have shaped Stimson's thinking about the atomic bomb, and it is difficult to imagine that it failed to be reflected in Stimson's conversations with the president.[23] Perhaps because of space limitations none of this appears in Lanouette's article.

In *The Myths of August*, Stewart Udall, the former congressman and cabinet member, referred to what Professor Bernstein considered the shifting numbers Truman used to justify the atomic bombings. Readers were told that President Truman's myth distracted attention from the military reality that potential casualties during an invasion would range from 20,000 to 46,000. Furthermore, General MacArthur and General Curtis LeMay believed that an invasion would not be necessary, and MacArthur was convinced that the Japanese would surrender by September 1 at the latest. "It is amazing," Udall wrote, "that the opinions of the men who were running the war in the Pacific were not solicited by Washington's decision makers in the summer of 1945."

The idea that the generals in the Pacific were ignored by Washington intimates that they would have objected to using the bomb. We do not know what their answer would have been if asked. Generals MacArthur and LeMay believed they could win using the tools they had, but on the available evidence MacArthur was unduly optimistic about what he could do if there was an invasion. More important, Udall, who served in the Air Force in 1944, ought to have known that LeMay and MacArthur were not advising the president and would not be expected to be consulted about using the bomb.

According to Udall, "One historian, Michael Sherry, has astutely adjudged that even if Truman had ideas of his own, it would have required 'exceptional intellectual and political courage' for him to have stopped Stimson's plan to use the bomb." One does not need to be a partisan of Truman to know that the stale story of a Truman who passively ratified the decision to drop the bomb is the stuff of historical fiction worthy of Gore Vidal.[24]

How the orthodox conventional wisdom of the historical profession continues to view the demise of the exhibit appeared some years later in a fine book on the development and purposes of Japanese victimhood. James Orr showed how this idea was played by Japanese political parties on both sides of the aisle and how it affected obtaining public acceptance of that nation's aggression in Asia. Portraying Japan as a victim of the A-Bombs was a way of minimizing or erasing war guilt. When he mentioned the *Enola Gay* controversy, however, Orr suggested that the veterans considered themselves victimized by having to compete for attention with the Japanese victims of the A-Bombs. "The inability of the Smithsonian Air and Space Museum to display the Enola Gay in a manner that honored Japanese victim sentiments shows that the United States has its own groups contesting the Hiroshima bombings and the privilege of victimhood." Fortunately this pop psychology, best left to the tabloids, came at the end of an otherwise serious book. How he came to that conclusion is evident in the endnote to this quote. Orr referred to several scholars who wrote "sensitive analyses of these contests over the place of the atomic bombings in America's history." These scholars included Barton Bernstein, Richard Minear, Edward Linenthal, Robert Jay Lifton and Greg Mitchell.[25]

IX

The Moral Question

The morality of the A-Bomb is mentioned toward the end of these essays, not because it may have been the last thing considered by decision makers, as some have suggested, or because of how it ranks in order of importance in discussions of the war's end. The morality of the bomb remains the most inconclusive and contentious issue surrounding atomics and one that brooks no compromise by parties to the debate. A common opinion of historians who write on the subject is represented by Professor Barton Bernstein, who is considered an authority on the subject of the A-Bomb. "No suggestion that the Pacific war, without the use of the A-Bomb, might have continued into the autumn or slightly beyond constitutes, necessarily, an ethical justification for the use of that weapon." As do many others who criticize the use of the A-Bomb, Bernstein hedged with a statement that is hardly a definitive, unqualified negative opinion about using the bomb. He left the door open for its use if the war continued into the autumn or beyond, intimating that if the war went on for the six months to a year anticipated by the American military after an invasion, the bomb could be used. In addition, by speaking of an undefined *ethical* justification for using the bomb he carefully avoided the problem of discussing whether there could be a *moral* justification for using the A-Bomb.

In an article written before the controversy, however, Professor Bernstein did refer to morality: "At minimum, then, the use of the bomb reveals the moral insensitivity of the President — whether he used it because the moral implications did not compel a reexamination of assumptions, or because he sought retribution, or because he sought to keep Russia out of Manchuria and the occupation government of Japan, and to make her more manageable in Eastern Europe. In 1945 American foreign policy was not innocent … nor was it characterized by high moral purpose or consistent dedication to humanitarian principles." In a thoughtful discussion

159

of U. S. strategic bombing during World War II, Ronald Schaffer did not hesitate to call it immoral. His review of the evolution of bombing policy in Europe that was a prelude to what happened in the Pacific suggests, as he said, "whether feelings for the welfare of enemy civilians can ever be compatible with military success." Posing the issue starkly, although leaving morality undefined, he provides a necessary background for considering the issue of the A-Bomb.

As part of that background, this is how two recent writers reacted to the A-Bomb. According to historian David Kennedy, "the great nuclear blast that obliterated Hiroshima hardly represented a moral novelty by this date in the conflict. The moral rules that had long stayed warriors' hands from taking up weapons of mass destruction against civilian populations had long since been violently breached — in the Allied aerial attacks on European cities, and even more wantonly in the systematic firebombing of Japan." Also writing in the *Atlantic Monthly* a few years later and using standard revisionist sources and arguments, Jonathan Rauch said, "the firebombing of Tokyo should be considered a war crime." He quoted what Professor John Dower wrote about a military aide of General Douglas MacArthur who said, "the firebombing campaign was one of the most ruthless and barbaric killings of noncombatants in all history." Turning to Hiroshima, Rauch noted Gar Alperovitz' claim that "modern scholarship and also governmental estimates at the time put likely U.S. casualties from an invasion of Japan, had one been necessary, in the range of 20,000 to 50,000." He went on to say that Hiroshima was targeted not for its "modest military value but mainly for psychological effect. Then, only three days later, the United States rushed — and it did rush — to bomb Nagasaki."

Professor Kennedy ignored the Axis aerial attacks on Guernica, Rotterdam, Coventry, London and other cities in France, Russia and China. Calling attention only to the Allies' actions breached the balance that one expects from historians. Telling the reader only part of the story of air warfare is advocacy and misrepresents what happened during a tragic time in history. Rauch obviously was impressed by Professors Alperovitz and Dower, and either was unaware or dismissive of contrary evidence, thus misleading his readers as an advocate of revisionist history. Such influential authors provide the context for the public, and especially younger readers are constrained to view World War II and provide skewed notions about the background for the use of the bomb.

Whether it was immoral to use the A-Bomb under any circumstances is a vitally important question. Theologians and philosophers, especially those in the Western tradition, have condemned its use, but their answers have not provided effective guidance for diplomats, the military, politicians or the general public. For those in the Judeo-Christian tradition a strong argument against any "terror" bombing can be found in Abraham's plea to his God not to destroy Sodom and Gomorrah if fifty innocent people could be found there. God agreed not to destroy the two cities, if the fifty could be found. Then Abraham begged that the cities be saved if forty, then thirty innocents could be found, and he finally succeeded in arguing the number down to ten innocents. The religious precedent appears obvious. (Genesis 18:20–32). Anyone aware of the awesome implications of the use of weapons of mass destruction ought to explore the thinking of those who question their use on moral grounds, as well as those who do so on the pragmatic grounds of mutually assured destruction, danger to the environment, and so forth. That might avoid much of the criticism of the use of such weapons that is essentially sanctimonious moralizing, as was the case during the *Enola Gay* controversy. On the other hand, in one of the few cases in which overt exception has been taken to the criticisms of churchmen and philosophers, Edward Luttwak argued that "the churchmen who hold that nuclear weapons are ipso facto immoral are guilty of a crude ethical illiteracy."

Although a number of other writers have compared the A-Bomb to Auschwitz, Professor Bernstein did not equate Hiroshima and Nagasaki with the Holocaust. "They were not moral equivalents, because intentional genocide and intentional mass killing of some noncombatants were not morally identical, but all were powerful testimonials to the fact of massive deaths organized by nation-states, implemented by modern warriors and endorsed by their civilian populations." He then said he judged the bombings by ethical standards usually abandoned during World War II, but does not ascribe those standards "to the leaders and citizens of the United States during the war [because to do so] is to distort the history of that terrible war and to misinterpret the important decisions made in it."[1]

The morality of the use of the A-Bomb is linked to that of the use of indiscriminate carpet bombing of cities, the use of toxic agents and other practices that have been common in twentieth century conflicts. While we know the destructiveness of these high-tech weapons, we ought not ignore the ease with which hundreds of thousands were killed with primitive weapons in Rwanda in the 1990s. Neither should we forget that the targeting of civilians is not a modern invention. Greece and Rome, Assyria and Egypt, made it a common practice, as it was in Europe during the Dark Ages, the Middle Ages, and into the 21st century. In Western Europe, to ameliorate the suffering of noncombatants, the medieval Church developed the concept of the "just war" to establish guidelines for the conduct of war. The guidelines were for public officials who were exercising legitimate decision making responsibilities. These rules were predicated on the assumption that public officials have a moral responsibility to seek justice, which includes the defense of the life and freedom of their constituents, and to seek at least a minimum of order in relations between contesting entities. The obligation of statecraft was the pursuit of justice, despite the risks that might be involved in that pursuit. That violence in war could be inevitable was recognized, and the tradition sought to reduce that violence to a minimum. It ruled out pacifism.

The criteria established by the just war tradition, called *jus ad bellum*, for making a war decision, included whether the cause was just, whether the war was to be conducted by a legitimate public authority, whether those authorities have a proper or right intention, and whether the proposed action was proportionate to the goal sought, that is, would the good to be accomplished be greater than the evil that would result by doing nothing? It was understood that these criteria would become effective after all other measures to avoid conflict were exhausted, or there was evidence that no other measures to avoid conflict would be viable.

If these criteria were met, they created the parameters for *jus in bello*, or the conduct of war. Then the question of proportion again had to be met, requiring that no more force than necessary be exerted to seek the goal of the conflict. Next there was the question of the immunity of noncombatants from violence to the extent possible. Nicholas Denyer took an absolutist position when he asserted that the principle of the immunity of the innocent to violence in war seems self-evidently true, adding any moral theory that denied this principle altogether would be something that only a knave or fool could accept. However, in the just war tradition it is fundamental that, although noncombatants may suffer, violence may be needed to achieve justice. The alternative to using these or similar guidelines can be a complete absence of rules of war or, at the other extreme, abdication of the obligation of public authority to defend the rights of its constituents. Those rights are no less a factor to be considered by public authority than the right to immunity of bystanders on the other side of a conflict.[2]

Professor John Rawls, an influential American philosopher, roundly condemned the bombing of Hiroshima, as did a prominent British philosopher, Professor Gertrude Anscombe, who objected to President Truman receiving an Oxford honorary degree because, she said, he murdered innocents in the bombing of Hiroshima and Nagasaki. Both Rawls and Anscombe give cogent reasons for their condemnation of the A-Bomb. Anscombe based her case on the just war tradition, while Rawls offered a case that draws heavily from the more secular tradition of Hugo Grotius, a founder of international law in the seventeenth century. That is not the case with moralizers like Robert Lifton, who present no clear rationale for their claims, assuming that everyone knows and accepts what is "moral."[3]

Thanks to "moral relativity," despite what John Rawls and others may have to say, while we in the United States may agree on certain democratic principles, agreement on principles of morality is another matter. Robert A. Orsi, for example, contended that "just as post colonial intellectual culture calls into question central tenets of Western thought, so a new kind of moral inquiry must be open to construals of the 'ethical' profoundly at variance with Christian ideals and formulations." When referring to the international arena it might be better to refer to Western ideals and formulations of ethics, but Orsi identifies the reality of differences that need attention when considering regime behaviors in a multi-cultural environment. A weapon of mass destruction that killed tens of thousands of civilians unquestionably is repugnant to most Americans, but repugnance does not necessarily mean that its use was immoral. Arguing that everyone knows when something is wrong is an insufficient answer; obviously everyone does not know or behave as if they know when an act is wrong. Mere rhetoric about morality provides no foundation for a meaningful discussion of the "morality" of the A-Bomb. Had the Allies been subjected to Japanese or German use of the bomb they would have roundly condemned it as immoral, but that would have been on our terms of morality, which were far from those of the Axis partners, who considered war from a very different viewpoint. Paul Nitze, who contended that the A-Bomb was unnecessary, nonetheless did not regret its use. He probably spoke for many when he said, "The whole idea of an apology is insane. There are no rules of morality in war that I am aware of."[4]

The morality of the bomb consistently has received considerable attention from religious leaders. In the United States, for example, the bomb has been strongly condemned by the National Council of Churches and the Roman Catholic hierarchy. A thoughtful argument against what he called obliteration or carpet bombing was made earlier in 1944 by John Lord. Characterizing it as "an immoral attack on the rights of the innocent. It includes a direct intent to do them injury. Even if this were not true, it would still be immoral, because no proportionate cause could justify the evil done; and to make it legitimate would soon lead the world to the immoral barbarity of total war." Such religious pronouncements are uncompromising about the use of atomic weapons and are based upon a clear rationale. In most cases, however, the discussion of morality assumes an agreement on what is "moral" or right, presuming that everyone understands the specifics of what would be moral actions. This is the case when Professors Michael Sherry and Barton Bernstein assert the immorality of the bombs. John Rawls parts company with such an approach. Unlike those who proceed from a religious, theological base, or those with vague appeals to morality, his tightly reasoned secular approach is predicated on what he calls the values of democratic peoples, although he does not trace the origins of those values. He rejected the notion that saving American lives was a valid reason for bombing, and believed we owed the Japanese people an opportunity to negotiate surrender before such a drastic step was taken.

Perhaps Professor Rawls was unaware that in authoritarian Japan decisions about surrender were made by a small group that had deliberately forfeited the opportunity to surrender until the last moment. If aware of that fact, however, it would have meant nothing to him, because he believed that all of the pragmatic considerations about using the bomb that faced Truman fell short of justifying the A-Bomb. Both the fire bombings of Japanese cities and the atomic bombing of Hiroshima were "very great wrongs," and he faulted Truman for failing in statesmanship that could have ended the war at "little cost in further casualties." What that statesmanship might have been was unstated. Although unstated, his reasoning closely resembles that of writers about the conditions for a "just war," such as the centuries old reasons that are explicated in Catholic writings on the subject and are the foundation of Anscombe's argument. At the end, Rawls called for Americans to recognize that we acted immorally in ending the war just as we expect that recognition from the Germans and Japanese. Rawls accepted many of the arguments against the bomb made by Barton Bernstein, Kai Bird, Gar Alperovitz and others, but they are incidental to the thrust of his argument that the institutions and laws, civil life and background culture of just and decent civilized societies depend absolutely on making significant moral and political distinctions in all situations.

Richard Posner showed how flimsy reliance on the idea of common values becomes when confronted with the harsh reality of multi-culturalism. "That the Germans killed millions of defenseless citizens is a fact; its truth is independent of what anyone believes. That the Nazi's actions were morally wrong is a value judgment: it depends on beliefs that cannot be proved true or false." In post modern Western societies morality is a pragmatic matter of multi-cultural opinion. In some non-western societies the differences are even more extreme. The American evidence for this relativism is how certain major "moral" issues, such as abortion, the death penalty, and euthanasia, are contested on "moral" grounds. Those grounds differ because proponents and opponents lack fundamental common principles on which they agree to even discuss such issues. The same problem exists in discussions about the morality of the A-Bomb that proceed as if everyone, even in a multi-cultural American society, let alone in a global one with contrasting if not conflicting values governing behavior, agreed on the ground rules for moral behavior.

An eminent British philosopher and authority on ethical theory, one who experienced war as a Japanese POW and survived the infamous Burma railroad, provided a way to think about the morality of bombing that differed from the absolutism of Anscombe and Rawls. According to R. M. Hare, "And there will also be cases which are so much outside the ordinary run of cases that we may feel impelled to ask whether the general principles, sound though they may be for general use, ought not to be scrutinized before they are applied to these unusual circumstances. Into this category come a great many political situations (such as some of those on which Professor Anscombe has commented, as for example Truman's dilemma about dropping the bomb). It is not to be supposed that the simple general principles which are the soundest guide in private life can always be safely employed in political situations; and this is so, not because political decisions lie outside morality and are to be made only for 'reasons of State', but because political situations differ in morally relevant respects from private situations, especially in their complexity and in the size of the calamities that it is possible to cause. But even in politics it is less often right to depart from the simple principles of good faith, restraint in the use of force, and the like, than many politicians deceive themselves into thinking. And in ordinary private life it is very seldom so." In another place, when comparing his position with that of another philosopher's do unto others as only what we accept when on the receiving end, Hare said, "I would include more people in the class of those whose sufferings are relevant to our moral decisions (for example, in the Hiroshima case, those that will die if the war is not ended quickly, as well as those actually killed by the bombing)." Professor Hare was considering the lesser of two evils; the thousands who would die at Hiroshima compared the hundreds of thousands more who would die if the war did not end. When evaluating Truman's decision to use the A-Bomb it is important to remember that the greater the temporal distance from that decision, the easier it becomes to judge it in the abstract terms one would use in the classroom. Hare suggests a way to understand what confronted Truman as he weighed what to do about the A-Bomb.[5]

After all is said about the morality of the A-Bomb it would be difficult to disagree with J. Samuel Walker's conclusion that the question of the morality of Truman's decision, which is an unstated part of the debate among historians, will not be solved. That was because individuals brought differing values, assumptions, and priorities to the subject and as a result, "The information that historians provide will not settle the moral issues."[6]

During the discussions about surrender, MAGIC heard the Japanese minister to Sweden cable Tokyo that America could be isolated morally and diplomatically by "emphasizing the extreme inhumanity of the Bomb."[7] Whether orchestrated or not, Minister Okamoto's suggestion has borne abundant fruit in the court of public opinion, but done nothing to clarify the question of why the bomb was used. Perhaps a consensus will evolve among nations and become part of accepted, enforceable international law, but until then the use of atomic and other exotic weapons will depend upon pragmatic decisions by interested parties, including rogue states and terrorists with access to such weapons. As interested parties to the use of such weapons, we can regret the bomb's use and work to insure it will not be used again. However, at least quietly, we also can appreciate that in the summer of 1945, Truman's decision made it possible for us to debate this issue. If the Axis had the opportunity to use the bomb, debating the issue would be moot for Americans.[8]

X

Epilogue

The purpose of these essays has been to show how the curators of the National Air and Space Museum of the Smithsonian Institution, one of the crown jewels of the nation's cultural institutions, ignored evidence and presented speculation as fact. Heavily influenced by the work of Professors Gar Alperovitz and John Dower, they followed the lead of a coterie of revisionist historians as they prepared *The Crossroads*. Portraying the controversy as a struggle between history and memory they could have learned from another battleground between history and memory, that was described by D. D. Guttenplan: "The struggle to find the right way to describe the destruction of European Jewry is sometimes depicted as a contest between history and memory. And as we have now all been taught, memory is a very unreliable guide to ... how it really was.... . Yet without witnesses, without human voices to put flesh on the facts, we have something that, while it may pass muster as history, can never tell the truth." The trick is not to see matters as either/or but as a meld of facts and their interpretation, and memory, which at its best is not mythical but can be as real and authentic as what can be found in the archives.[1]

The curators and their allies adopted a classic debater's trick: if you have a weak case attack the opposition and confuse the issues. Their failure to respond to the issues raised by critics prevented meaningful dialogue and led to unnecessary controversy. They approached the past as if they were producers of a modern adaptation of a play by Shakespeare. The language might need some changes to convey the Bard's thought to a modern audience and the actors might be in modern dress. Then another step is taken, imposing their vision of what Shakespeare ought to have meant when he wrote the play. In the theater that can make for excellent drama, although it hardly is Shakespeare as you like it. The advantage of such deconstruction is that it makes the playwright and the historian's task so much easier. No longer bound by yesterday's conventions or reality, one can roam freely, imagining what the text and its author would have meant had they been informed by the insights of today's scholar, who is contributing to the consensus of his peers.

With *The Crossroads* script defended by the historical associations and some well-known historians, at first glance there seemed to be prima facie evidence that the veterans were off base with their criticism of the exhibit. Reading the original script, however, leads one to question whether those historians bothered to read what they ardently defended. If they did, they would have seen the morass of obvious inconsistencies, misstatements and speculation passing for history that pervaded the script. Had the script been subjected to the peer review that is common in academia, those glaring faults would have been evident. Instead, because the progressive curators and their advisors were aligned with prominent factions of the historical and museum establishments, their positions were not challenged by their peers. Intellectual rigor and honesty may be prized in academia but whistle blowers seldom gain the respect of their peers. That is ironic because in a real sense, historians often are whistle blowers on the past. Instead it was left to a small band of veterans to ask for an authentic history of the war's end. As a result, at the hands of the exhibit's defenders, the word veteran almost became an epithet. Why that happened, and why the *Enola Gay* controversy stirred such strong feelings on both sides is for others to explore, if not explain. We were interested in documenting where the NASM's polemic fell afoul of history as it is, not as how the curators sought to corrupt it.

Going against the alleged "scholarly consensus" about the end of the Pacific war meant following Richard Evans' dictum that, "arguments and theories, however dominant in the intellectual life of their day, have to be assessed on their own merits, not accepted uncritically simply because they are espoused by the majority." To do that meant examining the script in detail, and also the authorities that the curators relied on as the basis for their narrative. Identifying their authorities was not difficult but it necessitated analyzing numerous books and articles to see if they substantiated what was said in the script. One example of the process involved a 1986 article in the *Bulletin of the Atomic Scientists* by Professor Bernstein about the exaggerated number of casualties if there was an invasion. Fortunately, that analysis already had been done by Professor Robert James Maddox, who showed that Bernstein doubted the recollections about casualty estimates by virtually all the major players in events at the war's end. He did so, of course, because those estimates differed from his own and therefore had to be dismissed as irrelevant. As we have seen, revisionists have an unfortunate tendency to ignore contrary evidence. To summarily dismiss, sometimes directly and at times by innuendo, the testimony of General Marshall, Secretary Stimson, President Truman and others as at best mistaken, and at worst as fabrications, might make lesser authorities than Professor Bernstein hesitate, but he was equal to the task.[2]

Although the exhibit was canceled, the Smithsonian's new Secretary did not disavow *The Crossroads*. Ira Michael Heyman, who became the Secretary of the Smithsonian Institution in September 1994 in the midst of the controversy, closed the exhibit in January 1995. Heyman said that the original script was deficient in that "Too much of the context for the use of the bomb was taken for granted. In this and other ways, the proposed exhibition was out of balance." He was adroit in calling the exhibit "flawed" in a public relations sense, claiming that it was such an emotional issue people would not have distinguished between the original draft and whatever emerged as the final script. In addition, he said, initially the exhibit was solely historical and went too deep into the analytical aspect, failing to commemorate the end of a tough war and the feelings of veterans.[3]

That was similar to Professor Dower's opinion that part of the problem with commemorating the fiftieth anniversary of the end of World War II was that "Participants in the events of a half century ago are still alive to tell their emotional personal tales." They are confronted by the skepticism and detachment of younger generations without memories of the war, and historians "who develop new perspectives on the dynamics and significance of what took place." That put-down enabled Professor Dower and Heyman to ignore the contested issues in the exhibit.

Thus in Heyman's opinion, *The Crossroads* was flawed, but only in a public relations sense. The curators were too historical and deeply analytical, and hurt the feelings of the veterans. Written as he intended, Heyman neatly ignored the substantive issues raised by critics, giving the curators a slap on the wrist, but with a wink, for doing their job too well, while attempting to salve the feeling of veterans. Heyman had been chancellor of the Berkeley campus of the University of California and said that he saw the Smithsonian as analogous to a public university. He must have known that the analogy was far fetched. A former professor should not have found it difficult to understand that serious intellectual issues were at stake, not the slighted emotions of veterans, whether or not aging. As an adept administrator, however, he knew when to fold his cards in the face of public outrage while not cutting ties to academia or the curators. By returning to the theme of emotional veterans who needed to be coddled, Heyman continued to demean their concerns and, with a wink and a nod, supported the curatorial staff.

Repeating Heyman's explanation in the Smithsonian's book *Exhibiting Memories* (1997), Steven Lubar found that the *Enola Gay* exhibit was controversial because the curators faced the "disjunction between memory and history... . Their first script moved too far for comfort from the veterans' memories." Lubar went on without referring to the issues involved: "the veterans had enough political clout to let the curators know it. The 'Enola Gay' exhibition that finally opened has exactly the opposite problem: it focuses almost solely on the object, the airplane, with little context to allow it to move the visitor's understanding beyond memory. Its technological and restoration history is given in loving detail. Technological details are safe; they do not assume any responsibility for moving visitors beyond where they were when they came to the museum."

With regard to another exhibit, Lubar said that "'The Enola Gay' exhibit was very much in our minds as we thought about 'World War II: Sharing Memories.' It was clear, in the political environment that the 'Enola Gay' controversy had brought to the Smithsonian, that we needed to move beyond the usual museum exercise of presenting history from a historian's perspective, beyond our usual techniques of displaying objects and providing explanations and interpretations: these techniques privileged historical analysis and depreciated the value of memory. We simply couldn't do that after the Enola Gay fiasco." As usual there was no reference to the substantive issues raised by the critics, only the continuing tendentious reference to memories versus history.[4]

A more recent comment in this regard by Arif Dirlik continued Heyman's demeaning view of veterans and warrants attention because it illustrates the intellectual context, not only of *The Crossroads* but of how that context continues in later writing about the war's end and the exhibit controversy. "The confounding of the structural causes of war with the experience of war of the rank and file who are dragged into it has played an important part in the controversies surrounding the commemoration of World War II in 1995. The cultural circumstances surrounding the commemoration have had the unfortunate consequence of trivializing those controversies into issues of 'political correctness,' for which both proponents and opponents must bear some responsibility... . More important is to recognize that the critique of such mythmaking-the critique of power, in other words-must take care not to erase the experiences of those who, dragged into war, nevertheless experienced it not as an abstraction or exercise in social criticism, but as a matter of life and death. The burden of memory surely lies more heavily on the living than on the dead. And it is important that their memories not be erased as other memories are exhumed from a buried past. If it is to avoid falling into the same exclusionary mentality of the White patriarchal nationalism that it would repudiate, critique must be tempered by a recognition that White male soldiers also die and suffer pain, and perhaps seek in commemorations not just the celebration of power, but some explanation for the suffering they have experienced. The relationship between nationalism and a postcolonial cosmopolitanism is not a zero-sum relationship. Recognition of its complexity ought to serve instead to bring forth the diversity of memory that is suppressed in a historiography that is bound to servitude under changing configurations of power." Despite the jargon, Dirlik joined Secretary Heyman in belittling "White male soldiers" unable to understand the grand drama in which they were pawns in a Pacific war reduced to a "White male patriarchal nationalism" power struggle.

The attitude of curator Thomas Crouch guaranteed confrontation when he told NASM Director Harwit that any morally responsible exhibit of the atomic bombing of Japan had to deal with the victims, and that an honest discussion of that topic would upset visitors. He also asked if Harwit wanted an exhibit that made veterans feel good or one that led visitors to consider the consequences of the atom bombing of Japan. By framing the issues in such a high minded manner he sought the high ground of morality against the (amoral?) veterans who only wanted to feel good about an exhibit. That patronizing attitude set the stage for confrontation with citizens who were not accustomed to being patronized. They began by petitioning for a redress of what they considered a grievance. They were given short shrift in a needless bureaucratic fumble, and then did what citizens do every day, they went public with eventual success. That others who objected to the exhibit became as shrill as its defenders, was not the fault of the veterans. The heated rhetoric that later developed on both sides of the controversy might have been avoided had the NASM responded collegially and respected the concerns of the petitioners.

Opposition to the use of nuclear weapons is not restricted to activists for peace and the abolition of the nuclear threat. Some of the most knowledgeable and determined opponents of nuclear arms are in the military because they know full well the dangers of nuclear war. Opposition to such weapons should not be based on scare tactics and willful distortion of the historical record. As a reminder of the thrust of the typical arguments used by opponents of the bombing of Hiroshima, one can turn to Kazuyo Yamane: "Veterans' groups and conservatives succeeded in using the exhibit to justify and glorify the use of the atomic bomb." Then, after asking why Truman used the atomic bombs, he answered: "The United States was aware of Japan's move for peace because it was intercepting and decoding the messages Foreign Minister Togo was sending to Ambassador Sato. Why did Truman advise Stalin to ignore Japan's plea for peace on 17 July? Perhaps he was afraid of losing an opportunity to use the atomic bombs, which had cost $2 billion to develop and produce? Another question is why Truman used the atomic bomb before 8 August when Russia declared war against Japan. According to *The Dictionary for Practicing Peace Education*, the United States wanted to display its power to the Soviet Union to exclude it from taking part in the settlement of postwar issues in East Asia. Nishijima pointed out that 'the atomic bombs were regarded not only as military weapons, but also political weapons whose great power would make Russia obey to the United States even before the bombs were made.' This is why Truman ignored, and even concealed, the Japanese proposal for peace." Gar Alperovitz was quoted as insisting that there had been no need for the use of the atomic bombs. "It is clear that alternatives to the bomb existed and that Truman and his advisers knew it… .Why then were the atomic bombs used?… . Some writers also suggest that because huge sums were spent, developing the new weapon, the US political leadership found it impossible not to use it. Most relevant to the Smithsonian flap is substantial scholarly acceptance of the once controversial idea that diplomatic issues— especially the hope of strengthening the West's hand against the Soviet Union — played a significant role in the decision." Yamane concluded, "The Japanese were guinea pigs for the first 'live' nuclear weapon experiments with two types of atomic weapon, using uranium and plutonium."[5]

Such tired arguments by true believers debase the debate about the use of atomics. Not satisfied with disagreeing with those who gave reasons for using the A-Bomb, they question their intellectual integrity, using arguments they either know or should know were concocted with no regard for the truth. Basing their position on such fraudulent "evidence" eliminates the possibility of open and honest communication between parties with equal devotion to the cause of peace.

It is an article of faith among revisionists that the Pacific war could have ended without the A-Bomb had Truman been patient after the Soviets entered the war and waited for conventional bombing and the blockade to weaken Japan's will to fight and forced surrender. The USSBS and others estimated that course of action, or inaction, would end the war within weeks or a few months after August 1945. That theory of how the war should or could have ended was translated for the public by James W. Loewen, who expressed his dismay that the Nimitz Museum of the Pacific War in Frederickburg, Texas, avoided the reality of war and tried to not to have its visitors think about its morality. "Army brass gave Truman low figures for American casualties in an invasion of Japan — perhaps partly so they would get the job and win the war. The Navy endorsed higher figures— perhaps partly to deter an invasion so they could win the with their naval blockade. Air Force leaders claimed no invasion would be necessary because air power would win the war by eliminating Japan's ability to fight on. Thus, the museum serves up what Gar Alperovitz ... calls 'American myth.'" Presented in this manner, the reader receives more than an impression that self serving military services competed for the honor of winning the war, and the army won. In fact, although Admiral King believed that blockade and bombardment might bring about Japan's defeat, he thought it might take a long time. General MacArthur, on the other hand, was definite in believing that an invasion would be needed. But the JCS discussions about how to end the war were far different than Loewen imagined. It is surprising that he was unaware that the discussions ended with General Marshall's reluctant decision that an invasion would be necessary. Loewen's misrepresentation is more dramatic and seemingly convincing only because he fails to acquaint the reader with what actually happened in 1945. That is precisely what he criticizes about historic sites across the country that fudge the truth about what happened and why.

While waiting for hunger and conventional bombing to work their will, large Japanese forces would require continuing military operations by the Allies. During those operations there would be American and Allied casualties. Advocates of the waiting game skip over those potential casualties as if they were irrelevant to planners, although they could have been as high as at Iwo Jima and Okinawa.[6] As an example of what allowing the war to continue could have produced, consider Operation ZIPPER, the massive post-surrender invasion of Malaya rivaling Normandy in size that was mentioned elsewhere. Another example of the problem posed by isolated Japanese garrisons was Luzon. General MacArthur had optimistically announced the official end of the Philippine campaign on July 4, 1945, except for "Some minor isolated action of a guerrilla nature in the practically uninhabited mountain ranges." Until after August 15, however, a large number of Japanese troops continued to hold out in the Philippines and could not be simply bypassed. By the end of June the American forces effectively controlled almost all of Luzon, except for about 50,000 Japanese holed up in the mountains who were difficult to dislodge. Four American and one Filipino division continued to fight them until the emperor's announcement of the surrender. That months long battle was far from MacArthur's "minor isolated action of a guerrilla nature," but was resistance by an experienced and organized Japanese corps. Had the war continued there would have been more American casualties on Luzon.

The cost of reducing pockets of Japanese resistance can be imagined by recalling what happened at the island of Betio, the principal island of the Tarawa atoll. Its garrison included 4,500 fighting troops and 2,200 construction troops and Korean laborers. The island was small, less than two miles long and no more than 600 yards wide, but was heavily defended by well dug in artillery and bunkers. The Americans attacked after heavy bombardment with about 18,000 troops, losing 1,009 KIA and 2,101 WIA. The tenacity of Japanese resistance is shown by the fact that only 146 Japanese survived.

Fighting also would have continued in China and Manchuria, but there most of the Allied casualties would be Russian and Chinese, something ignored by revisionists. The Soviets had a hard time taking Sakhalin island, where a fierce battle continued until August 25 with significant losses on both sides. That happened when the war formally was over and one can only imagine what would have happened elsewhere had the war dragged on until hunger took its toll. The Soviets were poised to invade Hokkaido and had the war continued might have done so, suffering heavy casualties but eventually overcoming Japanese resistance. Truman was able to stop Stalin's attempt to occupy part of Japan, but had the war continued a Soviet presence on Hokkaido could have led to a repetition of what happened in East Germany. If Japan ended as a divided country, the future of the Pacific Rim would have been more uncertain than actually developed, due to Soviet intervention in North Korea and North Vietnam.

Thanks to Japan's surrender American forces did not have to fight their way into South Korea. What could have happened there can be estimated from the early plan for an invasion of Korea as a stepping stone to the invasion of Japan. More than half a million Americans would be needed to execute that plan with resulting heavy casualties. The Soviets occupied the northern part of the country, and the world and the Korean people have lived with the consequences of that compromise. Unlike the Americans, who were unprepared to enter South Korea linguistically and politically, the Soviets "had trained cadres of Koreans in Moscow for their share of the occupation."

One cannot responsibly examine the situation in the Pacific without placing it in the context of the actual situation at the time, not the imaginary one favored by revisionists. They believe that, had Truman delayed and not used the bomb, the war would have ended quickly; but they are unwilling to say what could happen if that tactic was not successful, and the various scenarios mentioned above came into play. Would they have accepted joint American-Soviet occupation of Japan? Would they accept Hokkaido as a Soviet satellite and with what result? Those are questions revisionists refuse to discuss, although they are fully aware of the Soviet record in the Baltics, Poland, Czechoslovakia, Hungary and elsewhere.

Ceding all of Korea to the Soviets would have placed millions more behind an Asian Iron Curtain had the revisionist game plan been implemented in the real world of 1945. Some might not have objected to that outcome. Two months after the Korean War began in 1950, one apologist for North Korea said, "As soon as the reactionary and imperialist nature of the American occupation in South Korea and of its creature, the (Syngman) Ree clique, became clear, demonstrations, strikes, uprisings appeared once again. These appeared in South Korea only — not in North Korea.... In North Korea the people ruled — therefore no revolts." Professor Herbert Aptheker, a consistent Marxist, expressed that opinion in 1950. He was not alone then and others continue to share that essential position determined to ignore evidence of the harsh nature of North Korean repression of its people. Perhaps that is because as progressives they continue a residual faith in the USSR's seeming promise for its satellites. Quick to fault America's policies in 1945, they present no feasible alternate courses of action that would have kept Japan and South Korea out of the Soviet orbit to share the fate of Eastern Europe. The failure to do so implies a lack of concern for the future of those nations.

The appropriate concern that commentators express about "collateral damage," the euphemism for civilian casualties, should extend to more than the victims of bombing and more than Japanese civilians. Blockade caused widespread deaths from starvation and easily could have slowly killed hundreds of thousands more Japanese civilians. Allowing the war to continue at the pace before August 6th would have continued Japanese control of millions of Asian civilians, allowing them to starve and be subject to more atrocities, thus creating more candidates for "collateral damage." Why revisionists ignore the potential consequences of their so-called alternatives is unclear. When they plead humanitarian reasons for not using the bomb, they ignore the calculus of not ending the evil of conflict quickly. The known consequences of prolonging the war could have been many more deaths around the Pacific Rim than all the victims who died during the bombing of Japan. That stark reality should be faced without equivocation by anyone writing about the summer of 1945. Focusing on American deaths is understandable, but it is blinkered when writing about a global war. If the critics of American war policy were truly concerned about the suffering caused by the war, they would be less concerned about allegedly exaggerated American casualty figures and tell their readers about the human toll in Asia had Truman failed to act as he did in August 1945.

During the eight days after Hiroshima that it took for the Japanese to surrender, we only know how many people died at Nagasaki. There is not an exact count of those killed by the conventional bombing that continued after Hiroshima. Neither do we have a count of the local people killed in China, or in Manchuria after the Soviet attack, nor in Korea and other places in which fighting continued; nor do we know how many of the Japanese military died while the emperor and his Supreme War Council debated the issue of surrender. Unfortunately, we have no count of how many Allied troops, airmen and sailors died while the Japanese dithered about surrendering. The number of all those who died while waiting would be in the tens of thousands. Each day the war continued the Japanese government was responsible for those deaths. Those who would have tolerated continuing to wait for the Japanese to come to their senses are too casual about those unknowable but not unimaginable statistics.

Had there been delays and the November D-Day been kept, the enormous invasion fleet assembled for Kyushu would have encountered the violent typhoon "Louise" that devastated Okinawa on October 8 and 9, 1945. With the war ended many of the men and ships allotted to the invasion had returned to the United States, but substantial forces remained to support the occupation. The typhoon wrecked Okinawa, hundreds of men died and more than 250 ships were sunk or damaged beyond repair. The toll in lives and ships would have been immeasurably greater had the invasion force been en route to Kyushu. The fact of typhoon "Louise" has been known for a long time but it is never mentioned by those who advocated waiting and contending that the A-Bomb served no rational purpose.

From an Allied perspective, after Okinawa at the latest, Japan should have examined the cost/benefit ratio of continuing the war and decided that continuing to fight made no sense. But Japan did not surrender. Notwithstanding the efforts of Japanese specialists like former ambassador Grew and others to fathom Japanese behavior, they could not predict Japanese behavior, and that behavior had to be responded to as behavior, not an interesting case of multi-cultural difference. Unfortunately, even if Washington fully understood Japanese behavior, it would not have affected the outcome of the war. That is because the operative fact was that the Japanese were the ones to decide if and when to surrender. Then and now, when nations or people behave in certain ways, that behavior precipitates counter behaviors. *The Crossroads* and its defenders failed to understand that simple paradigm.

After the war, Hirohito's responsibility for the war was minimized, both by the Japanese and by the American occupation authorities, in order to mollify the population and the political groups that venerated the dynasty. The studies of Herbert Bix and Peter Wexler, however, reveal that Hirohito was much more than a figurehead. He actively participated in military planning and, according to Wexler, although he had the power to veto the decision to go to war, he did not because he feared doing so would cause the disintegration of the national polity. Although this did not mean he was responsible for starting the war he felt obliged to insure that the dynasty and the tradition it represented survived at any cost. The cost was that millions of Japanese and others were sacrificed for a polity that theoretically was intended to serve the people. In the hard nosed real world Washington faced, its choice must be evaluated in the long term outcome of that choice. A trial would have provided a semblance of justice, but at a cost that could only be estimated by having the revisionists continue to play with counterfactuals.[7]

When reviewing Bischof and Dupont's *The Pacific War Revisited*, Professor Bernstein commented on Kenneth Hagan's argument that, had American submarine warfare begun more vigorously in 1942 or early 1943, it would have destroyed "much of Japan's shipping and economy well before summer 1945; thus he implies (but never asserts) that Japan would have surrendered before August 1945 and without the atomic bombings." What Hagan did not imply was made explicit by British scholar Dan van der Vat, who held that, had there been 100 more submarines to concentrate on attacking Japanese tankers and merchantmen rather than warships, Japan would have been brought to its knees and the atomic bombs might not have been necessary. Dan van der Vat may have been correct in his surmise that more shipping and thus more of Japan's economy would have been destroyed, had life been different, but Professor Bernstein pushes beyond what Hagan and van der Vat hypothesized by suggesting yet another iffy reason for not using the A-Bombs. If Bernstein related his theory to wartime priorities for shipping and warships or to Daniel Blewett's chapter in *The Pacific War Revisited,* on how fuel shortages hampered American naval operations early in the war, he would have had a better understanding of the complexities of a global war, and especially warfare in the Pacific.

Ronald Spector's discussion of American submarine warfare in *Eagle Against the Sun* explains the problems that plagued the "Silent Service" early in the war, problems that included defective torpedoes, something well known for many years, and a slow learning curve about the best tactics to cope with the Japanese navy and merchant marine. Finally, with better torpedoes and unrestricted submarine warfare, the supply routes to Japan were mostly choked off in late 1944 and in 1945. Because of American merchant and naval ship building priorities and other factors, there is no way that could have happened earlier in the war, although one can imagine another Bernstein counterfactual. Given the objective situation and resources at the time, to suggest either implicitly or explicitly that unrestricted submarine warfare beginning in 1942 or early 1943 could have brought Japan to its knees before August 1945 and avoided the A-Bomb simply ignores the easily ascertainable records of the reality that existed at the time.[8]

Along with President Truman, Secretary of War Henry Stimson has been tried and convicted by revisionists for deliberately misrepresenting why the atomic bombs were used. If not for academic delicacy, critics might as well have accused them of mendacity. When Robert Newman reviewed the accusations, he concluded that the manner in which Stimson framed his explanation of the bombs' use as a choice between alternatives, such as an invasion, gave the critics an opening for their accusation of post facto misrepresentation. Instead of considering alternatives, Newman argued, Truman "confronted the necessity of using every legitimate means available to end a global war."[9] The bombs were used because Truman believed they would end the war sooner rather than later. Stimson was not a liar but he failed to clearly explain what happened. That would have been clear to the critics had they been willing to suspend their conspiratorial interpretation of his explanation. In his study of the Joint Chiefs of Staff during the war, Mark Stolar said, "Total victory over the Axis and its accomplishment as quickly as possible and with a minimum of U.S. casualties were political goals. They were also the fundamental political goals one would expect of a democratic society at war. Dictatorships may be capable of and willing to conduct long wars with enormous casualties, but they are neither possible nor desirable for a democracy given the nature of its public opinion and the emphasis it places on the importance and sanctity of individual life and freedom."

McGeorge Bundy described his work with Secretary Stimson as being his "scribe." Long after the fact he was critical, although understanding of the process that led to Hiroshima, but he ended his discussion as follows: "And if perhaps, or even probably, there were better courses, we must also recognize that we are measuring a real decision against might-have-beens. The bomb did not end the war, but it surely was responsible for its ending when it did…. The bomb did shorten the war; to those in charge of its development that had been its increasingly manifest destiny for years."

As a less complex and less charismatic person than the towering figure of Franklin Roosevelt, historians and political scientists did not expect much from Truman, and for years he received a poor press. Textbook writers continue to tell high school students that there is little to applaud in his domestic policies. As the new century began, and after a scathing review of Truman's background, Gus Russo left no doubt of his opinion when he wrote: "By any estimate, Truman's presidency was as mixed as his personal ethos. To his admirers, he defeated the Japanese and Germans in World War II, established the state of Israel, and organized NATO. To his detractors Truman was morally culpable for the decision to drop an atomic bomb on the population of Nagasaki after he had already done so on Hiroshima; his formation of NATO was a prime reason Soviet-American relations chilled, leading to the costly and dangerous Cold War; he unnecessarily committed U. S. troops to Korea, fifty thousand of whom returned in body bags." Despite that tirade, it is paradoxical that, as the years have gone by, President Truman is given increasingly good marks by political practitioners and, increasingly, by historians. Unfortunately for students, however, textbook authors continue repeating the conventional wisdom of the 1960s and 1970s. The notion that Truman was a small, insecure person controlled by advisors finds less support as distance makes it possible to entertain a more objective assessment of him as a man of character who fired the icon that was MacArthur, began the Marshall plan and ended the Pacific war the only way he knew how. As a dedicated student of history, President Truman could be said to have followed Sun Tzu's maxim to avoid a long war. Mrs. Eleanor Roosevelt, the late president's widow, who knew President Truman well and did not hesitate to advise him, remained his friend into his retirement. In a letter to him on August 12, 1959, she wrote: "as you know I have always said that you had no choice but to use the atomic bomb to bring the war to an end." What lends special emphasis to what she wrote is that, as someone who called the shots as she saw them, and as an activist for peace and reconciliation, Mrs. Roosevelt had no peer, and was closer to the events of 1945 than any of Truman's critics.[10]

In the ecclesiology of revisionism, the Cold War came about because President Truman had not been open enough with Stalin about the A-Bomb, excluded the USSR from Japan and sought a cordon sanitaire around the USSR. According to Gaddis Smith and other writers that 'confrontational' attitude polarized the relationship between the two nations. They are correct in describing what developed during Truman's tenure in office but failed to explain why that happened. Truman's attitude was a reaction to Soviet behavior and to explain it one must examine relations between the two nations almost from the beginning of their alliance against the Axis.

The paramount interest of the British and Americans was to keep the Soviets in the war against its former ally after June 22, 1941, when Germany invaded Russia, breaching the Molotov-Ribbentrop pact of 1939.

Every effort was made to placate Stalin, for example, when he called for a second front or complained about the slow delivery of Allied arms and supplies. The former was impossible until North Africa was invaded on November 8, 1942, and the latter, despite Soviet complaints, amounted to a too-little known heroic effort that delivered vast amounts of Lend Lease arms and supplies via Murmansk and Iran at a high cost of lost ships and men. Equipment that was badly needed elsewhere was diverted to Russia in order to maintain the Soviet effort, which was essential to Allied victory.

An important element of that equipment was highlighted by Isaac Deutscher in his biography of Stalin. "The weapons which the western powers supplied were a useful in some cases vital addition. But the lorries which carried the Russian divisions into Germany were most of American, Canadian and British make — more than four hundred thousand were supplied to Russia under Lend Lease. So were most of the boots in which the infantry proper slogged its way to Berlin, much of the army's clothing and of its tinned food were supplied under Lend Lease."[11] Although nothing can diminish the tremendous sacrifice and contribution Russia made to defeating the Nazis, neither should one forget something the revisionists overlook too easily, how the Allies aided the Soviets during the war.

However, due to Soviet suspicion, cooperation with its new allies often was problematic and grudging, according to Patrick Beesly. From the beginning of the alliance there was American concern about the distant behavior of the Soviets on the operational level. Despite the seeming endemic paranoia of the Soviets, the Roosevelt administration did everything it could to reassure Stalin and to provide Lend Lease supplies. Harry Hopkins advocated for the Soviets within the administration because he understood the importance of the Soviet effort against the Nazis. There certainly was recognition of Soviet bravery and sacrifices in the war they waged against Germany. However, there also was a litany of disturbing Soviet behaviors, although not even the massacre of Polish officers at Katyn with Stalin's approval disturbed the flow of supplies and the positive words of support for the Soviets. The denial of landing rights in Soviet territory to the Allies when seeking to aid the Polish Home Army during the Warsaw uprising in the summer of 1944 was overlooked. Stalin assured safe passage to representatives of the Polish Government in London to meet with the puppet Lublin government, and despite his pledge of free elections in Poland, proceeded to execute them. That also had to be overlooked. Stalin's tantrum over Operation Sunrise leading to the surrender of German forces in Italy finally irritated President Roosevelt enough to admonish Stalin in less than diplomatic language for his outburst, but to mollify him negotiations for the surrender of German forces were ended, at a cost to Allied soldiers and airmen. While the British and Americans were negotiating Bulgaria's surrender, the Soviets declared war on Bulgaria, notifying their Allies at almost the last minute. That enabled Soviet occupation of Bulgaria with all that followed. The list could go on and would continue to be ignored by the revisionists because it helps to account for the polarization during the Cold War. Critics of the real politic conducted by Roosevelt can suggest no alternative to the overriding imperative need to defeat the Axis, but although accepted as the price of victory, the Soviet confrontations could not be ignored by Washington.

Those episodes happened before Truman's watch began. He went to Potsdam with more or less an open mind and was charmed by Stalin. At the beginning of his administration there was not a confrontational attitude, but a continuation of the policy of conciliating Stalin. As students of the war know, the Soviets were confrontational as a matter of policy long before Truman entered office and continued it afterwards. This is not to disagree with the revisionist who would say that the United States provoked Stalin, especially and fruitlessly by reminding him of the provisions of the Atlantic Charter when he absorbed Eastern Europe.

Contrary to the impression created by some writers, who saw the American military as inordinately suspicious of the Soviets, there was no unanimity among top staff planners about how to relate to the Soviets. Some were suspicious of the Soviets and the threat they might hold to U.S. interests after the war. Others shared Roosevelt's more optimistic view of a future of collaboration with the Soviets. According to Mark Stoler, the Joint Chiefs shared the opinion of the president, and not merely as good soldiers because it was his opinion. "Indeed, the length of time the chiefs sided with the pro-Soviet and anti-British view is quite surprising in hindsight. Also surprising is the speed with which they then reversed themselves in the summer and fall of 1945." The JCS had maintained their former attitude "despite growing opposition and evidence to the contrary: they then shifted abruptly to a new one when the evidence and pressure for such a shift reached a critical point in mid-1945."[12] Why that happened is complex, as alluded to above, and examined in great detail by Stoler. What emerges from this is that Soviet-American relations deteriorated and then broke largely because of evidence of Soviet ambitions that conflicted with the perhaps naive hopes of sophisticated military leaders as well as practical politicians.

A word must be said about authors who resort to what purports to be a psychological interpretation of the actions of the figures in the wartime drama. This has become popular among political scientists and historians who seek to lend an interdisciplinary flavor to their work, assuming that thus they can "know" historical personalities from sketchy "evidence." It is one thing when persons with credentials in both history and psychology or psychiatry engage in psycho-history, and even then it is highly speculative; it is another when done casually by historians without credentials in another discipline. Skepticism about some practitioners of psycho history was expressed by the man who as much as anyone created the subject, Erik Erikson: "I would not wish to associate myself with all that is done in the name of this term." Erikson also said, "To a psychohistorian, for example, it might seem unnecessary to define what history was and is. Before long, then, his work may fuse with trends that may just as well be called psychojournalism or psychopolitics—and this is in one of the less savory connotations of these words."

In practicing a craft that relies heavily on conjecture, Professor Dower found that, as someone engaged in mass destruction, President Truman somehow blocked his knowledge that Hiroshima was not a military target and approved its destruction. Even the records of his actions, Dower said, are pervaded by such psychological blocking. When discussing the choice of Hiroshima as a target city, Professor Dower noted that Truman described it as a military target. Professor Dower did not consider it such a target and asked, "Had he (Truman) somehow persuaded himself to think otherwise? That is not at all implausible. Men engaged in mass destruction often find it expedient to deflect full acknowledgment of their actions through evasive and euphemistic language. Psychological blocking of this nature pervades the documentary record of the decision to drop the bomb on heavily populated urban targets." As a presumably expert witness, one wonders what qualifications for such distant analysis Professor Dower brings to the case. At times it is easier to place Truman on the analytic couch than to depend on the record of what he said and did. The dilemma, of course, is that with the record contaminated by "psychological blocking," that also cannot be trusted and the writer is left to shallow speculation. Although an otherwise fine historian, unfortunately Professor Dower is not alone in substituting pop psychology for historical analysis.

James Orr is another who tried to explain the *Enola Gay* controversy in psychological terms: "The inability of the Smithsonian Air and Space

Museum to display the Enola Gay in a manner that honored Japanese victim sentiments shows that the United States has its own groups contesting the Hiroshima bombings and the privilege of victimhood." Presumably in a deeply unconscious way the veterans were competing with the Japanese for the status of victims. But he had no explanation for the motivation of the other critics of the exhibit. Then there was Ronald Takaki, who found that Truman succumbed to the raging hate "rooted in a long history of animosity against the Japanese, as well as the fierce memory of Pearl Harbor."[13]

Like Professor Dower when practicing divination to understand Truman, Professor Bernstein said: "in what can only be interpreted as self deception, he had managed not to know that the A-bombs would slay many noncombatants." Bernstein went on to portray Truman as an uncertain and insecure president to whom General Marshall, "combining themes of martial values, national sacrifice, and patriotism, was clear and pungent: Be tough and decisive, endorse the Kyushu operation, and be a true leader." One can imagine bugles sounding in the background as that scene unfolds in a docudrama.[14]

Another revisionist with more of an apparent claim to expertise is professor of psychiatry Robert Jay Lifton, who diagnosed Americans as deeply conflicted and unconsciously guilty about Hiroshima. He discovered, for example, that "McCarthyism in the 1950s occurred precisely when the atomic-bomb terrors, now associated with the Soviet Union, spread throughout the American culture." That tenuous temporal association was not explained, nor did Lifton explain why he thought the bomb was related to Vietnam, Watergate and Iran Contra.

Professor Lifton subjected Harry Truman to long distance diagnosis in his chapter, "Harry Truman's Tragedy." Truman supposedly "was bedeviled by the image of being just a 'little man' ... and need to see himself as acting quickly, boldly and above all decisively ... remaining always vulnerable to a fear of unmanageable complexity, ineffectiveness, and even (as we shall see) of falling apart." At the time all this happened, unfortunately for history, Doctor Lifton was not available to provide the care he deemed the president needed to overcome these deficits. It should be remembered that in court trials, psychiatrists qualified as expert witnesses for either defense or prosecution have personal contact with the accused before testifying. Unfortunately, a few experts will tailor their testimony to fit an attorney's preference, much as psychologizing by purported historians tailor their testimony to fit a desired outcome. That makes a travesty of their supposed understanding of a personality who lived long ago. Although it may make for entertaining theater, it is not history.

Another who weighed in with a psychological assessment was Professor John Lewis Gaddis, who found that the NASM's aborted exhibit "provoked a raucous controversy among historians, veterans and politicians early in 1995, but in the end shed little new light on the actual decision to use the bomb." His conclusion was, " One ought not to minimize the guilt American leaders felt, if only subconsciously, over Hiroshima and Nagasaki, or the sense of responsibility—manifesting itself as a characteristic effort at reform and perhaps redemption—they drew from what they had done." Most of the actors in the summer of 1945 may have regretted the bombings, but Professor Gaddis presented no evidence of guilt feelings, subconscious or otherwise.

When explaining why the veterans criticized the exhibit, Lisa Yoneyama seemed to use group diagnostic skills to suggest that those who accused the veterans of being infatuated with their personal memories "prompted the return of what was repressed in such a counterfeit distinction between history and memory, reifying the originality and genuineness of the experiential truths advocated by many who witnessed the war." The resulting "amnesic hegemony" can reconstruct a version of the experienced past although not in its original form. The veterans "strove to memorialize the martyrs of their sacred war and to remember the atomic bombings through the mediation of the cold war paradigm, which justified the use of military power to achieve and maintain the doctrine of Pax Americana." Although Yaneyama might seem to have criticized the curators and others for posing the debate as one of history versus memory, but actually focused her diagnosis on a return of mistaken repressed feelings that led the veterans to justify force in the service of a Pax Americana. If nothing else the above examples reveal the gross misuse of psychology in the service of ideology.[15]

A small book written in 1965 by Herbert Feis explored the end of the war and the use of the A-Bomb. Feis covered the issues that later appeared in *The Crossroads* and concluded that "the decision to drop the bombs upon Hiroshima and Nagasaki ought not to be censured. The reasons were — under the circumstances of the time — weighty and valid enough." Obviously not happy with what happened, he added, "But a cluster of worrisome queries remain which the passage of time has coated with greater political, ethical and historical interest." He did not ignore those issues but after considering their pros and cons, he came to conclusions diametrically opposed to those of the curators. Whether the curators had considered what was written almost thirty years earlier is not known; they preferred to rely on the opinions of a coterie of revisionists and their advisory committee, none of whom would agree with Feis. Although the curators were not writing a book, a decent regard for the opinions of others like Feis, and for a balanced presentation of the events of the summer of 1945 for the public, might have saved them from the debacle that ensued.

Richard Kohn, a sympathetic supporter of the exhibit, considered the exhibit's cancellation "one of the worst tragedies to befall the public presentation of history in the United States in this generation." However, although he thought some material was taken out of context, the substance of his critique bears repetition. "The problems with the script lay in the omission of material, the emphasis on particular material, the order and placement of facts and analysis, and the tone and the mood. Taken as a whole and read with the emotional impact on viewers in mind, the exhibition was [*sic*] in fact unbalanced; it possessed a very clear and potent point of view. On a level of feeling that could be reached more powerfully through the senses of sight and sound than through the reading of words, the exhibit appealed to viewers' emotions, and its message could be read to be tendentious and moralizing; the exhibition script could be read to condemn American behavior at the end of World War II."

That critique by Kohn leads to the importance of considering what C. Behan McCullagh said when discussing bias in history. He believed that it was important for critics to protect the public from obviously false or misleading accounts of the past. "Only they can reveal ignorance or misuse of relevant evidence, failure to consider alternative, more plausible interpretations, and misleading descriptions of historical subjects. While free criticism and open debate among historians continues, the public will be protected from excessive misuse of history for the purposes of propaganda." The imbalance found in *The Crossroads* by Richard Kohn was not faulted, but instead defended by the historical establishment. If historians insist on consensus, who will protect the public from misleading accounts of the past?[16]

The coterie of historians who enlisted in defense of *The Crossroads* certainly were less interested in what actually happened in the summer of 1945 than in preserving what Kohn called a "tendentious and moralizing" account to condemn what happened to end the war. Found in the mainstream of contemporary history, their style accords with what Christopher Lasch once described as that of the "new left," a "drastic simplification of issues; synthetic contrivance of political and intellectual 'traditions' by reading present concerns into the past; strident partisanship." That can be added to what Richard Posner said about such academic "public intellectuals." Although he was not referring to these revisionists, we believe they qualify for that title, having "A proclivity for taking extreme positions, a taste for universals and abstraction, a desire for moral purity, a lack of worldliness, and intellectual arrogance work together to induce in many academic public intellectuals selective empathy, a selective sense of justice, an insensitivity to context, a lack of perspective, a denigration of predecessors as lacking moral insight, an impatience with prudence and sobriety, a lack of realism, and excessive self-confidence. The 'on the one hand, on the other hand' approach to politically or ideologically charged issues— the kind of approach that can understand slavery in its historical context, that sees the bad along with the good in abolitionists ... this approach is uncongenial to the academic temperament." That description helps to understand the revisionists obsessive desire to convict the dead white males led by Truman who planned the end of the Pacific war.[17]

The public will find that demonstrably misleading accounts of the past in our museums are not always easy to recognize, especially when they are promoted by academic public intellectuals like Noam Chomsky, and by prestigious national institutions with revisionist staffs supported by articulate and influential partisan interest groups. Nothing can falsify our understanding of what led to Hiroshima more than the denial of the evidence that decision makers had at hand in the summer of 1945. Appalled by Okinawa's and Iwo Jima's high casualty rates, and wanting to avoid an even more horrific bloodbath if there was an invasion of Japan's home islands, Washington saw the A-Bomb as the least costly alternative. Because the high ground in the history of this period is held by revisionists, the Smithsonian's trashing of the history of that summer was thwarted almost by accident when a small group of veterans alerted the Air Force Association to how the NASM proposed to mark the anniversary of the end of World War II. Our critique has documented several significant issues that were manipulated by the NASM in the hope that this account of one skirmish in the history wars will encourage others to go to the sources and meet the revisionists on a common intellectual ground without the heated rhetoric or the ad hominem attacks that too often characterized what happened in 1995. The last word can be left to historian I. B. Holley, who found the healing process between Japan and the United States to be long and slow, "but fair-minded citizens of both nations know that friendship and mutual understanding must be our goals. The Smithsonian scriptwriters impaired the healing by their failure to practice the objectivity and balance that is the hallmark of sound historical scholarship."[18]

Appendix A

Is Speculation History?

Content analysis studies the use of words and images in communication. The methodology used can range from basic and simple to highly sophisticated, depending upon its purpose. Even basic analysis can be informative and show how displays and documents manipulate content to influence a reader or viewer. As would any museum exhibit, the *Enola Gay* exhibit intended to present artifacts and photographs in addition to printed captions and brief explanations of some items. Director Harwit emphasized that the visual element of the exhibit was very important so, taking him at his word, the Air Force Association (AFA) examined the visual content considered important by Director Harwit in three versions of the script. In the original script the number of photos of Japanese casualties overwhelmed those of American casualties. Only 5.7 percent of the casualty photos featured Americans, something that hardly happened by chance. A few months later, the curators had increased the American casualty photos to 17.9 percent of all casualty photos and finally they made up 35 percent of the casualty photos. By design the original script barely referred to American casualties in a visual display deemed important by the curators.

CASUALTY PHOTOS IN THREE VERSIONS OF SCRIPT

Photos of	January	May	August
JAPANESE	49	32	26
AMERICANS	3	7	14

Not satisfied with counting the disproportionate attention given to Japanese casualties, the AFA carefully assessed the raw number of pages assigned to various topics and found the disproportion noted above pervaded the text for the exhibit. In what the museum called the emotional

heart of the exhibit, sustained and graphic attention was given to grue-
some photos of the aftermath of the bombings. That reality belonged in
the exhibit, but Harwit admitted that balance and context were lacking
when he charged the so-called "Tiger Team" to review and critique *The
Crossroads*. The report of this internal review on May 25, 1994 was carefully phrased, but despite the guarded language it was almost as critical of
the exhibit as the Air Force Association. Excerpts from the report are found
in the appendix.[1]

Analysis of a text can reveal whether the writer's conclusions are supported by qualifying words or phrases such as "might," "probably" and
similar words. Some leeway in using qualifiers must be left to the historian because much of the past is not known with certitude. However, when
supposition after supposition leads a writer to present the reader with a
firm conclusion, that conclusion rests on sand. Some will argue that
qualifiers are merely matters of style that do not affect the thrust of an argument. However, when a case is built on qualifiers, it is nothing less than
a counterfactual, and the frequency with which the writer uses them
reflects the writer's attitude toward the subject. The following is an example of sand castle building found in an excerpt from an article on the
bombing of Hiroshima and Nagasaki by a defender of the exhibit:

"Whatever one thinks about the necessity of the first A-bomb, the second — dropped on Nagasaki on August 9 — was almost certainly unnecessary. It was used because the original order directed the air force to drop
bombs 'as made ready' and, even after the Hiroshima bombing, no one in
Washington anticipated an imminent Japanese surrender. Evidence now
available about developments in the Japanese government — most notably
the emperor's then secret decision shortly before the Nagasaki bombing
to seek peace — makes it clear that the second bomb could undoubtedly
have been avoided. At least 30,000 Japanese and *possibly* almost twice that
number, as well as several thousand Koreans, died unnecessarily in Nagasaki."

When suggesting that at least 30,000 Japanese died at Nagasaki, Professor Bernstein was within the limits of acceptable speculation. The other
two qualifiers, almost certainly and could undoubtedly, are used to state
unequivocally that more than 30,000 died unnecessarily. In addition, the
final qualifier is based on "evidence now available" which was unknown
in 1945 and therefore irrelevant to the decision to drop the bomb. Although
Professor Bernstein is entitled to his opinion, his firm conclusion is not
supported by "almost certainly" and "could undoubtedly."[2]

Another simple analysis of the content of an article by Professor Alperovitz gave similar results. "As early as April 18 the Joint Planners had

reported that a clarification of the surrender terms in itself might be all that was needed to achieve surrender. Throughout May this judgment was continuously reinforced so that by June it was clear to American leaders that either a Russian declaration of war or a change in the surrender terms *was likely* to bring capitulation. *Almost certainly* a combination of the two measures would stop the fighting immediately" (italics added). One of the persons cited for that conclusion was Admiral Leahy, who had serious reservations about an invasion. However, Professor Alperovitz was stretching what Leahy reported in his memoirs to support his statement that it was clear to American leaders what was likely to bring about capitulation. It would have been more accurate to say that it was clear to some but obviously not all American leaders.[3]

Although unmentioned by Professor Alperovitz in the document he cited, the other planners referred to the problem posed by unconditional surrender: "The concept of 'unconditional surrender' is foreign to the Japanese nature. Therefore 'unconditional surrender' should be defined in terms understandable to the Japanese, who must be convinced that destruction or national suicide is not implied. This could be done by the announcement on a governmental level of a 'declaration of intentions' which would tell the Japanese what their future holds. Once convinced of the inevitability of defeat, it is possible that a government could be formed in Japan that would sign and could enforce a surrender instrument. Unless a definition of unconditional surrender can be given which is acceptable to the Japanese, there is no alternative to annihilation and no prospect that the threat of absolute defeat will bring about capitulation." It went on to say that a campaign of blockade and bombardment would not assure unconditional surrender or defeat.... "Therefore, the invasion of Japan is considered the most suitable strategy to accomplish unconditional surrender or ultimate defeat."

Ignoring the planners' warning, Professor Alperovitz said, "(It is not my purpose to argue whether either or both of these measures would, in fact, have ended the war. What I wish to show is that American leaders believed [*sic*] such a result was likely. Hence, their decision to use the atomic bomb was made at a time when the best intelligence and military advice indicated there were other ways to end the war without an invasion. As will be shown, the bomb was used not because there were no alternatives, but precisely because American policy makers wished to avoid the political consequences of these alternatives.)" (Parentheses in the original.)

One can make a case that Professor Alperovitz' assertions ignore the evidence, but we will remain with the fact that, in an excerpt of 174 words, eight of them significantly modify the credibility of the author's conclusion that there were ways to end the war without an invasion. Arguing that point is fair, but it is hardly supported by what the author wrote. The weight of the voluminous, almost overwhelming apparent evidence cited in Professor Alperovitz' book seems to lend credibility to the overall work and thus to conclusions such as the one mentioned above, unless one analyzes what actually is said by the author. In addition, contrary to what Alperovitz wrote, the alternatives were considered and rejected for reasons that are well known to revisionists and that made sense to decision makers in 1945. One may believe them mistaken, but ignoring or suppressing that information is not playing fair with the reader. However, it made the curators task easier, and that may be why they singled out an Alperovitz book as the only one mentioned by *The Crossroads* for possible inclusion in the exhibit.[4]

How conditional terms can lead to a firm conclusion also is shown in Professor Bernstein's opinion of how the war could have ended. The following article and several of his other writings on the end of the war were examined to determine how qualified they were. In one article he said that a combination of alternatives made it "seem very likely, although not definite, that a synergistic combination of guaranteeing the emperor, awaiting Soviet entry, and continuing the siege strategy would have ended the war in time to avoid the November invasion. And quite possibly Soviet entry amid the strangling blockade and the heavy bombing of cities could have accomplished that goal without dropping the atomic bomb. There was, then more probably than not, a missed opportunity to end the war without the A-bomb and without the November invasion. And it is virtually definite, had the Kyushu invasion occurred with these other strategies, and without the A-bomb, that Japan would have surrendered well before the March 1946 invasion" (emphasis added). His case was made by moving from "seems very likely" to "quite possibly" to "more probably" and finally to "virtually definite." Courts would banish testimony based on such evanescent "evidence," but apparently some judges (editors) in the court of history represented by professional journals saw no problem with crystal gazing.

Another example of using qualifying phrases to produce the appearance of certainty: "The main analysis in this essay does not depend upon the evidence of this discussion at a Potsdam meeting, although the inferential evidence suggests that such a discussion was *somewhat likely*." As will be seen later, the more than frequent use of such qualifiers reveals how Professor Bernstein edges toward deconstructionism.[5] In many fields of study deconstruction remains an approach to teaching, research and academic writing. The ubiquitous use of qualifiers enables one to deconstruct a document and achieve a unique interpretation that can be the opposite of what others commonly held it to mean, or its creator intended it to mean. The presumed evidence of the validity of the interpretation rests on a footnote, as if that authenticated the new interpretation, no matter how off the wall and spurious it might be.

Allied to the freedom to impose one's own interpretation on texts is the tendency to exercise one's creative imagination An article in the *Pacific Historical Review* by Professor Bernstein is a good example of this creative approach to history, using a large number of qualifying terms to guide the reader. Opinions may differ about a few of these words, and his extensive references to archives creates an impression of credibility, but the sheer volume of these words impugns the credibility of what is presented in the article.

apparently (2)	seem(s) (+4)
seems questionable	likely (+14)
suggests that (+ 7)	undoubtedly
probable	might be
probably	would have been
presumably (3)	often view
quite possible	might prove
certainly possible	could further weaken
could well have	not seem to know
could have	undoubtedly
may well have been	seemed to be
might also have been	may even have been
might have been,	undoubtedly
perhaps (+ 12)	could conceivably
apparently	was at best a possibility
might have done	definitely possibly
might have	quite likely
apparently imply	would undoubtedly
seemed to be suggesting	might well have
undoubtedly	might be
presumably indicated	unstated implication
perhaps	would have been
implied	seems unlikely
might have	undoubtedly
inclined some analysts to believe	plausible inference
some analysts speculate	possible
implicit	might

necessarily quite possible   might well have

Struck by the extensive use of qualifiers in the above articles, we became interested in the extent to which the author might have done the same in his other writing. As a prolific author, only a few of Professor Bernstein's many articles could be covered, so several articles that directly addressed the end of the Pacific war were examined to see if they contained qualifying words such as: probably, likely, unlikely, perhaps, seemed, suggests, and possibly. The 1999 article in *The Pacific Historical Review* had 147 qualifiers in 47 pages of text. Professor Bernstein's 1999 review essay, a hatchet job on an article by Norman Polmar and Thomas Allen, appeared in *Peace and Change*. In about 19 pages of text there are 101 qualifiers similar to those in the first article examined. In the 23 pages of a 1998 article in *The Journal of Military History*, 76 similar qualifiers appeared. The author concluded with several obvious ones that added up to another "might have been."

Discussing the final phase of the war he questioned whether the A-bomb would have been used truly on a military target, and not on substantially noncombatants: "*if* Marshall had pleaded such a case with the President, *if* Leahy had affirmed such values, and *if* Stimson had also joined them. Then, quite probably, Truman could have written, correctly in his Potsdam diary 'that military objectives and soldiers and sailors are the target and not women and children.'" How easily an iffy counterfactual led the author, if not Truman, to the "correct" decision.

Another 17 page article on the A-Bomb, this time in *Foreign Affairs*, had 36 of those pesky qualifiers as the author explored the morality of the A-Bomb. *Diplomatic History* carried a densely argued 37 page article in 1993, this one with only 60 qualifiers. In that article Professor Bernstein aptly remarked that the effort to understand and explain the dropping of the A-Bomb "has raised issues about evidence and interpretation and about the purposes and assumptions of many authors." Professor Bernstein might recall the words of the poet Robert Burns "O wad some Power the giftie gie us, to see oursels as others see us."[7]

Imagine what the response to a journal article would be if, after developing a new medicine, a researcher concluded that quite likely, presumably or perhaps, it would be safe to use, and that undoubtedly or conceivably it could be used to treat some disease. Although history may not be able to reach the level of assurance that is required and can be achieved in the physical sciences, surely more can asked of it than the squishy comments about events found in the examples mentioned above. When discussing matters of state, or anything in Clio's realm, we could profit by insisting that "Opinions are to be stated so as to be clear in their meaning. Wording should not be such that inferences are drawn which are not valid, or that slant the opinion in a particular direction." That is from the code of ethics of the Midwest Association of Forensic Scientists, which points out that to do otherwise can result in a miscarriage of justice. The same can happen in history. If a beginning graduate student used such conditional statements in a seminar to buttress a position, it would not be tolerated; much less should it be tolerated in the public arena.[8]

Conditional statements are not the only problem the reader faces when assessing written material. The following is an example of a writer's seemingly plausible claim that shows how the shifting of a time frame misrepresented the situation in the war's final phase. When ostensibly discussing how the attitudes of both sides changed after the war, Professor Dower said, "the dominant wartime stereotypes on both sides were wrong ... the Japanese were more diversified and far more war-weary than their enemies had been led to believe. The analysts in the Foreign Morale Analysis Division of the Office of War Information, ignored by men in power while the war raged, proved to be more accurate in their predictions of both Japanese exhaustion and Japanese adaptability. Liberal and leftist scholars in the West, who had tried with little success during the war to call attention to democratic and progressive traditions in prewar Japan, also turned out to have been more perceptive than the propagandists and most of the war planners. The Japanese people — unlike their militarist leaders— welcomed peace."[9]

An unwary reader might not notice a temporal shift in Professor Dower's well written counterfactual. The time frame for what was to be a discussion of the post war situation in Japan shifted to what happened during the war. Professor Dower's reference to the analysts' reports and the failed efforts of liberal and leftist scholars to get a hearing during the war intimates that had they been heeded they might have changed the outcome for Japan. Although the analysts may have been right about Japanese exhaustion, that was no revelation considering what was known from intercepts about the effectiveness of the blockade. Surely Professor Dower knew that war-weary or not, public opinion made no difference in a nation whose repressive military used secret police to control the population as effectively as the Gestapo did in Germany. As early as July 1946 the U. S. Strategic Bombing Survey had reported that until the end, "national traditions of obedience and conformity, reinforced by the police organizations, remained effective in controlling the behavior of the population.... It is probable that most Japanese would have passively faced death in a continuation of the hopeless struggle, had the Emperor so ordered." Thus, although it is nice to know that there were "democratic and progressive" traditions in Japan, Professor Dower did not tell readers that these traditions were shared by a very small number of marginalized individuals including "progressive" members of the Communist party who surfaced during the occupation. None of those traditions could have played a role in persuading Japan's rulers to end the war. Although the Japanese people welcomed peace after August 14, contrary to what Professor Dower clearly implied, they could have had no part in bringing it about because their militarist leaders had mobilized them to fight to the last. Speculation seemingly buttressed by the paraphernalia of scholarship has been deployed by too many revisionists in their obsessive efforts to change the history of the end of the Pacific war.[10]

Appendix B

The "Tiger Team" Report

In response to growing criticism of the exhibit Director Harwit asked a small group of NASM staff who had not worked on the exhibit to review *The Crossroads* script and prepare a report for him. This was the so-called "Tiger Team." Because of limited space the complete 22 page executive summary of the Tiger Team report is not reproduced. However, we believe that the several pages that are reproduced here fairly represent the content of the report and show how five experienced persons close to the NASM, but not involved in preparing the exhibit, reacted to the original script. In sending the report to Director Harwit the team said, "This Report is intended to complement the more specific and detailed entries contained in the Master Script." There is a tantalizing hint that those more specific entries could be even more critical of the exhibit than the report itself.[*]

NATIONAL AIR AND SPACE MUSEUM EXHIBIT SCRIPT
"THE CROSSROADS: THE END OF WORLD WAR II, THE ATOMIC BOMB AND THE ORIGINS OF THE COLD WAR"
REVIEW AND RECOMMENDATIONS

I. UNIT 100: "A FIGHT TO THE FINISH"

A. *REVIEW OF UNIT 100.* Unit 100 contains a number of imbalances with respect to text, photos and quotations which are likely to be perceived as being more sympathetic to Japanese versus American views of the War. Additionally, several important historical themes are not adequately developed.

1. *Depictions of Japanese as victims.* This unit appears overly sympa-

---

[*] *The Tiger Team Report of May 25, 1994 can be found in* Revisionism Gone Wrong, Analysis of the Enola Gay Controversy, Part II. *Arlington, VA., The Air Force Association, March 2000.*

thetic to the Japanese, seen as suffering, desperate defenders of their home-land and unique culture (i.e., "100 Million Hearts Beating as One"). In contrast, the U.S. will likely be perceived as motivated by vengeance and a desire to destroy the Japanese empire and its people.

2. Depictions of Japanese pre-war aggression and brutality. There is insufficient development of Japan's extensive pre-war aggression through-out Asia, atrocities and brutality inflicted upon Asian cities, civilian pop-ulations, forced laborers and prisoners of war.

3. *Japanese attack on Pearl Harbor.* The surprise attack against the U.S. Naval Base at Pearl Harbor is the pivotal event from which sprang "A Fight To The Finish." As such the attack should be covered in a separate section (with title) and with considerably more text, photos and quota-tions than currently accorded.

II. UNIT 200: THE DECISION TO DROP THE BOMB

A. REVIEW OF UNIT 200.

1. *History and development of the Bomb.* Unit 200 successfully traces the history of the Manhattan Project, the development of the atomic bomb, and key U.S. and Japanese leaders and decision makers.

2. *Characterization of Truman and Groves.* Through various infer-ences and quotations, President Truman appears as not entirely in com-mand of the decision process regarding use of the atomic bomb. References to Major General Groves~ the Manhattan Project leader~ show him as eager to use the bomb, fighting to restore Kyoto, the historic capital of Japan, to the target list, and worried that the war would end before his bomb was ready. These impressions appear to be somewhat overstated and could be misleading to the public.

3. *Unattributed title and subtitle quotations.* Several titles of Unit sub-headings are carried as quotations which contain no reference or attribu-tion, nor of the context in which they were originally stated.

4. *Japan seeks a negotiated surrender.* The text's descriptions of Japan's efforts to modify the Allies' demand for unconditional surrender and to guarantee the Emperor's post-war status is generally well covered. The text does, however, appear to convey the impression that Japan was seek-ing peace, while the U. S. was seeking to obstruct means for a negotiated settlement. This could be misleading to the public.

5. *"Historical Controversies."* The unit contains a number of sidebars titled "Historical Controversies" relating to the decision to drop the Bomb and/or possible alternatives to using the Bomb. Because most of these "Historical Controversies" were found to contain a fair amount of spec-

ulation, their stature as "controversies" was considered somewhat diminished. As presently written, these controversies could lead the viewing public to conclude that the decision to drop the A-Bomb was questionable (perhaps unjustified?) rather than debatable (still open to discussion).

B. RECOMMENDED REVISIONS TO UNIT 200.

Recommendations for changes regarding Unit 200 consist generally of minor editing and other adjustments, with the exception of the "Historical Controversies." Most of these were recommended for revision and rewrite, in order to appear less speculative and more closely aligned with acknowledgments and judgments to which most historians generally subscribe. A rewrite would also increase the public's understanding of these controversies....

III. UNIT 300: DELIVERING THE BOMB

A. REVIEW OF UNIT 300.

1. *Development of the B-29.* The development of the B-29 bomber and the resultant mechanical and technological difficulties experienced is generally well presented.

2. *Pressure to bomb Japan.* The early pressure from President Roosevelt on military leaders to bomb Japan "heavily and relentlessly" requires additional explanation, in order to emphasize the many early difficulties in mounting effective aerial attacks against Japan.

3. *Change in B-29 bombing tactics and weapons.* In the section entitled "Burning Japan," there is insufficient explanation and development of the rationale for the change in B-29 bombing tactics and weapons in March 1945 — the only explanation being "... poor results achieved by EXIST Bomber Command...."

4. *Imbalance: Japanese cities as "targets."* There are several references in this and subsequent sections to "burning cities," "attacking cities" and "razing cities." There are no references to industrial complexes, war-producing industries or other "targets" of military value in and around these cities. References only to the firebombing of cities and "Burning Japan" convey an erroneous impression that cities per se, rather than military/industrial targets, were the focus of the B-29 raids against Japan.

Appendix C

Why Not Full Disclosure?

Journalists have the unique privilege of reporting information without the responsibility of identifying the source. Writing about the role of Paul Nitze in arms control, Strobe Talbot said that if journalism is the first draft of history, his book complete with end notes was a second draft in which he "necessarily leaves many sources who must remain anonymous." Professors do not have Talbot's leeway. The source, whether a document, an individual or an artifact must be identified for the benefit of other researchers and to insure that the source exists and can be checked for accuracy and relevance. That is why historians and other scholars use footnotes, often to the distress of the general reader. Footnotes may intrude on the flow of a narrative, but they are indispensable to preserve the integrity of the research process.

This is a suggestion that historians and other social scientists should take an additional step, and along with their footnotes tell their readers who paid for their research, if it received funding. Why do this? For the same reason the public wants to know if there is a relationship between academic researchers in the health sciences and pharmaceutical companies. In such cases there can be the appearance of a conflict of interest, or of special pleading by the researcher. If there was disclosure by historians then, without implying anything sinister, one could ask about the complete provenance of a book by Professor Alperovitz. He was generous in expressing his appreciation to the large staff of what can only be called a major research project that led to the book, *The Decision to Use the Atomic Bomb*. On the title page he named seven individuals who assisted in the research, some for several years and perhaps full time. About twenty others are named for their legal and research contributions to the project. In addition there were fourteen volunteer researchers and graduate interns and fourteen persons who did typing and other research assignments. Managing, compiling and integrating the work of so many individuals was no small or inexpensive task, and the project could not have proceeded without generous funding.[1]

Research projects receive funding from organizations that have an interest in their purpose. Fund raising is not easy and anyone interested in raising money looks for sympathetic donors. In the hard sciences less ideology is involved in grantsmanship than in the softer social sciences. Academics know that liberal foundations support projects with a liberal cast and that the many fewer conservative donors support projects with a conservative cast. It also is true, although fervently denied, that even federal grants in the social sciences often follow the private liberal philanthropic pattern.

When acknowledging those who contributed to the preparation of the book, Professor Alperovitz thanked ten foundations and named other financial supporters who provided money, then added that other persons contributed anonymously. Does that anonymity matter? We believe that it does. It is appropriate for researchers to make full disclosure not only in their end notes but also of their funding sources. An unknown benefactor who donates a building to a hospital may not influence public policy, but many social science grants have that goal and as long as researchers are open about donors there is no problem when the reader is alerted to a possible advocacy agenda. Storm signals arise when we learn that university researchers testing new drugs have received money from pharmaceutical companies, because it suggests a possible conflict of interest. It should be no less true for the social sciences. It is unlikely that money came from an off-shore foundation interested in a possible favorable spin to the outcome of research by someone with a known agenda. But the nagging question remains, why not full disclosure?

Related to the idea that funding ought to be fully disclosed is the question of who, if anyone, is responsible for a book beyond the person's name on the cover. In the aftermath of the admission about "borrowing without attribution" by two well known historians who blamed it, at least in part, to relying on assistants and sloppy note taking, Professor James Giles wondered whether "plagiarism was the tip of the iceberg in the book world. We might compare the use of shortcuts in the form of research assistants to athletes' use of steroids. Or, less harshly, the use of researchers might be compared to the atelier system in which assistants were routinely responsible for many parts of a finished painting. Either way, one must ask who is responsible for the finished product. In evaluating a book, should reviewers take into account whether it was researched and written by a single individual or by a team of researchers working for the person who is named as the author? Should readers be fully informed of the precise nature and extent of the researchers' contribution?" Giles went on to say that "we need to rethink what we mean by 'author' and reconsider how we should evaluate these books." What Giles suggests has little chance of implementation, but apart from the issue of the responsibility of the name on the cover, it raises a serious intellectual question about the authenticity of authorship.

More thought along the line of transparency was stimulated by what Professor Bernstein said in a slashing 1999 critique of an article by Thomas Allan and Norman Polmar. Referring to them as "journalistic/historians," (although they are "respected military writers" who appear in a popular, generally respected military publication), Bernstein claims that they misread sources, relied on dubious materials and indulged in questionable reasoning. He also proposed to discuss the social/political functions of the article and raise questions about standards in scholarship and publishing that allowed their article to find its way into print.[2]

Say what you will about Bernstein's critique, his introduction of the legitimacy of questioning the social/political dimension of the Allen/Polmar article is a contribution to a transparent consideration of the sociopolitical narratives that have flowed from the controversy about the atomic bombing of Japan, as well as other debated issues in history. The presumably more "authentic" scholarship in contemporary history, often conflated with so-called "revisionism," has been negatively criticized outside the academy for its deconstruction of the "myths" of past history, but there have been relatively few rebuttals within the academy. When they occur they are dismissed under the rubric of being socio-politically "conservative," a word that carries a lot of baggage among academics and public intellectuals. Equity makes it appropriate to ascertain the socio-political dimensions of historians who may not be writing "popular history" but presumably real history, like that of Gar Alperovitz, Kai Bird and Howard Zinn, not in terms of a catch-all word like liberal or radical or conservative or reactionary, but in terms of the "dimensions" of their thought. After all, fairness is (or should be) the watchword of academics when discussing issues in any field. When reviewing a book by Steven Ross, Professor Bernstein, for example, thought it was unfortunate that the author chose "not to discuss the identities and backgrounds of the war planners, and how, if at all significantly, they differed by about 1949 from their Second World War counterparts." Although it would be difficult to document any shift, it could be useful to make the attempt and his shrewd observation ought to be taken to heart by scholars. Furthermore, what is sauce for the goose....

Not many historians have followed the example of Richard and Dale Newman, who told the reader "We acknowledge at the outset a left-liberal bias." Few revisionists have been as frank as one of the earliest and most influential who became a model and icon for those who followed. William Appleman Williams wanted students to become their own historians: "Being one's own historian does not mean being an anarchist or a devil-take-the hindmost kind of capitalist — or communist. The truth of it is that the most difficult and challenging prospect is to be a democratic socialist. To achieve that objective it is first necessary to be a historian." And not many are inclined to follow the path of Richard Bosworth, an Australian historian whose survey of European historians places them in their socio-political context by examining their backgrounds and not hesitating to categorize their approach to history in terms of their political beliefs. This classifying of historians can be helpful, especially to those lacking familiarity with their foreign colleagues. In the United States, although retrospectively Charles Beard or Frederick Jackson Turner are identified in ideological terms, there is little to alert readers of contemporary history to the historian's thought. With experience the defining code words may be learned, although some are subtle and fortunately few are as shopworn as those found in Marxist writing.[3]

It may be argued that requiring disclosure about funding sources could lead to an accusation of a kind of guilt by association. As in the example of the attack by Professor Bernstein mentioned above, such guilt already happens. Conservative sources can be prejudicial to a fair hearing, but all sides should run the same risks, or none. If campaign ads identify their source, and milk containers and food cans reveal their provenance, should less be expected of intellectual fare?

Contemporary historians stress the importance of understanding the ideological stance of those they study. There is insistence on the importance of ascertaining the subjectivity of the reasoning and actions of individuals and groups under study. Bernstein is correct when he suggests that the same is true for the journalist/historians, and he ought to add just plain historians, in order to evaluate their work. Is it important to ask about their personal agendas and their goals? If such questions are appropriate when examining political appointees, including Supreme Court Justices, are they any less appropriate when seeking to understand what lies behind the scholarly facade of a book or article?

Thus, not only documents from archives or private collections and in libraries, articles in journals, newspapers, videos, etc., need to be identified. We ought to know who gathered the material and why, because there are enough clever forgers of paintings, artifacts and documents (including Hitler's diaries) to suggest that one must be prudent when assigning authenticity, especially when dealing with documents. The revelation that historian David Irving deliberately mistranslated documents and falsified his reports of archival discoveries is a cautionary tale for researchers. Typically, researchers rigorously follow the canons of their craft, not for fear of exposure, but because honest reporting is drilled into them in their education, and the integrity of the research process is their Holy Grail. Because checking to validate every citation and reading every document in a distant archive that is mentioned in a book is often difficult and sometimes impossible, what a footnote says must be accepted on faith. That is why tampering with evidence, or even a gentle massaging of it to fit it into a pattern, is such a serious betrayal of the canon.

We wish to return briefly to the matter of financial support for research, an element of the scholarly process that has not received as much attention as it deserves. An example from the distant past illustrates the point. As Fascist Italy prepared for the passage of the infamous "racial" laws of 1938 based on spurious anthropology and history, some university faculty who were subsidized by the regime produced articles and books proving that Jews were racially different than Italians. Their pseudo science was used to justify the draconian laws that excluded Jews from public life. Today that junk science seems almost comic but at the time it helped Mussolini emulate Germany's Nuremberg laws.

It may be argued that the peer review panels of government agencies and foundations ensure objectivity and non-discrimination in the allocation of grants, but insiders know that panels can be stacked and grants "wired" to preferred recipients. Someone is sure to cry that to open such questions implies favoritism or guilt by association. But association corrupted the work of fascist scholars, as well as that of Soviet scholars during the heyday of communism. Their scholarship often was tainted because inevitably, given their education and the atmosphere in which they worked, they hewed to the party line. That it why it can be important to ask the provenance of the researcher, and the source of funding. That does not warrant a crude and reckless accusation of censorship or McCarthyism. It does suggest a prudent, common sense way of assessing the credibility of the author, just as authors study the backgrounds of their subjects to assesses their credibility.[5]

Notes

Chapter I

1. Harwit, Martin. *An Exhibit Denied: Lobbying the History of the Enola Gay.* New York, Springer Verlag, Inc., 1996. Allen, Thomas B. and Norman Polmar. *Code-Name DOWNFALL: The Secret Plan to Invade Japan — and Why Truman Dropped the Bomb.* New York, Simon & Schuster, 1995. Frank, Richard B. *Downfall: The End of the Imperial Japanese Empire.* New York, Random House, 1999. Newman, Robert P. *Truman and the Hiroshima Cult.* East Lansing, Michigan State University Press, 1995.

For one analysis of the controversy, see Hubbard, Bryan and Marouf A. Hasian Jr., "The Generic Roots of the Enola Gay Controversy." *Political Communication,* vol. 15, 4, Oct.-Dec. 1998. The attitude displayed by curator Thomas Crouch guaranteed confrontation. He sought the high ground of morality against the (amoral?) feel-good veterans. That patronizing attitude set the stage for confrontation with citizens who began by petitioning for a redress of what they considered a grievance. Given short shrift in a needless bureaucratic fumble, they did what citizens do every day, they went public with eventual success. That others who objected to the exhibit became as shrill as its defenders was not their fault. The heated rhetoric that developed on both sides of the controversy might have been avoided had the NASM responded collegially and respected the concerns of the petitioners.

2. Re Challinor, see Harwit, ibid. 33. "The Exhibition Planning Document," Adam's memo and Crouch's memo are found in *Revisionism Gone Wrong, Part II.* Arlington, VA, Air Force Association. 2000.

3. *The Crossroads: The End of World War II, the Atomic Bomb and the Origins of the Cold War,* January 12, 1994. An all too common example of imbalance is found in the exhibit's title. While the curators spoke of the origins of the Cold War they named no others "origins" in the script. In their absence the visitor would carry away the impression that the A-Bomb had a primary role in creating the Cold War. Harwit, Martin. "Academic Freedom in "The Last Act" in the *Journal of American History,* December 1995. op. cit., 1075, 1064, 1069. Correll, John. Memo for Record, August 17, 1994, in "Enola Gay Archive," available at http://www/afa.org/media/enolagayu/02–01.html. Lifton, Robert Jay and Greg Mitchell. *Hiroshima in America, Fifty Years of Denial.* New York, G. P. Putnam's Sons, 1995. 172, 278. ERIC, ED 401218. A copy of *The Crossroads* is at the Air Force Association according to *First Search,* a data base of books and articles held by libraries in the United States and elsewhere. The NASM may have what it called a "clean copy" in remote storage in the Smithsonian's archives, however, it was unable to supply a copy of the original script according to a letter from NASM, June

27, 2001. A trio of Columbia University journalism students prepared an award-winning documentary on the *Enola Gay* controversy called "A Plane Hanging." A revealing comment in the *Columbia University Record* was that one of their biggest problems was: "The Smithsonian shut us out, shut everyone out. We had to do a story about a place that wouldn't let us in." *Columbia University Record*, vol. 21, no. 21, March 29, 1996. Nobile, Philip, ed. *Judgment at the Smithsonian.* New York, Marlowe & Company, 1995. By publishing the script Nobile provided a service to readers who otherwise could not readily obtain a copy. He obtained his copy from the Air Force Association. In 1995 a copy of the fifth script was available from the Smithsonian for $35. For a revisionist version of the Cold War see the entry by Michael Meeropol in Buhle, MariJo and Paul Buhle, et al. *The Encyclopedia of the American Left.* New York, Garland Publishing Company, 1990, 145–146. The historian Robert Conquest aptly characterized the revisionist coterie: "academics of the middle generation whose political and general judgment was negligible were able to build reputations as experts by minor studies and then be consulted as to broader matters in which they had little competence, though much to say." Conquest, Robert. *Reflections on a Ravaged Century.* New York, W. W. Norton & Company. 2000, 221.

4. What is called the "original" script by the NASM is found on microfiche in the Educational Resources Information Center (ERIC). This 1995 ERIC copy is misrepresented to the public as "original," when it is actually the much edited version prepared just before the exhibit was canceled. The introduction says, "This material offers the educator material to stimulate discussion, analysis and critical thinking in world history, modern history or United States history courses." An unwary historian could be deceived by that copy. Reading this script after it was sanitized by removing the vengeance statement and other disputed elements of the *original* script, could lead one to ask what all the fuss was about. The accompanying "Enola Gay" microfiche that covers the B-29 was funded by the U. S. Office of Education, Office of Educational Research and Improvement (OERI) in 1995. The most available copy is in Nobile, Philip, *Judgment at the Smithsonian,* op. cit.

5. Hogan, Michael J., ed. *Hiroshima in History and Memory.* Cambridge, Cambridge University Press, 1998, 210, 231; Goldberg, Stanley. "Smithsonian suffers Legionnaire's disease." *Bulletin of the Atomic Scientists,* vol. 51, no. 3, May 1995, 28–33. Goldberg, Stanley. "The Enola Gay Affair: What Evidence Counts When We Commemorate Historical Events?" *Orbis,* Annual 1999, 17. Goldberg had prepared a 1985 exhibit for the 40th anniversary of the bombing of Hiroshima and Nagasaki. At a meeting with the American Legion, Harwit also stressed that *The Crossroads* was a first draft and asked not to be judged by it. Harwit, Martin. *An Exhibit Denied: Lobbying the History of Enola Gay,* op. cit., 327. The exhibit's advisory committee members were: Edwin Bears, chief historian, National Park Service; Barton J. Bemstein, professor of history, Stanford University; Victor Bond, radiation physiologist, Brookhaven National Laboratory; Stanley Goldberg, historian of science and biographer of Gen. Leslie Groves, who headed the Manhattan Project; Richard Hallion, military historian in charge of the United States Air Force's Center for Air Force History; Akira Ilriye, professor of history at Harvard University and past president of the American Historical Association; Edward T. Linenthal, professor of Religious Studies at the University of Wisconsin, Oshkosh; Richard Rhodes, author of a Pulitzer Prize-winning book on the atomic bomb; and Martin J. Sherwin, director of the John Sloan Dickey Center for International Understanding, Dartmouth College. An added member of the panel was historian Herman S. Wolk, attached to the United State's Air Force Center for Air Force History.

6. Nash, Gary B., Charlotte Crabtree and Ross E. Dunn. *History on Trial: Culture*

Wars and the Teaching of the Past. New York, Alfred A. Knopf, 1997, 125. Nash was co-director of the project that prepared the national history standards. He was quoted by National Public Radio as saying that the manual the project prepared was frankly aimed at revising the teaching of history: "We really need to open up the mental prison that we've created, to get away from the top-down, hero-driven history full of great generals and great politicians, to emphasize that ordinary people are important in creating history, to try to promote active learning rather than passive memorizing." National Public Radio transcript #1095–12, October 30, 1994.

7. Kohn, Richard H. "History at Risk: The Case of the Enola Gay" in Linenthal, Edward T. and Tom Engelhart, ed. *History Wars, The Enola Gay and Other Battles For The American Past.* New York, Metropolitan Books, 1996, 146, 149. See Linenthal, "Anatomy of a Controversy," 9–62, ibid. Linenthal, Edward T. *Sacred Ground, Americans and Their Battlefields.* Urbana, University of Illinois Press, 1993, 184, 242. Jacques Derrida's "deconstructionism," a faddish French import about thirty years ago, has lost momentum in the last decade as it fell somewhat behind the curve of intellectual fashion. So-called postmodernists who favor deconstruction continue to be influential in literature, art, political science, critical legal studies in law, philosophy, and other fields of knowledge, including history. Although rarely applied to the words on currency, or to the meaning of warning signs on high tension lines, it remains an important force in academia, as is evident from Linenthal's comment. According to Derrida, "My hope as a man of the left, that certain elements of deconstruction will have served — because the struggle continues particularly in the United States— will serve to politicize or repoliticize the left with regard to positions which are not simply academic." Quoted in Lilla, Mark. *The Restless Mind, Intellectuals in Politics.* New York, New York Review Books, 2001, 185. See also: Derrida, Jacques. *Deconstruction in a Nutshell: A Conversation with Jacques Derrida.* New York, Fordham University Press, 1997.

8. Henderson, Amy and Andrienne L Kappler. "Introduction." in Henderson, Amy and Andrienne L Kappler, ed. *Exhibiting Dilemmas, Issues of Representation at the Smithsonian.* Washington, Smithsonian Institution Press, 1997, 7. Yeingst, William and Ionnie G Bunch. "Curating the Recent Past" in *Exhibiting Dilemmas,* op., cit. 145, 152, 153, 154. Their idea of "manipulating history to deal with the present" recalls the unhallowed Soviet approach to history. *Air Force Magazine,* Arlington, VA. Harwit, Martin. *An Exhibit Denied: Lobbying the History of Enola Gay.* op. cit. The supposed conflict between history and memory finds expression in the museum world's criticism of "heritage centers," theme parks and recreating a deceptive past in Williamsburg and elsewhere. They are seen as efforts to create a common, popular, nostalgic memory of the past that ignores the accounts of genuine analytical history. The defenders of the exhibit saw the final Enola Gay display as mere "heritage" while the original exhibit was seen as genuine history.

9. Hogan, Michael J. op. cit. Linenthal, Edward T. "Anatomy of a Controversy" in *History Wars,* op. cit.

10. Lifton, Robert Jay and Greg Mitchell. *Hiroshima in America, Fifty Years of Denial.* New York, G. P. Putnam's Sons, 1995, 256, 296.

11. Harwit, Martin. "How Lobbying Changed the History of Enola Gay." *Japan Quarterly* 44, no. 3, July-September 1997, 57.

12. Piehler, G. Kurt. *Remembering War the American Way.* Washington, DC, Smithsonian Institution Press, 1995, 185. Smith, Geoffrey S. "Feature Review." *Diplomatic History,* vol. 22, no. 1, Winter 1998, 121–130. Those calling the story of World War II mythical appropriate the ideas of scholars of ancient myths such as those of the Greeks, Egyptians, Mayans and others, hoping to lend authenticity to their claims and create the impression that their critics were also lost in the mists of antiquity. Unfortunately

208
Notes — Chapter I

for their claims, World War II is close enough to allow us to assess their claims using the factual record, and not speculation based on ideology.

13. Walker, J. Samuel. *Prompt & Utter Destruction: Truman and the Use of Atomic Bombs Against Japan.* Chapel Hill, University of North Carolina Press, 1997, 107; Thelen, David. "History after the Enola Gay Controversy: An Introduction" in *The Journal of American History*, vol. 82, no. 3, 1031, 1035. Mayr, Otto. "The Enola Gay Fiasco: History, Politics, and the Museum." *Technology and Culture*, vol. 39, no. 3, 1998, 462. Mosse, George L. *Fallen Soldiers, Reshaping the Memory of the World Wars.* New York, Oxford University Press, 1990, 7. Dubin, Steven C. *Displays of Power, Memory and Amnesia in the American Museum.* New York, New York University Press, 1999, 216. *The New York Times*, Wednesday, April 25, 2002, E 2. Miller, James Edward. Book Review, *The International History Review*, vol. 24, no. 2, June 2002, 474.

14. Hubbard, Bryan and Marouf A. Hasian. "The Generic Roots of the Enola Gay Controversy." *Political Communication*, vol. 15, no. 4, Oct.-Dec. 1998, 497–513. Sherry, Michael S. *The Rise of American Air Power, The Creation of Armageddon.* New Haven, Yale University Press, 1987. Mark Stoler began with that attitude: "As a member of the 1960s generation, I deeply distrusted those forces for their activities and stated views during the Vietnam War. Indeed, some of my scholarly interest in the wartime Joint Chiefs arose from my desire to trace the origins of what I considered not only incorrect but also extremely dangerous military influence and views. I was at that time totally ignorant of military modes of thinking, however, and victimized by simplistic stereotypes about military officers—and about military history." Stoler, Mark. *Allies and Adversaries: The Joint Chiefs of Staff, The Grand Alliance, and U. S. Strategy in World War II.* Chapel Hill, The University of North Carolina Press, 2000, xv-xvi.

15. Harwit, Martin. "Academic Freedom in 'The Last Act.'" *The Journal of American History.* December 1995, 1064, 1069, 1975, 1082. For a definition of academic freedom, see "1940 Statement of Principles on Academic Freedom and Tenure with 1970 Interpretive Comments" available at www.aaup.org. Lifschultz, Lawrence and Kai Bird. ed. *Hiroshima's Shadow.* Stony Creek, CN, The Pamphleteer's Press, 1998, xxxiii. In 2001–2002 Kai Bird was a fellow at the Woodrow Wilson Center for Scholars preparing a biography of J. Robert Oppenheimer with Martin Sherwin. His quote of Vidal is in the Wilson's International Center for Scholars web site. Sherry, Michael S. "Patriotic Orthodoxy and American Destiny," in Hein, Laura and Mark Selden, ed. *Living with the Bomb: American and Japanese Cultural Conflicts in the Nuclear Age.* Armonk, NY, M. E. Sharpe, 149.

16. Although deconstruction purportedly seeks the hidden or latent meaning of texts, that effort is hardly new or exceptional. Theologians, philosophers and other scholars have engaged in that effort for ages. What made deconstruction different, and attractive to many intellectuals, was the political spin that Jacques Derrida and his followers placed on their analysis. Claiming that no text actually has a sure meaning, any interpretation of a text is acceptable. Applied to the work of poets Ezra Pound or James Joyce that may be relatively harmless, except to impressionable students, but applied to historical and other texts deconstruction can falsify what happened in the past. See Kurin, Richard. *Reflections of a Culture Broker: A View from the Smithsonian.* Washington, DC, Smithsonian Institution Press, 1997, 80. Cmiel, Kenneth. "Talking It Over" in *Reviews in American History*, vol. 27, no. 1. 1999, 160. Cmeil referred to Fox, Richard Wrightman and Robert B. Westbrook. ed. *In the Face of the Facts: Moral Inquiry in American Scholarship.* Cambridge, Cambridge University Press and Woodrow Wilson Center Press, 1998. Despite a few remarks about critical race theorists and feminism, the tenor of a book with the Wilson Center's imprint lacks balance. Robert A. Orsi, one of the authors, contended that "just as post colonial intellectual culture calls into

question central tenets of Western thought, so a new kind of moral inquiry must be open to construals of the 'ethical' profoundly at variance with Christian ideals and formulations." That is a widely held viewpoint among critics of American cultural imperialism but it was not balanced by any other viewpoints, especially in a book issued by a press funded partly by federal dollars, 216. The Woodrow Wilson International Center For Scholars is a federally supported adjunct of the Smithsonian Institution.

17. Alperovitz, Gar. "Hiroshima: Historians Reassess." *Foreign Policy*, vol. 99, Summer 1995, 15. Alperovitz, Gar. "Why the United States Dropped the Bomb." *Technology Review*, vol. 93, no. 6, 22. Hogan, Michael J. "The Enola Gay Controversy: History, Memory, and the Politics of Presentation" in *Hiroshima in History and Memory*. op. cit. 220–221.

18. NPR transcript #1092–10, October 9, 1994; NPR Transcript #1009–12, February 5, 1995. ABC News Special, July 27, 1995, Transcript # 63.

19. Cleland, Robert A. Letter to the Editor. *Wilmette Life*. December 7, 2000.

20. Werrell, Kenneth P. *Blankets of Fire: U. S. Bombers over Japan during World War II*. Washington, DC, Smithsonian Institution Press, 1996, 251. McCullagh, C. Behan. *The Truth of History*. London, Routledge, 1998, 307–309.

21. Giovenetti, Len and Fred Freed. *The Decision to Drop the Bomb*. New York, Coward-McCann, 1965, 319. Kagan, Donald. "Why America dropped the bomb." *Commentary*, vol. 100, no. 3, September 1995, 23. van der Vat, Dan. *The Pacific Campaign, World War II: The U.S.— Japanese Naval War 1941–1945*. New York, Simon & Schuster, 1991, 15. Davis, Jack E. "New Left, Revisionist, In-Your-Face History" in Toplin, Robert Brent. ed. *Oliver Stone's USA, Film, History, and Controversy*. Lawrence, University Press of Kansas, 2000, 136.

Chapter II

1. *Revisionism Gone Wrong: Analysis of the Enola Gay Controversy, Part II*. Arlington, VA, Air Force Association, March 2000. The letter writer was William A. Rooney. The "five old men" included W. Burr Bennett, Ben Nicks, Frank Rabbitt, Donald C. Rehl and William A. Rooney. Many other veterans, and non veterans, played important roles in the "battle" but the five helped spearhead the confrontation with the Smithsonian. Oliver Wendell Holmes (1809–1895) wrote "Old Ironsides" in September 1830.

2. Harwit, Martin. *An Exhibit Denied: Lobbying the History of Enola Gay*. New York, Springer Verlag, 1998. Re 1989 "wreak havoc" memo: Harwit, ibid, 93. Correspondence and other papers of W. Burr Bennett and William A. Rooney relating to the *Enola Gay* are archived at the University of Texas at Dallas. Harwit, Martin. *An Exhitit Denied*. "A wreck," op. cit, 9. Victor Agather, who had been involved in the B-29 project almost since it was a design on paper in Dayton, Ohio, had served as a troubleshooter for General Arnold throughout the war. He became concerned about the aircraft when he received a letter from a souvenir thief with a picture of the ashtray in the tail gunner's compartment that was for sale for a four figure amount. When the NASM argued that the plane could not be displayed in the museum because it was too large, Agather visited the museum and stepped off one of the galleries, determining that, with the judicious shifting of some exhibits, the plane could indeed be shown completely assembled in one of the galleries. Harwit agreed that with some shifting of exhibits the plane would fit inside the NASM, but then said that the foundations of the gallery would not carry the weight of the plane unless it was heavily jacked up from the garage immediately below. That was reasonable because of the aircraft's great

weight, but Harwit's account revealed that the aircraft could have been installed had there been the will to do so. The Smithsonian's lack of interest in the *Enola Gay* from the mid 1950s until the early 1980s led some veterans to suspect that, as a derelict, it would be written off and thus pose no problem for Secretary Adams or the Smithsonian. Thanks to public pressure, that did not happen, but they wondered if, without pressure, the *Enola Gay* would find a home at the NASM.

3. *The Crossroads*, EG: 100, 3; Wallace, Mike. *Mickey Mouse History and Other Essays on American Memory*. Philadelphia. Temple University Press, 271. An earlier version is "The Battle of the *Enola Gay*" in *Radical Historians Newsletter*, May 1995. Re: Sherwin, see Yoneyama, Lisa. "For Transformative Knowledge and Postnationalist Public Spheres: the Smithsonian *Enola Gay* Controversy" in Fujitani, T. Gregory M. White and Lisa Yoneyama, eds., *Perilous Memories: The Asia-Pacific War(s)*. Durham, NC, Duke University Press, 2001, 336, 337. Goldberg, Stanley. "Smithsonian suffers Legionnaire's disease," *Bulletin of the Atomic Scientists*, vol. 51, no. 3, May 1995, 28–33. Linenthal, Edward. "Anatomy of a Controversy" in Linenthal, Edward T. and Tom Englehardt. eds., *History Wars: The Enola Gay and Other Battles for the American Past*. New York, Metropolitan Books, 1996, 28. Neufeld, Michael quoted in *History Wars*, op. cit., 18. Linenthal, Edward T. *Sacred Ground: Americans and Their Battlefields*, 2d ed. University of Illinois Press, 1993, 184. Blackett, P. M. S. *Fear, War, and the Bomb*. New York, McGraw-Hill Book Company, Inc., 1949, 139. Alperovitz, Gar. *The Decision to Use the Atomic Bomb and the Architecture of an American Myth*. New York, Alfred A. Knopf, 1995, 128. There is a remarkable affinity between the work of Blackett and Alperovitz who thanked Blackett for his help in the acknowledgments of *Atomic Diplomacy: Hiroshima and Potsdam* (1985 ed). Although he has only one footnote referring to Blackett (page 160) it seems evident where Alperovitz found inspiration for his work. "Progressive" is a code word ranging from politically liberal to radical. As used by Yoneyama it edges toward the radical. In contemporary use it has no relation to what it meant in the early 20th century. The original progressives included Theodore Roosevelt and historian Charles Beard, who would be scandalized by revisionists who referred to Cuba and East Germany as "progressive" states. Revisionist scholars have approached World War II without any sense of what confronted decision makers in 1945 and a mind set that is unable to accept the context of the events about which they write. Just one example epitomizes how they reflect a contemporary sensibility about war that conditions their writing. Professor Bernstein, one of the most prominent members of the coterie that defended the exhibit, denounced the ROTC on the Stanford campus because it was "preparing students for war and training them to kill." *STANFORD*, op. cit., January/February, 2002, 64–65.

4. Dower, John. *War Without Mercy* op. cit. Wallace, Mike. *Mickey Mouse History and Other Essays on American Memory*. Philadelphia. Temple University Press, 273. Because the themes in Professor Dower's book are important in *The Crossroads*, frequent reference will be made to his work .

5. Steinfels, Margaret O'Brien. "The Vatican and the Holocaust." *Dissent,* Summer 1998, 15. Lathem, Edward Connery, ed. *The Poetry of Robert Frost*. New York, Holt, Rinehart and Winston, 1968, 399. The poem first appeared in the *Atlantic Monthly* in December 1946.

6. Hogan, Michael. *Hiroshima in History and Memory*, op. cit., 226. Bernstein, Barton J., ibid., 5. Bernstein has been adept at giving the benefit of the doubt to the Soviets on almost every issue relating to the Cold War. In 1970, long after Soviet behavior was well documented, Bernstein wrote as if unaware of the early problems with the Soviets over the Baltic republics, Soviet behavior during the Warsaw revolt in the summer of 1944, other minor matters such as the disappearance of the London Polish del-

egation that was to negotiate entering a new government with the Lublin Poles, or the tactics of the Communists in France and Italy. Ignoring such context and following the lead of William Appleman Williams who saw the Cold War as a product of rapacious American capitalism, Bernstein could select evidence he needed to bulwark his multiple hypotheses of why Truman dropped the bomb and of heavy American culpability for the Cold War. For an explication of responsibility for the Cold War, see Alperovitz, Gar and Kai Bird. "A Theory of Cold War Dynamics: U. S. Policy, Germany and the Bomb." *The History Teacher*, vol. 29, no. 3, May 1996, 281–300. Messer, Robert L. *The End of an Alliance: James F. Byrnes, Roosevelt, Truman and the Origins of the Cold War.* Chapel Hill. The University of North Carolina Press, 1982, 237–238. Williams, William Appleman. *Americans in a Changing World: A History of the United States in the Twentieth Century.* New York, Harper & Row, 1978. Buhle, Paul. "William Appleman Williams: Grassroots Against Empire" in Hunter, Allen. *Rethinking the Cold War.* Philadelphia, Temple University Press, 1998, 296.

   7. Alperovitz, Gar. *Atomic Diplomacy: Hiroshima and Potsdam: The Use of the Atomic Bomb and the American Confrontation with Soviet Power.* Rev. ed. London & New Haven, CT, Pluto Press, 1994. "Remote possibility," xi. "By June," 158. Alperovitz, Gar. *The Decision to Use the Atomic Bomb and the Architecture of an American Myth.* New York, Alfred A. Knopf, 1995, 650–651 (a revision of a book published in 1965). The only book named for possible inclusion in the exhibit was that of Gar Alperovitz; see *The Crossroads* script, EG: 200, 39. Professor Alperovitz believed that the A-bomb was used to intimidate the Soviet Union. McGeorge Bundy wrote that the claim that impressing the Soviets with the bomb was a major factor in deciding to use the bomb: "… is false, and the evidence to support it rests on inferences so stretched as to be a discredit to the judgment of those who have argued in this fashion and the credulity of those who have accepted such arguments. There is literally no evidence whatsoever that the timetable for the attack was ever affected by anything except technical and military considerations; there is no evidence that anyone in the direct chain of command from Truman to Stimson to Marshall to Groves ever heard or made any suggestion that either the decision itself or the timing of its execution should be governed by any consideration of its effect on the Soviet Union." See Bundy, McGeorge. *Danger and Survival: Choices About the Bomb in the First Fifty Years.* New York, Random House, 1988, 88. Apparently the curators were not aware of Bundy's 1988 criticism of the theory touted by Alperovitz and others, including P. M. S. Blackett who wrote about the A-bomb. Bundy called Alperovitz work "sloppy and tendentious" and driven by a "fantastically Machiavellian view of Truman," op. cit., 650–651.

   8. Hogan, op. cit., 212, 230.

   9. Crouch, Tom. See *Revisionism Gone Wrong, Part II.* Arlington, VA, Air Force Magazine, Air Force Association, 2000. Buhle, Paul. "Book Review." *The Journal of American History*, vol. 88, no. 2, September 2001.

   10. Lomax, Eric. *The Railway Man: A POW's Searing Account of War, Brutality and Forgiveness.* New York, W. W. Norton & Company, 1995, 105. Ienaga, Saburo. *The Pacific War: World War II and the Japanese, 1931–1945.* New York, Pantheon Books, 1978. Tanaka, Yuki. *Hidden Horrors: Japanese War Crimes in World War II.* Boulder, CO, Westview Press, 1996, 218. Cook, Haruko Taya and Theodore F. Cook. *Japan at War: An Oral History.* New York, The New Press, 1992, 158, 145, 155. Goldenhagen, Daniel Jonah. *Hitler's Willing Executioners: Ordinary Germans and the Holocaust.* New York, Alfred Knopf, 1996. Harris, Sheldon H. *Factories of Death, Japanese Biological Warfare 1932–45 and the American Cover-up.* London, Routledge, 1994, see chapter 9. When introducing Tanaka's book, Professor John Dower attributed a lack of interest in documenting Japanese behavior during the war to the fact that "sanitizing the Japanese

past quickly became a collaborative Japanese-American undertaking. Certain egregious Japanese war crimes were covered up to serve American interests," xiv. In the immediate aftermath of the war that may have happened, but to suggest that the United States prevented American scholars from exploring the anecdotal evidence of POWs and the mountain of evidence accumulated during the American occupation of Japan for the Tokyo war crimes trials, as well as the mass of documentation gathered by the Australians and British after the war, is nonsense. Other nations did their own investigations, but in the case of China, Indonesia and Korea, language may have been a barrier to their exploitation by Americans. Although the United States government was not eager to embarrass a new ally, that would not have deterred scholars long before the Pentagon Papers appeared. Some quarters in a less open Japanese society might have been hostile to such inquiries, but that would not have been the case if progressive American scholars sought to document how ideals allegedly were compromised, for example, by the suppression of facts about Japanese medical experimentation on POWs. Soon after the war there was no silence about the employment of German rocket expert Wernher Von Braun and his colleagues, or about the U. S. employing the German Gehlen organization for its spycraft to counter the Soviets during the early days of the Cold War. Whatever the reasons American scholars failed to explore this terrain, there was no governmental firewall between them and the facts of Japanese behavior. Dower, John. *War Without Mercy*, op. cit., 58–59.

11. Harper, Stephen. *Miracle of Deliverance: The Case for the Bombing of Hiroshima and Nagasaki*. New York, Stein and Day Publishers, 1986, 182.

12. Moon, Tom. *This Grim and Savage Game. OSS and the Beginning of U.S. Covert Operations in World War II*. Los Angeles. Burning Gate Press, 1991, 301. Also see Daws, Gavan. *Prisoners of the Japanese: POWs of World War II in the Pacific*. New York, William Morrow and Company, Inc., 1994. Lerner, "Making History Her Story Too." *The New York Times*, July 20, 2002, A-17. Professor Lerner began the graduate program in women's history at the University of Wisconsin-Madison.

13. Nobile, Philip. *Judgment at the Smithsonian*, op. cit., lxx. Foner, Eric, ed. "Introduction" in the *New American History*. Philadelphia. Temple University Press, 1990, vii. Farber, David. "War Stories" in *Reviews in American History*, vol. 23, no. 2, 1995, 318.

14. Farrell, Michael. *National Catholic Reporter*, February 18, 2000, 2. Sweeney, Charles W. *War's End: An Eyewitness Account of America's Last Atomic Mission*. New York, Avon Books, 1997, 217–220. Pierce, Frank. "A Memorable Trip to Nagasaki in 1946." *On Station*, vol. 5, no. 1, 2001, 3. On August 18, 1946, three American naval officers— Armin A. Richter, Harold Davis and Frank Pierce — visited Nagasaki on a Sunday afternoon. "Our most impressive visit of the afternoon was into the major Mitsubishi factory area, where all kinds of munitions had been produced in quantity throughout the war. Included were the deadly and feared "long Lance" torpedoes which sank a number of our over-matched cruisers.... These huge, strongly-constructed war plants were located close to the bomb's epicenter. Now their haunting roofless remains stood as twisted blackened iron skeletons...." Tree, Sanho. "Book Review," *Journal of American History*, 83, 4, 1997, 1475–1476. MacEachin, Douglas J. *The Final Months of the War with Japan: Signals Intelligence, U. S. Invasion Planning, and the A-Bomb Decision*. Central Intelligence Agency, Center for the Study of Intelligence, 1998. Document 17, Enclosure "A" Alternatives to "OLYMPIC."

15. Lifschultz, Lawrence and Kai Bird, ed. *Hiroshima's Shadow*. Stony Creek, CT. The Pamphleteer's Press, 1998.

16. Truman, Harry. *Memoirs*, op. cit.

17. Alperovitz, Gar. op. cit., 240.

18. Holloway, David. *Stalin and the Bomb: The Soviet Union and Atomic Energy 1939–1956.* New Haven, Yale University Press, 1994, 131. Messer. Robert L. *The End of an Alliance: James F. Byrnes, Roosevelt, Truman and the Origins of the Cold War.* Chapel Hill. The University of North Carolina Press, 1982, 120. Millis, Walter. *The Forrestal Diaries.* New York, The Viking Press, 1951, 68; Truman, *Memoirs,* op. cit., 440–441. What happened at Hokkaido was reminiscent of General De Gaulle's attempt to annex Italy's French-speaking Val D'Aosta at the end of the war in Italy. Contrary to prior agreements the French occupied the area, installed French officials and threatened to expel American troops by force. DeGaulle was rebuffed by Truman, who cut off Lend Lease to the French until they withdrew, at which time the French termed the confrontation a misunderstanding. DeGaulle, Gen. Charles. *The Complete War Memoirs of Charles DeGaulle,* New York, DaCapo Press, 1984, 873–877.

19. Feis, Herbert. *Between War and Peace, The Potsdam Conference.* Princeton, NJ, Princeton University Press, 1960, 39.

20. Bernstein, Barton J. "Truman and the A-Bomb: Targeting Noncombatants, Using the Bomb and his Defending the 'Decision.'" *Journal of Military History,* vol. 62, no. 3, 1998, 269.

21. Playfair, I. S. O., C.I.C. Molony. *The Mediterranean and Middle East, Vol. IV. The Destruction of the Axis Forces in Africa.* London, His Majesty's Stationery Office, 1966, xvi, op. cit., 508–509. The impasse continued until it was resolved by the atomic bombs with an assist from Soviet intervention. In the opinion of John Skates, "Those who still search for an explanation of why the atomic bombs were used against an already defeated Japan need look no further than the conflict between America's rigorous insistence on unconditional surrender and the irrational, suicidal, and hopeless nature of Japan's last defenses." Skates, John Ray. *The Invasion of Japan, Alternative to the Bomb.* Columbia. University of South Carolina Press, 1994, 257.

22. Mayr, Otto. "The Enola Gay Fiasco: History, Politics and the Museum." *Technology and Culture,* vol. 39, no. 3, 1998, 462–473.

Chapter III

1. *The Crossroads,* EG; 200, 46. MacArthur, Douglas. *Reminiscences.* New York, McGraw-Hill Book Company, 1964, 260. Leahy, William. *Now It Can Be Told.* op. cit., 410. For MAGIC, see Lewin, Ronald. *The American Magic: Codes, Ciphers and the Defeat of Japan.* London, Farrar, Straus and Giroux, 1982. Even earlier than 1945, in mid-1944, the Marine Corps commandant was prepared for a war that would continue until the fall of 1946. See Sherrod, Robert. *History of Marine Corps Aviation in World War II.* Washington, DC, Combat Forces Press, 1952, 327.

2. Butow, Robert J. C. *Japan's Decision to Surrender.* Stanford, CA, Stanford University Press, 1954, vi. *The Crossroads,* EG:200; 63.

3. *The Crossroads,* EG: 200; 28. Robertson, David. *Sly and Able: A Political Biography of James J. Byrnes.* New York, W. W. Norton & Company, 1994, 431.

4. Maddox, Robert James. *Weapons for Victory: The Hiroshima Decision Fifty Years Later.* Columbia, University of Missouri Press, 1995, 189.

5. Minear, Richard H. "Atomic Holocaust, Nazi Holocaust: Some Reflections." *Diplomatic History,* vol. 19, no. 2, 1995, 360. Quigley, Martin S. *Peace Without Hiroshima: Secret Action at the Vatican in the Spring of 1945.* Lanham, MD, Madison Books, 1991. The dates of Harada's messages to Tokyo are in a letter Quigley sent to Robert Graham, June 20, 1985. Graham's papers are in the library of *Civilta Cattolica* in Rome. Quigley's papers are at Georgetown University.

6. VESSEL was the code name for a purported Vatican source who provided detailed, authentic sounding information about Vatican policies. OSS purchased this information until doubts arose about its veracity. The source was Virgilio Scattolini, a journalist and for years a successful con artist who sold "news" to major American newspapers including the *New York Times*, as well as British papers, German intelligence and a host of Italians who wanted insider Vatican information. See Graham, Robert A. S. J. "Il Vaticanista falsario. L'incredibile successo di Vergilio Scattolini." *Civilta Cattolica.* 124, III, 15 September 1973, 467–478.

7. Alperovitz, Gar. *Atomic Diplomacy: Hiroshima and Potsdam, the Use of the Atomic Bomb and the American Confrontation with Soviet Power.* New Haven, CT, Pluto Press, 1994, 315. See also Alperovitz, Gar and Robert L. Messer and Barton J. Bernstein. "Correspondence, Marshall, Truman and the Decision to Drop the Bomb." *International Security*, vol. 16, 3, Winter 1991–1992, 204–221. Robert Smith Thompson either was unaware of or ignored a distinction long known to other historians. In any event he mislead his readers by relying on Kai Bird's misleading account of the meaning of Japanese peace feelers. In their eagerness to show that Hiroshima was unnecessary, revisionists disinform readers by telling only that part of the story that suits their agenda; this is a fatal flaw in a historian. Thompson, Robert Smith. *Empires on the Pacific: World War II and the Struggle for the Mastery of Asia.* New York, Basic Books, 2001, 369–370.

8. Annan, Noel. *Changing Enemies: The Defeat and Regeneration of Germany.* New York, W. W. Norton & Company, 1995, 102. Nitze, Paul. *From Hiroshima to Glasnost, at the Center of Decision: A Memoir.* New York, Grove Weidenfeld, 1989, 30. Gray, J. Glenn. *The Warriors: Reflections on Men in Battle.* New York, Harper & Row Publishers, 1970, 215.

9. General Andrew Goodpaster, remarks commemorating V-E Day, V-E Day Conference, Eisenhower Center, University of New Orleans, New Orleans, Louisiana, May 8, 1995; Walters, Vernon. *Silent Missions*, Garden City, New York, Doubleday & Company, 1978, 135.

10. Ohl, John K. *Supplying the Troops: General Somervell and American Logistics in World War II.* DeKalb, Northern Illinois Press, 1994. The debate over reconversion to civilian goods is treated in Polenberg, Richard *War and Society: The United States 1941–1945.* Philadelphia, J. B. Lippincott Company, 1972, 226–237. See also Robertson, David. *Sly and Able: A Political Biography of James F. Byrnes.* New York, W. W. Norton & Company, 1994, 368–374. Bernstein, Barton J. "America in War and Peace: the Test of Liberalism." in Barton J. Bernstein, ed., *Toward a New Past, Dissenting Essays in American History.* London, Chatto & Windus, 1970. Professor Barton Bernstein saw those opposed to industrial reconversion as engaged in "a cunning maneuver to protect the prewar oliogopolistic structure of the American economy." His attribution of class interest to the actions of the dollar-a-year men ignored the needs of the men in battle and revealed his ideological position, complete with the appropriate terminology of the 1960s, 295. Indeed in 1969, as a Stanford University faculty member, Professor Bernstein helped lead a successful movement against ROTC. At the height of student turmoil on campuses, a student referendum favored keeping ROTC but the faculty senate voted against it with Professor Bernstein arguing that none of the ROTC faculty had Ph.Ds. More recently, in a discussion of whether the university should again offer ROTC, he claimed to be intellectually embarrassed by the program because it "represents a group of pseudo-faculty preparing students for war and training them to kill." *STANFORD*, January/February 2002, 64–65. At about the same time Professor Bernstein expressed his opinion of the ROTC and military, another university also was thinking about its ROTC program. About ten years earlier, ROTC, which enrolled

about ten percent of the students, was unsuccessfully targeted for removal by activists. With some activists again questioning the moral appropriateness of ROTC, one of the university's alumni, Malham Wakin, presented the case for officer preparation on a private university campus. "Unless the world we live in changes very dramatically (which seems unlikely) we are going to need the profession of arms at least as critically as we continue to need the medical, legal, educational and clerical professions. Military leaders must be men and women who are both intellectually competent and morally sensitive." Reflecting that the service academies cannot and should not be expected to meet all these needs, he continued, "The University of Notre Dame and other distinguished colleges and universities should continue to prepare men and women of significant competence and character to lead our nation's military services ... when we want a correct moral decision to be made, our best hope is that a person of decent moral character is in command." Wakin, Makin M. "Fighting Right." *Notre Dame Magazine.* Spring, 2001, 32–37.

11. MacEachin, Douglas J., op. cit., Appendix C, Document 1. The brutal, costly fighting on Okinawa is best described by George Feifer's *Tennozan.* op. cit. Another good account is by Gerald Astor, *Operation Iceberg: The Invasion and Conquest of Okinawa in World War II.* New York, Donald I. Fine, Inc., 1995.

12. Meyer, Cord. *Facing Reality: From World Federalism to the CIA.* New York, Harper and Row, 1980, 49. Tuchman, Barbara W. *The First Salute.* New York, Alfred A. Knopf, 1988, 191.

13. "Japanese Imperial Government will ignore" quotation from Werrell, Kenneth P. *Blankets of Fire: U. S. Bombers over Japan during World War II.* Washington, DC, Smithsonian University Press, 213. Iriye, Akira. "Continuities in U.S. Japanese Relations 1941–1945" in Nagai, Yonosuke and Akira Iriye, eds. *The Origins of the Cold War in Asia.* New York, Columbia University Press, 1977, 295–296. Alperovitz, Gar. op. cit., 233. Bix, Herbert. *Hirohito and the Making of Modern Japan.* New York, HarperCollins, 2000. See his "Delayed Surrender," chapter 13. Rees, David. *The Defeat of Japan.* Westport, CT. Praeger, 1997, 146. Mansonari, Nakamura. *The Japanese Monarchy, Ambassador Joseph Grew and the Making of the "Symbol Emperor System," 1931–1991.* Armonk, NY, M.E. Sharpe, Inc., 1992. Mokusatsu, The Pacific War Research Society. *Japan's Longest Day.* Tokyo, Kodansha International, 2002, 16–17. The alleged ambiguity of the phrase was emphasized by William Coughlin in 1953. His account of the final days in Tokyo are similar to those of later writers. See Coughlin, William. "The Great Mokusatsu Mistake: Was This the Deadliest Error of Our Time?" *Harper's,* vol. 206, no. 1234, March 1953.

14. Murakami, Hoye. *Japan: The Years of Trial, 1919–1952.* Tokyo, Kodansha International LTD, 1983, 175; implacable, 179. Butow, Robert J. C. *Japan's Decision to Surrender.* Stanford, CA. Stanford University Press, 1954, 127. Iriye, Akira. *Power and Culture, The Japanese-American War, 1941–1945.* Cambridge, MA, Harvard University Press, 1981, 263.

15. Butow, Robert J. C. *Japan's Decision to Surrender.* op. cit. Ugaki, Matome. *Fading Victory, The Diary of Admiral Matome Ugaki. 1941–1945.* Pittsburgh, PA. University of Pittsburgh Press, 1991. Ugaki was Admiral Yamamoto's chief of staff and accompanied Yamamoto on another plane when both planes were shot down by American fighters in 1943. Ugaki was one of the few survivors.

16. Dower, John. *Embracing Defeat, Japan in the Wake of World War II.* New York, W. W. Norton & Company, 1999. 44. Nitze, Paul H. *From Hiroshima to Glasnost.* op. cit., 44–45. Feis, Herbert. *The Atomic Bomb and the End of World War II.* op. cit., 191. Newman, Robert P. "Ending the War with Japan: Paul Nitze's 'Early Surrender' Counterfactual." *Pacific Historical Review,* vol. 64, no. 2, 1995, 167–194. Speaking of the SBS

European study, the AAF said, "Its verdict that air power had been the decisive factor in the defeat of Germany did not meet with universal endorsement." Craven, Wesley Frank and James Lea Cate. *The Army Air Forces in World War II, The Pacific: Matterhorn to Nagasaki, June 1944 to August 1945.* Washington, Office of Air Force History, Washington, DC, 1983, 737. Reischauer, Edwin O. *Japan: The Story of a Nation.* New York, Alfred A. Knopf, 1970, 216. Alperovitz, Gar. *Atomic Diplomacy: Hiroshima and Potsdam.* op. cit., 315–316. Although not fully referenced by Alperovitz, the report was a memo from R. F. Innis, Chief, Intelligence Group, Chief Strategic Policy Section, Strategy and Policy Group, OPED. "Use of Atomic Bomb on Japan, 30 April 1946." National Archives Project, Marshal Library, Lexington, VA. Bernstein, Barton J. "Compelling Japan's Surrender Without the A-Bomb, Soviet Entry, or Invasion: Reconsidering the US Bombing Survey's Early Surrender Conclusions." *The Journal of Strategic Studies,* vol. 18, no. 2, 1995, 101–148.

17. Reischauer, Edwin O. *The United States and Japan.* 3d ed. Cambridge, MA, Harvard University Press, 1965, 240–241. Harper, Stephen. op. cit., 210.

18. Skates, John Ray. *The Invasion of Japan, Alternative to the Bomb.* Columbia, University of South Carolina Press, 1994, 251. Talbot, Strobe. *The Master of the Game, Paul Nitze and the Nuclear Peace.* New York, Alfred A. Knopf, 1988. In the mid-1960s, Nitze served as secretary of the navy.

19. Sigal, Leon V. *Fighting to a Finish: The Politics of War Termination in the United States and Japan, 1945.* Ithaca, NY, Cornell University Press, 1988, 278–279. Marx, Joseph Laurence. *Nagasaki: The Necessary Bomb?* New York, The Macmillan Company, 1971, 223. Butow, Robert J. C. *Japan's Decision to Surrender.* Stanford, CA, Stanford University Press, 1954, 231.

20. Sadao, Asada. "The Shock of the Atomic Bomb and Japan's Decision to Surrender — A Reconsideration." *Pacific Historical Review,* vol. 67, 1998. Walker, J. Samuel. *Prompt and Utter Destruction: Truman and the Use of Atomic Bombs Against Japan.* Chapel Hill, The University of North Carolina Press, 1997, 96.

21. Bix, Herbert P. *Hirohito and the Making of Modern Japan.* New York, Harper Collins Publishers, 2000, 521. Drea, Edward J. *In The Service of the Emperor: Essays on the Imperial Japanese Army.* Lincoln, University of Nebraska Press, 1998, 215; *The Crossroads,* EG: 100, 54; Rose, Lisle. *Dubious Victory: The United States and the End of World War II.* Kent, OH, Kent State University Press, 1973, 355–366. Rose complained about how the war was handled in Europe, contending that Operation SUNRISE was "the clandestine surrender of Nazi forces in northern Italy to Western representatives." Apparently he was unaware that the Japanese and the Soviets knew about Sunrise, and so did the Germans. Rose also echoed Professor Bernstein's unrealistic criticism of Allied tardiness in opening a second front: "Prior to the invasion of Normandy the Allied Armies had engaged no more than eleven German divisions in their peripheral probes of the Nazi Empire. The Soviets had engaged over ten times that number." Unaware of the facts, and overlooking the global nature of the war, Rose overlooked the 141 German divisions the British faced in France before Dunkirk, other German divisions in Norway, Italian Axis divisions in Africa and Greece and Japanese divisions in Asia. Rose, Lisle R. *The Long Shadow: Reflections on the Second World War Era.* Westport, CT, Greenwood Press, 1978, 90, 78. Frank, Richard B. *Downfall.* op. cit., 359–360.

Chapter IV

1. Spiedel, Gen. Hans. *Invasion 1944: Rommel and the Normandy Campaign* Chicago: Henry Regnery Company, 1950, 16. Campbell, A. E. "Franklin Roosevelt and

Unconditional Surrender" in Langhorne, Richard, ed. *Diplomacy and Intelligence during the Second World War.* Cambridge: Cambridge University Press, 1985, 219–244. Hull, Cordell, op. cit., chapter 103; "Unconditional Surrender." Stephen Ambrose has a useful discussion of the policy in *The Supreme Commander: The War Years of General Dwight D. Eisenhower.* New York, Doubleday & Company, Inc., 1970. For a discussion of the pros and cons of the policy of unconditional surrender, see Armstrong, Anne. *Unconditional Surrender: The Impact of the Casablanca Policy Upon World War II.* New Brunswick, NJ, Rutgers University Press, 1961. Military leaders on the scene were concerned that "unconditional surrender" could create serious problems. Eisenhower feared that it might lead to the scuttling of the Italian Fleet. See Coles, Harry L. & Weinberg, Albert K. *Civil Affairs: Soldiers Become Governors.* Washington, D.C., Office of The Chief of Military History, Department of the Army, U.S. Government Printing Office, 1964, 236. Truman, Harry S. *Memoirs of Harry S. Truman, Volume One, Years of Decision.* Garden City, New York, Doubleday & Company, 1957, 90.

3. O'Reilly, Charles T. *Forgotten Battles: Italy's War of Liberation 1943–1945.* Lanham, MD, Lexington Books, 2000, 52–54.

4. Millis, Walter. *The Forrestal Diaries.* New York, The Viking Press, 1951, 74–75. Roosevelt quoted in Frank, Richard B. *Downfall: The End of the Imperial Japanese Empire.* New York, Random House, 1999, 337. *Entry of the Soviet Union Into the War Against Japan: Military Plans, 1941–1945.* Washington, U.S. Department of Defense, 1955, 74. Skates, John Ray. *The Invasion of Japan, Alternative to the Bomb.* Columbia, University of South Carolina Press, 1994, 257.

5. Walzer, Michael. *Just and Unjust Wars: A Moral Argument with Historical Illustrations.* 2d ed. New York, Basic Books, 1992, 103. Walzer was the editor of *Dissent,* which describes itself as "The Leading Magazine of the American Left." Walzer seems to have relied on the analysis of the use of the bomb by Martin Sherwin. Sherry, Michael S. *The Rise of American Air Power: The Creation of Armageddon.* New Haven, CT, Yale University Press, 1987, 234–235. Bundy, McGeorge. *Danger and Survival.* op. cit., 652, en 91. Professor Walzer might consider the relevance to Japan of what Professor Richard Pipes wrote about Soviet history: "… how futile it is to study Soviet history 'from below,' as the 'revisionist' school of historians would have it. In the Soviet regime the population at large had as much influence on events as the chorus in a Greek tragedy" in *The New York Times,* March 26, 2003, E7.

6. Reischauer, Edwin O. Introduction to Butow, Robert J. C. *Japan's Decision to Surrender.* Stanford, CA, Stanford University Press, 1954, vi. Hamby, Alonzo L. *Man of the People: A Life of Harry S. Truman.* New York, Oxford University Press, 1995, 325. Villa, Brian. "The U.S. Army, Unconditional Surrender, and the Potsdam Proclamation." *Journal of American History,* vol. 63, no. 1, June 1976, 66–92. A lengthy discussion of the revisionist and other historians' approach to Potsdam and Byrnes supposed using the bomb to coerce the Soviets is in David Robertson, *Sly and Able: A Political Biography of James F. Byrnes.* New York, W. W. Norton & Company, 1994, 390–413, 414–439. He presents the revisionist view fairly, then demolishes it.

7. Ienaga, Saburo. *The Pacific War,* op. cit., Chapter 6, "The War at Home, Democracy Destroyed." Walker, J. Samuel. *Prompt & Utter Destruction.* op. cit., 120; Walker, J. Samuel. "Origins of the Cold War in United States History Textbooks" in *The Journal of American History,* vol. 81, no. 4, 1995, 1659. Chappell, John D. *Before the Bomb: How America Approached the End of the Pacific War.* Lexington, The University Press of Kentucky, 1997, 130, 131, 147. The length to which some detractors of Truman go appeared when Paul Buhle wrote in *Radical History* in 1994 that Truman was "America's Stalin." See Kleher, Harvey and John Earl Hayes "Radical History." *The New Criterion,* June 2002, 19.

8. Reischaur, Edwin. op. cit., 216–217.

9. *The Crossroads*, EG: 100: 29.

10. Masonari, Nakamura. *The Japanese Monarchy: Ambassador Joseph Grew and the Making of the Symbol Emperor System, 1931–1991.* Armonk, NY, M. E. Sharpe, Inc., 1992, 71–73; Millis, Forrestal *Diaries*, op. cit., 66.

11. *The Crossroads. EG: 200, 31;* Feis, Herbert. *The Atomic Bomb and the End of World War II. rev. ed.* Princeton, NJ, Princeton University Press, 1966, 179.

12. *The Crossroads.* EG: 200, 31. Bix, Herbert J. "Japan's Delayed Surrender: A Representation." *Diplomatic History,* vol. 19, no. 2, 1995, 222–223. Bix, Herbert J. in Masanori, *The Japanese Monarchy,* op. cit., viii.

13. Bix, Herbert P. *Hiroshima and the Making of Modern Japan.* New York, Harper-Collins Publishers, 2000, 523.

14. Harper, op. cit., 208. Frank, Richard B. *Downfall.* op. cit., 343. Dower, John W. "Three Narratives of Our Humanity" in Linenthal, Edward T. and Tom Englehardt. *History Wars: The Enola Gay and Other Battles for the American Past.* New York, Metropolitan Books, 1996, 265, 266, 267. The military/political turmoil in Tokyo during Japan's final days is described in Brooks, Lester. *Behind Japan's Surrender: The Secret Struggle That Ended an Empire.* New York, McGraw-Hill Book Company, 1968. Based on interviews and documents in Japan, the readable narrative broadly corresponds to what others reported but it lacks the footnotes that would be useful to scholars.

15. That was when Washington crossed the Delaware River to win the battle of Trenton and capture 918 Hessians, many of whom eventually decided to remain in North America.

Chapter V

1. *The Crossroads*, EG: 100: 15, 38; Allan Nevins, 43; racism, 4.

2. Dower, John W. *War Without Mercy: Race and Power in the Pacific War.* New York, Pantheon Books, 1986. Nevin's quote, 33. Dower, John W. "Triumphal and Tragic Narratives of the War in Asia" in *Journal of American History,* vol. 82, no. 3, 1997, 1027, 1028. Dower, John W. *War Without Mercy.* op. cit., 145, orgy of bloodletting, 11. In an interview with the *New York Times,* regarding the fire bombing of Tokyo, Professor Dower said, "The American reaction at the time was that they deserved it. There was almost a genocidal attitude on the part of the American military, and it extended to the American public." *New York Times,* March 14, 2002, A4. For the turmoil in Tokyo in the last days, see Brooks, Lester. *Behind Japan's Surrender,* op. cit. Racism is an ill-defined word. Writers assume that everyone agrees on what the word means, but this value-laden word is often loosely used for political advantage to condemn certain opposing beliefs, behaviors and attitudes as "racist." Often the word is used inappropriately to refer to ethnic and religious conflict. Professor Dower tends to use the word loosely to refer to what others would call prejudice or stereotypes which may or may not represent racism. For analytical purposes, a term that covers every kind of prejudice or discrimination means nothing. For a concise review of current writings about racism, see Solomon, John and Lee Back. "Race and Racism" in Krueger, Joel, ed., *The Oxford Companion to Politics of the World. 2d ed.* Oxford, Oxford University Press, 2001, 710–712.

3. Ambrose, Stephen E. *Americans at War.* Jackson, University Press of Mississippi, 1997, 99. Ambrose also pursued the racism theme in "Racism, the Atomic Bomb and the Transformation of Japanese-American Relations." in Ambrose, Stephen E. and Brian Loring Villa. Bischof, Gunter and Robert L Dupont. eds. *The Pacific War Revis-*

ited. Baton Rouge, Louisiana State University Press, 1997. Trotsky, Leon. *The Revolution Betrayed*. New York, Pathfinder Press, 1972, 222.

4. Walker, Samuel J. "The Decision to Use the Bomb: A Historiographical Update" in Hogan, Michael J., ed. *Hiroshima in History and Memory*. Cambridge, Cambridge University Press, 1996, 25. Walker, Samuel. *Prompt & Utter Destruction, Truman and the Use of Atomic Bombs Against Japan*. Chapel Hill, The University of North Carolina Press, 1997, 96. See also his "The Origins of the Cold War in United States History Textbooks." *The Journal of American History*, March 1995, 1652– 1661. Sherry, Michael S. *The Rise of American Air Power, The Creation of Armageddon*. New Haven, CT, Yale University Press, 1987, 253. Falk, Stanley L. "Burma Memories and the Reality of War." *Army History*. Winter 2003, 12–13.

5. Linenthal, Edward T. *Sacred Ground*. op. cit., 178. West, Philip and Steven I. Levine and Jackie Hiltz. ed. *America's Wars in Asia: A Cultural Approach to History and Memory*. Armonk, NY, M. E. Sharpe, 1998, 8. Johnson, Sheila K. *American Attitudes Toward Japan, 1941–1945*. Washington, DC, American Enterprise Institute, 1975.

6. Takaki, Ronald. *Hiroshima: Why America Dropped the Atomic Bomb*. Boston: Little, Brown and Company, 1995; racialization of the war, 71; Truman's mother, 95; raging hate, 146. Piehler, G. Kurt. *Remembering War the American Way*. op. cit., 132. Robertson, David. op. cit., 426–427. Robertson, David. *Sly and Able: A Political Biography of James F. Byrnes*. New York, Norton, 1994.

7. Bergerud, Eric. *Touched by Fire: The Land War in the South Pacific*. New York, Viking, 1996, 403–425. Falk, Stanley L. "Burma Memories and the Reality of War." *Army History*. Winter 2003, 12.

8. *The Crossroads*. op. cit. EG 100: 38, 53.

9. Sherry, Michael S. *The Rise of American Air Power, The Creation of Armageddon*. New Haven, CT, Yale University Press, 1987, xi.

10. McGeorge, Bundy and Vannevar Bush quoted in Alperovitz, Gar. *The Decision to Use the Atomic Bomb and the Architecture of an American Myth*. New York, Alfred A. Knopf, 1995, 661. Marx, Joseph Laurence. *Nagasaki: The Necessary Bomb?* New York, The Macmillan Company, 1971, 219. Groves, Leslie B. *Now It Can Be Told: The Story of the Manhattan Project*. New York, Harper Brothers, 1962.

11. Powaski, Ronald J. *March to Armageddon: The United States and the Nuclear Arms Race, 1939 to the Present*. New York, Oxford University Press, 1987, 13. Alexander Sachs was a New York banker with Lehman Brothers, and a long time, trusted advisor on financial matters to President Roosevelt. His access to the president was important. See: Jungk, Robert. *Brighter Than a Thousand Suns*. New York, Harcourt Brace, 1958. 84–85.

12. Budiansky, Stephen. *The Battle of Wits: The Complete Story of Codebreaking in World War II*. New York; The Free Press, 2000, 333. Barney quote in Terkel, Studs. *"The Good War": An Oral History of World War Two*. New York, Pantheon Books, 1984, 530. Having read Terkel's books and listened to his dark views of American policies, I have the impression that calling it the "good war" was more of the sarcasm that sprinkles his commentaries on the radio: General Paul Tibbets in a telephone conversation with William Rooney, May 31, 2002. Even Budiansky may have tended toward some simplification. On that topic Admiral Henry E. Eccles, a naval logistics expert, said: "historians and analysts may be tempted to ascribe success or failure to a single element, decision or circumstance. Actually, it was extremely difficult to prove such a contention because in war we were not running controlled laboratory experiments nor did we have instruments for precise measurement. Instead we were dealing with extraordinary complexities of matter, mind and spirit where the so-called intangibles may dominate." Eccles quoted in Blewett, Daniel K. "Fuel and U. S. Naval Operation in the Pacific,

1942" in Bischoff, Gunter and Robert L. Dupont. ed., *The Pacific War Revisited*. Baton Rouge, Louisiana State University Press, 1997, 75–76.

13. The Crossroads, op. cit., EG 200: 15. Groves, Leslie. *Now It Can Be Told*, op. cit.

14. Groves, Leslie. Ibid., 187.

15. Dower, John W. *Japan in War and Peace*. New York, New Press, 1993. "'NI' and 'F' Japan's Wartime Atomic Bomb Research," 55–100. Shapley, Deborah. "Nuclear Weapons History: Japan's Wartime Bomb Projects Revealed." *Science*, vol. 199, no. 13, January 1978, 152–157. See also Wilcox, Robert K. *Japan's Secret War*. New York, William Morrow and Company, Inc., 1985. Dower, ibid. 56–57. Dower reacted strongly to Shapley's article, claiming that it was distorted, sensationalistic and anti-Japanese. See 88–89. He also cited General Groves as repudiating the idea there was a remote possibility that Japan could build an a-bomb. As noted elsewhere, however, Groves hedged on his doubts about Japanese ability to build a bomb and during the war did not dismiss the possibility they might have a "sizeable program" (89).

16. With regard to Joliot, see Groves, Leslie R. *Now It Can Be Told: The Story of the Manhattan Project*. op. cit., 34. Sherwin, Martin J. *A World Destroyed: Hiroshima and the Origins of the Arms Race*. New York Vintage Books, 1987, 132. At a meeting in Ottawa in July 1944, members of the French team informed General DeGaulle about the A-bomb. See Bundy, McGeorge, *Danger and Survival*. New York, Random House, 1988, 474.

17. *New York Times*, Dec. 16, 1945. See Bernstein, Barton J. ed., *Politics and Policies of the Truman Administration*. Chicago, Quadrangle Books, 1970, 46. Bernstein, Barton J. "The Dropping of the A-Bomb: How Decisions Are Made When a Nation Is at War." *The Center Magazine*. March-April 1983, 7–15.

18. Talbot, Strobe. *The Master of the Game, Paul Nitze and the Nuclear Peace*. New York, Alfred A. Knopf, 1988, xiv-xv. Bundy, McGeorge. *Danger and Survival*. op. cit., 88. Bundy called Alperovitz's argument "excellent polemics but bad history," 650, en 78.

19. Holloway, David. *Stalin and the Bomb: The Soviet Union and Atomic Energy 1939–1956*. New Haven, Yale University Press, 1994; bomb group, 106; some evidence, 398. Fekisov, Alexander and Sergei Kostin. *The Man Behind the Rosenbergs*. New York, Enigma Books, 2001. 64. Schecter, Jerrold L. and Vyacheslav V. Luchkov. *Khrushchev Remembers: The Glasnost Tapes*. Boston, Little, Brown and Company, 1990, 193–194. Julius and Ethel Rosenberg were executed in 1953 for conspiracy to pass atomic secrets to the Soviet Union.

20. Wedemeyer, Albert C. *Wedemeyer Reports.*, op. cit., 236. Drea, Edward J. *In the Service of the Emperor: Essays on the Imperial Japanese Army*. Lincoln, University of Nebraska Press, 1998, xi. Ickes, Harold. *The Secret Diary of Harold L. Ickes, Volume 3: The Lowering Clouds, 1939–1941*. New York, Simon and Schuster, 1953, 203. O'Reilly, Charles T. *Forgotten Battles: Italy's War of Liberation 1943–1945*. Latham, MD, Lexington Books, 2001. Aldrich, Richard J. *Intelligence and the War Against Japan, Britain, America and the Politics of Secret Service*. Cambridge, Cambridge University Press, 2000, 64.

21. Bernstein, Barton J. "Reconsidering Truman's Claim of 'Half a Million American Lives' Saved by the Atomic Bomb: The Construction and Deconstruction of a Myth." *Journal of Strategic Studies*, vol. 22, no. 1, March 1999, 69. Hersey, John. *Hiroshima*. Knopf, 1946. Marx, Joseph Laurence. *Nagasaki: The Necessary Bomb?* New York, The Macmillan Company, 1971, 80. Rhodes, Richard. *The Making of the Atomic Bomb*. New York, Simon & Schuster, Inc., 1986, 713. Craven, Wesley Frank and James Lea Cate. *The Army Air Forces in World War II, The Pacific: Matterhorn to Nagasaki, June 1944 to August 1945*. Office of Air Force History, Washington, DC, 1983, 657. Spec-

tor, Ronald H. ed. *Listening to the Enemy: Key Documents on the Role of Communications Intelligence in the War with Japan*. Wilmington, DE Scholarly Resources, 1988. Dower, John. *War Without Mercy*. op. cit., 295–301, 120.

22. Holloway, David. *Stalin and the Bomb*. op. cit., 122. A review of the Interim Committee is found in David Robertson's *Sly and Able*, op. cit., 397–419; racist, 396. Alperovitz, Gar. *The Decision to Use the Atomic Bomb*. op. cit., 661.

23. Bernstein, Barton J. "Truman and the A-Bomb: Targeting Noncombatants, Using the Bomb and His Defending 'The Decision.' *Journal of Military History*, vol. 62, July 1998, 569; Bernstein, Barton J. "Hiroshima and Nagasaki: The Atomic Bombings Reconsidered." *Current*, no. 372, 1995, 13. Re "only about 20,000 ... deaths," Bernstein, Barton J. "An Analysis of 'Two Cultures': Writing about the Making and the Using of the Atomic Bombs." *The Public Historian*. vol. 12, no. 2, 1990, 96. From his detailed familiarity with the documentary record, Bernstein knew that Truman's Interim Committee specifically recommended targets of military importance. Instead he virtually ignored the fact that there were large, legitimate military targets in Japanese cities, while emphasizing the risk to civilians. Urban places were important to the Japanese war effort, thus it was unfortunate that such places housed the Mitsubishi factories and naval shipyards in Nagasaki, and that 40,000 troops, an army headquarters and naval headquarters were in Hiroshima. As did their adversaries, the Japanese did not locate their munitions factories, steel plants, naval shipyards and military headquarters in rural areas.

24. Neal, Steve. *Eleanor and Harry*. New York, Simon and Schuster, 2002.

Chapter VI

1. Frank, Richard B. *Downfall*. op. cit., 131–148. Harper, Steven. *Miracle of Deliverance: The Case for the Bombing of Hiroshima and Nagasaki*. New York, Stein and Day Publishers, 1986, 89. Rees, David. *The Defeat of Japan*. Westport, CT. Praeger, 1997, 2; Dower, John. *War Without Mercy*. op. cit., 246. Truman, Harry S. *Years of Decision*. *Vol I*. Garden City, NY, Doubleday, 1955, 10.

2. *The Crossroads*. Eg: 200, 66.

3. Kohn Richard H. "History at Risk: The Case of the Enola Gay" in Linenthal, Edward T. and Tom Engelhart, ed. *History Wars: The Enola Gay and Other Battles for the American Past*. New York, Metropolitan Books, 1996, 161. Quoted in Linenthal, Edward T. "Anatomy of a Controversy," *History Wars*, 58. Kohn had been chief of air force history for the United States Air Force and since 1986 served on three advisory committees for the NASM. Hein, Laura and Mark Selden. "Commemoration and Silence: Fifty Years of Remembering the Bomb in America and Japan" in Hein, Laura and Mark Selden, eds., *Living with the Bomb: American and Japanese Cultural Conflicts in the Nuclear Age*. Armonk, NY, M. E. Sharpe, 1997, 19.

4. Alperovitz, Gar. *Atomic Diplomacy: Hiroshima and Potsdam, the Use of the Atomic Bomb and the American Confrontation with Soviet Power*. Rev. ed. East Haven, CT., Pluto Press, 1994, xi.

5. Truman, *Memoirs*. op. cit., 417. MacEachin, Douglas J. *The Final Months of the War with Japan;* op. cit. "Truman to Cates Jan. 12, 1953." Document 18F and Document 18D. Test in the box, ibid., page 7. Re signals intelligence, iii. Cray, Ed. *General of the Army: George C. Marshall Soldier and Statesman*. New York, W. W. Norton & Company, 1990.

6. Bernstein, Barton J. "Writing, Righting, or Wronging the Historical Record: President Truman's Letter on His Atomic-Bomb Decision" in *Diplomatic History*, 16,

Winter 1992, 163–173. If General Marshall used the figure of 250,000 casualties, then the ratio of one death in every four casualties would have resulted in 61,666 fatalities, substantially more than the claimed "under fifty thousand American dead." When reviewing Richard Rhodes, *The Making of the Atomic Bomb*, Professor Bernstein acknowledged the counsel of nine individuals plus members of the Peace Studies group and Nuclear History group at Stanford, the Japan Fund and the MacArthur Foundation. See: *The Public Historian*, vol. 12, no. 2, 1990. 83.

7. Chandler, Alfred D. *The Papers of Dwight David Eisenhower. The War Years, III*. Baltimore, The Johns Hopkins University Press, 1970, 1563. Piehler, G. Kurt. "Finding the Best Plan to Win the 'Good War.' in *Reviews in American History*, vol. 29, no. 3, 2001, 447–454. Stoler, Mark A. *Allies and Adversaries: The Joint Chiefs of Staff, the Grand Alliance, and the U.S. Strategy in World War II*. Chapel Hill. University of North Carolina Press, 2000, 106. Cray, Ed. *General of the Army: George C. Marshall Soldier and Statesman*. New York, W. W. Norton & Company, 1990, 558–559; casualties, 442. Biennial Report of The Chief of Staff, July 1, 1943 to June 30, 1945, to the Secretary of War, 87. Leahy quoted in McCullough, David. *Truman*. New York, Simon & Schuster, 1992, 400.

8. Kolko, Gabriel. *The Politics of War: The World and United States Foreign Policy, 1943–1945*. New York, Random House, 1968, 621. It is useful to note what some peers said about Kolko. With reference to his reliability, Lisle Rose said: "In Kolko's world of policy and diplomacy the war never really occurs, but merely serves as a backdrop for the 'real' struggle between predatory capitalism and social realism." Rose, Lisle. *The Long Shadow: Reflections on the Second World War Era*. Westport, CT. Greenwood Press, 1978, 25. And in relation to his view of Operation Crosswords, Harriette L. Chandler wrote: "Kolko has quoted his sources irresponsibly, … tried to change the facts to fit his own interpretation of the event." Chandler, Harriette L. "Another View of Operation Crosswords: A Revision of Kolko." *Military Affairs*, 42, April 1978, 70. Walker, J. Samuel in Hogan, Michael J., ed. *Hiroshima in History and Memory*. Cambridge, Cambridge University Press, 1996, 24. Smith, Gregory S. "Beware, the Historians! Hiroshima, the Enola Gay and the Dangers of History." *Diplomatic History*, vol. 22, no. 1, Winter 199, 125; Bernstein, Barton J. in Nobile, Philip, ed. *Judgment at the Smithsonian*. op. cit., 167. O'Reilly, Charles T. *Forgotten Battles: Italy's War of Liberation*. op. cit., 288–290.

9. Miles, Rufus E. Jr. "Hiroshima: The Strange Myth of Half a Million American Lives Saved." *International Security*, vol. 10, no. 2, Fall 1985; 20,000 lives, 121; expected deaths, 134; conclusion, 140. MacEachin, Douglas, op. cit., document 5, 7. Miles also mentioned the impressive American kill ratio on Okinawa and elsewhere as if it was somehow related to the expected number of American deaths. That kind of ratio was essentially irrelevant then and was a precursor of the reliance on body counts in Vietnam. According to Deborah Shapley, "MacNamara's statistical control was the ratio of enemy killed in relation to the number of friendly deaths. Progress could be occurring over time if the number of enemy dead increased in relation to the number of friendly dead." Shapley, Deborah. *Promise and Power: The Life and Times of Robert McNamara*. Boston, Little, Brown and Company, 1993, 250. For mandarins enamored of statistics, counting the enemy dead was modern management by bean counters but it proved to be a futile exercise they pretended had meaning, and too late, knew better. An enemy uncaring of its losses can frustrate the MBA approach to warmaking. Cray, Ed. *General of the Army: George C. Marshall Soldier and Statesman*. New York, W. W. Norton & Company, 1990, 534. Craven, Wesley Frank and James Lea Cate, eds. *The Army Air Forces in World War II. Volume Five, The Pacific: Matterhorn to Nagasaki, June 1944 To August 1945*. Washington, DC, Office of Air Force History, 1983.

10. Maslowski, Peter. "Truman, the Bomb, and the Numbers Game." *Military History Quarterly*, vol. 7, Spring 1995, 105.

11. MacEachin, Douglas J. op. cit., Document 5, 15 June 1945, Joint War Plans Committee. "Details of the Campaign Against Japan."

12. Ambiguity about the meaning of casualties is found in Truman's letter to Professor James Cates on January 12, 1953. "I asked General Marshall what it would cost in *lives* (emphasis added) to land on the Tokyo Plain and other places in Japan. It was his opinion that such an invasion would cost a minimum of one quarter of a million casualties and might cost a million on the American side alone." See MacEaclin, op. cit., Document C, D, E, F.

13. Skates, John Ray. *The Invasion of Japan, Alternative to the Bomb*. Columbia, University of South Carolina Press, 1994. 227–232. De Gaulle, Charles. *The Complete War Memoirs of Charles De Gaulle, 1940–1946*. New York, Da Capo Press, 1984, 325. De Gaulle said that he was asked, but according to Truman, at about the time the French unsuccessfully attempted to annex part of Italy's Val D'Aosta in May 1945, De Gaulle demanded to have French troops participate in the war with Japan. See Truman's *Memoirs*, op. cit., 240.

14. For the Japanese treatment of the population of Malaysia, see Kratoska, Paul H. ed. *Malaya and Singapore During the Japanese Occupation*. Singapore, National University of Singapore, 1995, especially, Frei, Henry P. "Japan Remembers the Malaya Campaign." op. cit. 148–168. Harper, Stephen. *Operation ZIPPER*, op. cit.

15. Nalty, Bernard C. *The United States Marines on Iwo Jima: The Battle and the Flag Raising*. Washington, D.C., Historical Branch, G-3 Division, Headquarters, U.S. Marine Corps. 1967.

16. Craven, Wesley Frank and James Lea Cate. *The Army Air Forces in World War II, The Pacific: Matterhorn to Nagasaki, June 1944 to August 1945*. Washington, Office of Air Force History, Washington, DC, 1983. Map based on MacEachin, Douglas, op. cit., Doc. 5, Tab E, p. 15, JWPC to JCS, 15 June 1945.

17. Yahara, Hiromachi. *The Battle for Okinawa*. New York, John Wiley & Sons, Inc., 1995. Introduction by Frank B. Gibney, 23. Yahara was the senior operations officer (G-3) of the Japanese army on Okinawa. Chandler, Alfred D. *The Papers of Dwight D. Eisenhower. The War Years, III*. Baltimore, The Johns Hopkins University Press, 1970; Soviet doctrine, 1767. Von Clausewitz, Carl. *On War*. New York, Penguin Books, 1968. See chapter VII, "Friction in War," 164–167.

18. MacEachin, Douglas J. *The Final Months of the War with Japan*, op. cit., "Appendix C, Selected Archival Documents. Langley, VA, Center for the Study of Intelligence, Central Intelligence Agency, 1998. Other American casualty figures for Okinawa were, Army 64,700; Navy 9724, for a total of 74,424 of which 12,513 or 16.8 percent were killed. Drea had 49,151 battle casualties and 31,000 non battle casualties. Drea, Edward. op cit., 153. See also, Yahara, Hiromichi. *The Battle for Okinawa*. New York, John Wiley & Sons, Inc., 1995, 156. "Preliminary Report To Pacific Order Of Battle Conference, 15 August 1945, War Department, Pacific Order of Battle Conference, 15 August 1945" in Spector, Ronald H. *Listening to the Enemy*. op. cit., 249–259; Ross, Steven T. *American War Plans 1941–1945: The Test of Battle*. London, Frank Cass, 1997, 159.

19. Bernstein, Barton J. "American Foreign Policy and the Cold War" in Bernstein, Barton J., ed. *Politics and Policies of the Truman Administration*. Chicago, Quadrangle Books, 1970, 67. Lifton, Robert J. and Greg Mitchell. *Hiroshima in America: Fifty Years of Denial*. New York, G. P. Putnam's Sons, 1995, 274.

20. Takaki, Ronald. *Double Victory: A Multicultural History of America in World War II*. Boston, Little, Brown and Company, 2000. 166.

21. Sherwin, Martin J. *A World Destroyed: Hiroshima and the Origins of the Arms*

Race. New York, Vintage Books, 1987; "grossly exaggerated," xxii. The chart on casualties is on page 342.

22. MacEachin. Douglas J. op. cit., Document 5, 7. MacEachin, ibid., Document 5, 7.

23. MacEachin, Douglas. op. cit., Document 15–1. See also Astor, Gerald. *Operation Iceberg,* op. cit.

24. In September 1955, in response to requests from members of Congress and the press, the Department of Defense issued *The Entry of the Soviet Union into the War Against Japan: Military Plans, 1941–1945.* U. S. Department of Defense, September 1945. Dower, *War Without Mercy.* op. cit., 331; British airmen, 73. Manchester, William. *Goodbye Darkness: A Memoir of the Pacific War.* Boston, Little Brown and Company, 1979, 248. Yoshida, Mitsuru. "The Sinking of the Yamato" 487, in Evans, David C. ed. *The Japanese Navy in World War II in the Words of Former Japanese Naval Officers.* 2d ed. Annapolis, MD, Naval Institute Press, 1986. Feifer, George. Tennozan, *The Battle of Okinawa and the Atomic Bomb.* New York, Ticknor & Fields, 1992, 207.

25. Kemp, Paul. "Decima MAS," 348–361, in Cowley, Robert. ed. *No End Save Victory: Perspectives on World War II.* New York, G. P. Putnam's Sons, 2001. The X-MAS that remained with the Germans and Mussolini after the Armistice became one of the most notorious units in Mussolini's Fascist Army. Neo-Fascists and other revisionists have worked hard to rehabilitate the reputation of the X-Mas and Mussolini's Army of Salo. See O'Reilly, Charles. *Forgotten Battles: Italy's War of Liberation.* Latham, MD, Lexington Books, 2001, 276–277. The efforts to rehabilitate them is akin to those of Americans dedicated to revising the story of the Abraham Lincoln Brigade.

26. Warner, Denis and Peggy Warner with Commander Sadao Seno. *The Sacred Warriors: Japan's Suicide Legions.* New York, Van Nostrand Reinhold Company, 1982, chapter 17, 286–304. Bauer, K. Jack and Alan C. Coox. "Olympic vs Ketsu-Go." *Marine Corps Gazette,* vol. 49, no. 8, August 1965. As early as July 1946, the U.S. Strategic Bombing Survey noted that at the surrender the Japanese had 9,000 planes available for kamikaze attacks. Referring to Kyushu it said, "Had the Japanese been able to sustain an attack of greater power and concentration they might have bee able to cause us to withdraw or to revise our strategic plans." United States Strategic Bombing Survey, *Summary Report (Pacific War) Washington, D.C. 1 July 1946.* United States Government Printing Office, Washington; 1946, 10.

27. Sherrod, Robert L. *Marine Corps Aviation,* op. cit., 272–273, 418–420. Yoki, Toshiyuki. "Kamikazes in the Okinawa Campaign," 453–473. in Evans, David C. ed. *The Japanese Navy in World War II.* Annapolis, MD, Naval Institute Press, 1986. Information about the effect of kamikaze attacks was available soon after the war but it may have been dismissed by revisionists unfamiliar with the minutiae of war. It is little known that the Japanese KI-77, a large experimental plane with a range of 10,000 miles, was intended for use as a suicide bomber against cities in the United States. See: Warner, Denis and Peggy Warner. *The Sacred Warriors.* op. cit., 337.

28. Giangreaco, D. M. and Kathryn Moore. "Half a Million Purple Hearts: Why a 200-year-old decoration offers evidence in the controversy surrounding the Hiroshima bombing." *American Heritage.* December-January 2001, 81–83. Also with regard to the order for more Purple Hearts, see Allen, Thomas B. and Polmar, Norman. *Code-Name Downfall: The Secret Plan to Invade Japan — and Why Truman Dropped the Bomb.* New York, Simon and Schuster, 1995. "Epilogue" EN 292.

29. *Surgery in World War II: Activities of Surgical Consultants, Volume II.* Washington, D.C. Office of the Surgeon General, Department of the Army, 1964. 856 Larson, George A. *The Road to Tinian: The Story of the 135th USNCB.* ND, 84.

30. *Surgery in World War II.* op. cit., 745; *Building the Navy's Bases in World War*

II: History of the Bureau of Yards and Docks and the Civil Engineer Corps 1940–1946. Volume II. Washington, United States Government Printing Office, 1947; engineers, 408; hospitals, 406, 410–410. *Surgery in World War II.* op. cit., 155; Bernstein, Barton J. in Nobile, Philip, *Judgment at the Smithsonian.* op. cit., 139. Craven, Wesley Frank and Cate, James Lea, eds. *The Army Air Forces in World War II.* op. cit., 692.

Chapter VII

1. Bernstein, Barton J. "A Postwar Myth: 500,000 U. S. Lives Saved." *Bulletin of the Atomic Scientists*, June-July 1986, 38–40. Bundy, McGeorge. *Danger and Survival.* op. cit., 647. Giangreco, D. M. "Casualty Projections for the U. S. Invasion of Japan, 1945–1946: Planning and Policy Implications." *The Journal of Military History*, vol. 61, no. 3, July 1997, 521–582. Bernstein, Barton J. "Truman and the A-bomb: Targeting noncombatants, using the bomb and his defending the 'Decision'" in *The Journal of Military History*, vol. 62, no. 3, July 1998, 547–570. Among his other criticisms of Giangreco's article, Professor Bernstein complained that despite repeated requests to Giangreco for documents he used to substantiate his claims about a steady continuation of the "Saipan ratio" for U. S. casualties, he did not do so. Bernstein wanted Giangreco to do his work for him, forgetting that in the grown-up world, if Bernstein considered something "questionable" about another's work, nothing stopped him or one of his assistants from checking those documents. MacEachin, op. cit., Document 17, Enclosure "A." Bernstein, Barton J. "The Struggle Over History" in Nobile, Philip, ed. *Judgment At The Smithsonian.* New York, Marlowe & Company, 1995, 140.

2. Cray, Ed. *General of the Army: George C. Marshall Soldier and Statesman.* New York, W. W. Norton & Company, 1990. Byrnes, James F. *Speaking Frankly,* New York, Harper & Brothers, 1947, 261–262.

3. Bernstein in Nobile, op. cit., 139.

4. Ferrell, Robert. *Harry S. Truman, A Life.* Columbia, University of Missouri Press, 1994, 194–195. Sherwin, Martin J. *A World Destroyed: Hiroshima and the Origins of the Arms Race.* New York, Vantage Books, 1987, 352, 354. See also Allen, Thomas B. and Norman Polmar. *CODE-NAME DOWNFALL: The Secret Plan to Invade Japan — and Why Truman Dropped the Bomb.* New York, Simon & Schuster, 1995, 215–216, 323. The former president's visit to the White House was not a spur of the moment decision by President Truman. On May 1, 1945, Navy Secretary Forrestal and Secretary Stimson had discussed whether Hoover would be useful regarding the food crisis facing Europe. Although they had some reservations, all agreed that his general knowledge and clearness of thought ought to be available. Forrestal, op. cit., 52. The sequence of events that brought Hoover and Truman together is detailed in Smith, Richard Norton. *An Uncommon Man: The Triumph of Herbert Hoover.* New York, Simon & Schuster. 1984. 344–346. Hoover was well aware of events in Washington because Stimson had him briefed by some of his staff. Capaccio, Tony "Pentagon A-Bomb Exhibit Includes Suspect Casualty Claims." *Defense Weekly*, August 7, 1995. McCullough, David. *Truman.* New York, Simon & Schuster. 1992. 401.

5. Wallace, Mike. *Mickey Mouse History.* op. cit., 316; Minear, Richard H. "Atomic Holocaust, Nazi Holocaust: Some Reflections." *Diplomatic History*, vol. 19, no. 2, Spring 1995, 347–365. McCullough, David. Truman. op. cit., 400–401. Saburo, Ienaga (translated and introduced by Minear, Richard H). *Japan's Past Japan's Future: One Historian's Odyssey.* Lanham, MD, Rowman & Littlefield Publishers, Inc., 2001, x. Walker, J. Samuel. *Prompt & Utter Destruction*, op. cit., 107, also has an account of this tempest in a teapot. Sherry, Michael S. *The Rise of American Air Power: The Creation of*

ington, DC, 1983, 732. Sherry, Michael S. *The Rise of American Airpower*, op. cit., 341, 297. Cray, Ed. *General of the Army: George C. Marshall Soldier and Statesman*. New York, W. W. Norton & Company, 1990, 525. Pogue, Forrest C. *George C. Marshall: Organizer of Victory, 1943–1945*. New York, The Viking Press, 1973, 569.

7. Bernstein, Barton J. ed. *Politics and Policies of the Truman Administration*. Chicago, Quadrangle Books, 1970, 34. Dower, John W. in *Days of Destiny*. op. cit., 309. Cranston, Alan. "The Non-event: Dropping the A-Bomb." *The New Republic*, vol. 213, no. 8–9, August 21, 1995, 10. Lifschultz, Lawrence and Kai Bird, ed. *Hiroshima's Shadow*. Stony Creek, CT, The Pamphleteer's Press, 1998, xxxvi. Bernstein, Barton J. "Misconceived Patriotism." *The Bulletin of the Atomic Scientists*, vol. 51, May-June 1995, 4. In a 1996 article, Professor Bernstein noted that "not even Leahy, who, alone among the group, probably ethically disliked the use of the A-Bomb, had ever said that it should not be used" (page 65). Bernstein, Barton J. "Understanding the Atomic Bomb and the Japanese Surrender: Missed Opportunities, Little-Known Disasters, and Modern Memory" in Hogan, Michael J., ed. *Hiroshima in Memory and History*. Cambridge, Cambridge University Press, 1996, 65. Alperovitz, Gar. *Atomic Diplomacy*, op. cit. Spector, Ronald H. *Eagle Against the Sun: The American War with Japan*. New York, The Free Press, 1985. Spector, Ronald H. ed. *Listening to the Enemy: Key Documents on the Role of Communications Intelligence in the War with Japan*. Wilmington, DE, Scholarly Resources, 1988.

8. *The Crossroads*. EG: 200, 48, 49. Sweeney, Charles W. *Wars End*. op. cit., 279. Leahy, William D. *I Was There: The Personal Story of the Chief of Staff to Presidents Roosevelt and Truman Based on His Notes and Diaries Made at the Time*. New York, McGraw Hill Book Company, Inc., 1950, 441, 442. Bundy, McGeorge. *Danger and Survival*. op. cit., 71–74. Bernstein, Barton J. "Misconceived Patriotism." *The Bulletin of the Atomic Scientists*, vol. 51, May-June 1995, 4. He also faulted the NASM of a generation earlier for failing to mention the wastefully competitive program of rival military services, or the militarization of U.S. science and technology during World War II. Cray, Ed. *General of the Army: George C. Marshall Soldier and Statesman*. New York, W. W. Norton & Company, 1990, 549. Fogelman, Edwin. *Hiroshima: The Decision to Use the A-Bomb*. New York, Charles Scribers Sons, 1964, 53. Compton also reported that when 150 men who worked on the bomb at the Metallurgical Laboratory at Chicago were polled on the use of the bomb, and given five alternatives ranging from no use in war to its military use in the manner most effective in bringing prompt Japanese surrender, 87 percent voted for its military use, at least if, after other means were tried, this was found necessary to bring surrender (page 56). Bundy, McGeorge. *Danger and Survival*. op. cit., 649, en 59.

9. *The Crossroads*. EG: 200, 63. Dower, John W. *Days of Destiny*. op. cit., 318, 320.

10. Bernstein, Barton J. ed. *Politics and Policies of the Truman Administration*. Chicago, Quadrangle Books, 1970, 5. Bernstein Barton J. "The Dropping of the A-Bomb: How Decisions are Made When a Nation is at War." *The Center Magazine*. March-April 1983, 7–15. Leffler, Melvyn P. *The Specter of Communism: The United States and the Origins of the Cold War, 1917–1953*. New York, Hill and Wang, 1994. De Jonge, Alex. *Stalin and the Shaping of the Soviet Union*. Glasgow, Fontana/Collins, William Collins & Co. Ltd., 1987. Mastny, Vojtech. *The Cold War and Soviet Insecurity, the Stalin Years*. New York, Oxford University Press, 1995, 194.

11. Hogan, Michael J. "The Enola Gay Controversy: History, Memory, and the Politics of Presentation" in Hogan, Michael J. ed. *Hiroshima In History and Memory*. Cambridge, Cambridge University Press, 1998, 216, 221, 227.

12. Noam Chomsky, quoted in *Revisionism Gone Wrong, Part II*, Arlington, VA, Air Force Association, op. cit. Chomsky's attitude was not new. According to Shelia John-

son, "Chomsky's argument is that Japan was not fascist and expansionist in the 1930's, but that the United States was, and is." Johnson, Shelia K. *American Attitudes Toward Japan, 1941–1975.* Washington, DC, American Enterprise Institute, 1975, 102, 103. Chomsky, Noam. *9–11.* New York, Seven Stories Press, 2001, 101. *The New York Times,* May 4, 2002, page A-17. A short survey of Chomsky's political thinking is found in Chomsky, Noam. "The Cold War and the University" in Montgomery, David. ed. *The Cold War and the University: Toward an Intellectual History of the Postwar Years.* New York, The New Press, 1997, 171–194. A short, sympathetic review of Chomsky's work is found in Paul Buhle's entry on Chomsky in Buhle, MariJo, Paul Buhle, et al. *The Encyclopedia of the American Left.* New York, Garland Publishing Company, 1990, 130–131.

13. Sherwin, Martin quoted by Michael Hogan in "The Enola Gay Controversy: History Memory, and the Politics of Presentation" in Hogan Michael, ed. *Hiroshima in History and Memory.* Cambridge, Cambridge University Press, 1996, 226. Hogan re McCullough, 230–232. Posner, Richard A. *Public Intellectuals: A Study in Decline.* Cambridge, MA, Harvard University Press, 2001, 392.

14. Nobile, Philip. *Judgment at the Smithsonian.* op. cit. Nobile accused John Correll, the editor of *Air Force,* of a lack of journalistic ethics and foul play for misquoting *The Crossroads* script, xxxi-xxxii. An article in *Air Force* by Correll quoted *The Crossroads*: "'For most Americans,' the script says, 'it was a war of vengeance. For most Japanese it was a war to defend their unique culture from Western imperialism." He did not include the words "this was fundamentally different than the one waged against Germany and Italy." Allegedly Correll's quote "was torn out of context and suspiciously cropped" (xxxi). In a strange and tortured interpretation of the sentence that made no sense, Nobile said that the complete sentence clearly referred to events in the summer of 1945, although how he reached that conclusion is unclear (xxxi-xxxii).

15. Hogan, Michael J. *A Cross of Iron: Harry S. Truman and the Origins of the National Security State, 1945–1954.* Cambridge, Cambridge University Press, 1998. Is the title an allusion to William Jenning Bryan's famous "Cross of Gold" speech at the 1896 Democratic convention? Perhaps as Bryan confronted the monied interests in his speech, Hogan was confronting the military-industrial complex (pages 463–464, 478). Blum, John Morton. ed. *The Price of Vision: The Diary of Henry A. Wallace, 1942–1946.* Boston, Houghton Mifflin Company, 1973. Kennan, George F. *The Nuclear Delusion: Soviet-American Relations in the Atomic Age.* New York, Pantheon Books, 1983, x.

16. Bernstein, Barton J. "American Foreign Policy and the Cold War," 16–17, in Bernstein, Barton J. *Politics and Policies of the Truman Administration.* Chicago, Quadrangle Books, 1970; Modus vivendi, 16–17; invasion, 17.

17. Alperovitz, Gar. *The Decision to Use the Atomic Bomb and the Architecture of an American Myth.* New York, Knopf, 1995, 315. Castle preceded Joseph Grew as ambassador to Japan.

18. Alperovitz, Gar. *Atomic Diplomacy: Hiroshima and Potsdam: the Use of the Atomic Bomb and the American Confrontation with Soviet Power. 2nd ed.* East Haven, CT, Pluto Press, 1994, 179.

19. According to Nikita Khrushchev: "Togliatti ... was ready to start an armed insurrection. It might have occurred had it not been for the presence of American troops. Stalin restrained Togliatti. He warned that an insurrection would be crushed by American forces" in *Khrushchev Remembers: The Glasnost Tapes.* op. cit., 100. For an account of Soviet intervention after the assassination attempt, see O'Reilly, *Forgotten Battles,* op. cit., 334. Colville, John. *The Fringes of Power: 10 Downing Street, Diaries, 1939–1945.* New York, W. W. Norton & Company, 1985, 505.

20. Holloway, David. *Stalin and the Bomb: The Soviet Union and Atomic Energy 1939–1956.* New Haven, Yale University Press, 1994, 370.

21. Saburo, Ienaga (translation & introduction by Minear, Richard H.). *Japan's Past Japan's Future, One Historian's Odyssey.* Lanham, MD, Rowan & Littlefield Publishers, Inc., 2001, 10, ix, x. Fujitani, T. Gregory M. White and Lisa Yoneyama. "Introduction." in Fujitani, T. Gregory M. White and Lisa Yoneyama, eds. *Perilous Memories: The Asia-Pacific War(s).* Durham, NC, Duke University Press, 2001, 6. Foner, Eric *Who Owns History? Rethinking the Past in a Changing World.* New York, Hill and Wang, 2002, xii, 22.

22. Davidson James West and Mark Hamilton Lytle. *After the Fact: The Art of Historical Detection. Fourth Edition.* Boston, McGraw Hill, 2000; Nagasaki, 308; historians we respect, xv, 308–309. Cray, op. cit., 351.

23. Lanouette, William. "Why We Dropped the Bomb." *Civilization,* vol. 2, no. 1, Jan/Feb 1995, 13, 16–17, 35. Bernstein, Barton J. "Understanding the Atomic Bomb and the Japanese Surrender: Missed Opportunities, Little-Known Disasters and Modern Memory" in Hogan, Michael J., ed. *Hiroshima in History and Memory.* Cambridge, Cambridge University Press, 1996, 70. Newman, Robert P. "Hiroshima and the Trashing of Henry Stimson" in the *New England Quarterly,* March 1998, 21. As George Feifer showed in *Tennozan,* the Japanese defense of Okinawa was prolonged and brutal. See Feifer, George. *Tenozan, the Battle of Okinawa and the Atomic Bomb.* New York, Ticknor & Fields, 1992. According to Alvin D. Coox, however, "Waged only a few months before the atomic bomb was tested at Alamagordo, was Operation Iceberg (the American invasion of Okinawa) worth the price and the agony?" Coox ignored the fact that there was uncertainty as to whether the A-Bomb would work. So the answer by reasonable people at the time would be to continue the long standing plan to take Okinawa as a launching pad for the planned invasion of Japan. See Coox, Alvin D. book review in *Journal of American History,* March 1995, 1814. It should be remembered that even Admiral Leahy told President Truman that the A-Bomb would not work.

24. Udall, Stewart L. *The Myths of August: A Personal Exploration of Our Tragic Cold War Affair with the Atom.* New Brunswick, NJ, Rutgers University Press, 1998, 99–100. Originally published in 1994, *The Myths of August* appeared during the *Enola Gay* controversy and, although not specifically addressing that debate, used the arguments for the exhibit by its defenders. That is why it is included here. Drea, Edward. *MacArthur's Ultra: Codebreaking and the War against Japan, 1942–1945.* Lawrence, University Press of Kansas, 1992, 99, 100, 210.

25. Orr, James J. *The Victim as Hero: Ideologies of Peace and National Identity in Postwar Japan.* Honolulu, University of Hawaii Press, 2001, 179, 241.

Chapter IX

1. Kennedy, David. M. "Victory at Sea." *The Atlantic Monthly,* March 1999, 76. Rauch, Jonathan. "Firebombs Over Tokyo, America's 1945 attack on Japan's capital remains undeservedly obscure alongside Hiroshima and Nagasaki." *The Atlantic Monthly,* July-August 2002, 22. Bernstein, Barton J. "Understanding the Atomic Bomb and the Japanese Surrender: Missed Opportunities, Little-Known Near Disasters, and Modern Memory" in Hogan, Michael J. ed. *Hiroshima in Memory and History.* Cambridge, Cambridge University Press, 1996, 39. Professor Bernstein did not explain why his judgment about the A-Bomb was based on ethics instead of morality, unless he did not distinguish between them. However, the distinction is significant. Nagasaki and Hiroshima, 79. Bernstein, Barton J. "American Foreign Policy and the Cold War,"

15–77, in Bernstein, Barton J. *Politics and Policies of the Truman Administration.* Chicago, Quadrangle Books, 1970; Moral insensitivity, 35. Schaffer, Ronald. "U. S. Strategic Bombing was Immoral" in Chambers, John Whiteclay and G. Kurt Piehler, eds. *Major Problems in American Military History.* Boston, Houghton Mifflin Company, 1999, 360. Luttwak, Edward N. *On the Meaning of Victory: Essays on Strategy.* New York, Simon and Schuster, 1986, 65.

2. Denyer, Nicholas. "Just War," 137–152, in Teichmann, Roger, ed., *Logic, Cause & Action: Essays in Honour of Elizabeth Anscombe.* Cambridge, Cambridge University Press, 2000. Denyer's reasoned analysis of the laws of war showed how the development of the theory of the just war (*jus ad bellum*) and the conduct of war (*jus in bello*) had medieval origins that led to much later international codification in the Paris declaration on maritime law in 1865 and in subsequent international treaties embodied in the various Hague and Geneva Conventions.

3. Rawls, John. "Fifty Years After Hiroshima." *Dissent,* vol. 42, no. 3, 1995, 323–327. Anscombe, G. E. M. *Ethics, Religion and Politics: The Collected Philosophical Papers of G. E. M. Anscombe, Volume III.* Oxford, Basil Blackwell, 1981. Chapter 7, "Mr Truman's Degree." 62–71. An excellent discussion of the just war tradition and its evolution in modern times: Manzo, Louis A. "Morality in War Fighting and Strategic Bombing in World War II.' *Air Power History,* vol. 39, no. 3, Fall 1992, 35–50.

4. Quoted in Nobile, Philip. op. cit., lxxv. Orsi, Robert in Fox, Richard Wrightman and Robert B. Westbrook, eds. *In the Face of the Facts: Moral Inquiry in American Scholarship.* Cambridge, Cambridge University Press and Woodrow Wilson Center Press, 1998, 216.

5. Lord, John C. S. J. "The Morality of Obliteration Bombing." *Theological Studies,* vol. 3, September 1944, 308–309. Posner, Richard as quoted by Gertrude Himmelfarb. "Judging Judge Posner." *Commentary,* vol. 103, no. 2, 2002, 43. In a review of Posner's *Public Intellectuals: A Study in Decline.* Cambridge, MA, Harvard University Press, 2001. Hare, R. M. *Essays in Ethical Theory.* Oxford, Clarendon Press, 1989, 59. Hare, R. M. *Essays on Political Morality.* Oxford, Clarendon Press, 1989, 61. Rawls, John. op. cit., 326.

6. Walker, J. Samuel. *Prompt and Utter Destruction: Truman and the Use of Atomic Bombs Against Japan.* Chapel Hill, The University of North Carolina Press, 1997, 109.

7. Weintraub, Stanley. *The Last Great Victory: The End of World War II. July/August 1945.* New York, Truman Talley Books, Dutton, 1995, 656.

8. Albert Speer, who was involved in the German effort to create an atomic bomb, wrote: "I was sure that Hitler would not have hesitated for a moment to employ atomic bombs against England." Speer, Albert. *Inside The Third Reich.* New York, The Macmillan Company, 1970, 227. As McGeorge Bundy reviewed proposals for control of atomic weapons that appeared soon after its first use, he said that "The most noted political argument ... was an extended appeal by Walter Lippmann for a system of law enforceable against individuals, the argument is lucid and the solution extraordinarily irrelevant in the real world of nation-states—especially, if not uniquely, the real world of Soviet Russia." Bundy, McGeorge. *Danger and Survival.* op. cit., 656. Early in 1950 George Kennan wrote in a memo to the Secretary of State: "We deplore the existence of all weapons of indiscriminate mass destruction. We regret that we were ever obliged to make use of one. We hope never to have to do so again. We do not propose ever to do so, unless forced to it by the use of such weapons against us. Meanwhile, we remain prepared to go very far, to show considerable confidence in others, and to accept a certain risk for ourselves, in order to achieve international agreement on their removal for international arsenals; for we can think of nothing more dangerous than continued international competition in their development." Kennan, George F. *Memoirs*

1925–1950. New York, Pantheon Books, 1983, 473–74. More than half a century later that goal still proves elusive.

Chapter X

1. Guttenplan, D. D. *The Holocaust on Trial.* New York, W. W. Norton & Company, 2001, 307–308.

2. Maddox, Robert James. "Casualty Estimates for the Invasion of Japan: The "Postwar Creation Myth." *Continuity*, vol. 24, Fall 2000, 10–32. Evans, Richard J. *In Defense of History.* New York, W. W. Norton & Company, 1999, 12.

3. "Installation address," I. Michael Heyman, September 19, 1994. *The Electronic Smithsonian.* Heyman quoted in Stuteville, Joe. "An American Institution." *American Legion Magazine*, vol. 144, no. 3, March 1998, 28–29.

4. Dower, John W. "Triumphal and Tragic Narratives of the War in Asia" in *Journal of American History*, vol. 82, no. 3, 1997, 8, 1024. Lubar, Steven. "Exhibiting Memories" in Henderson, Amy and Adrienne I. Kaeppler. ed. *Exhibiting Dilemmas: Issues of Representation at the Smithsonian.* Washington, Smithsonian Institution Press, 1997, 17.

5. An available resource for the effects of the bombings is: *Hiroshima and Nagasaki: The Physical, Medical, and Social Effects of the Atomic Bombings.* The Committee for the Compilation of Materials on Damage Caused by the Atomic Bombs in Hiroshima and Nagasaki. New York, Basic Books, Inc. 1981. Yamane, Kazuyo. "Hiroshima and Nagasaki: The Beginning of the Nuclear Age" in Holdstock, Douglas and Frank Barnaby, eds. *Hiroshima and Nagasaki: Retrospect and Prospect.* London, Frank Cass, 1995, 12. Dirlik, Arif. "'Trapped in History' on the Way to Utopia: East Asia's 'Great War' Fifty Years Later" in Fujitani, T. Gregory M. White and Lisa Yoneyama. eds. *Perilous Memories: The Asia Pacific War(s).* Durham, NC, Duke University Press, 2001, 320.

6. Loewen, James W. *Lies Across America: What Our Historic Sites Get Wrong.* New York, The New Press, 1999. 191–192. From a speech by Major General Heywood Hansel, 58th Wing Reunion, Ft. Lauderdale, FL. 1985.

7. MacArthur, Douglas. *Reminiscences.* New York, McGraw-Hill Book Company, 1964. 259. van der Vat, Dan. *The Pacific Campaign, World War II: The U.S.–Japanese Naval War 1941–1945.* New York, Simon & Schuster. 1991. 299–300. Wexler, Peter. *Hirohito and War: Imperial Tradition and Military Decision Making in Prewar Japan.* Honolulu, University of Hawaii Press, 1998. Weingraub, Stanley. *The Last Great Victory: The End of World War II. July / August 1945.* New York, Truman Talley Books Dutton, 1995, 672. Herbert Aptheker quoted in "Letters to the Editor," *The Journal of American History*, vol. 87, no. 4, 2001.

8. Bernstein, Barton J. "*The Pacific War Revisited*" (book review) in *Pacific Historical Review*, vol. 67, no. 4, 642. Hagan, Kenneth J. "American Submarine Warfare in the Pacific, 1941–1945, Guerre de course Triumphant" in Bischof, Gunter and Robert L. Dupont, eds., *The Pacific War Revisited.* Baton Rouge, Louisiana State University Press, 1987. Van der Vat, Dan. *The Pacific Campaign: World War II, The U.S.-Japanese Naval War, 1941–1945.* New York, Simon & Schuster, 1991. Spector, Ronald H. *Eagle Against the Sun.* New York, The Free Press, 1985; see Chapter 21, "War of Attrition." Blewett, Daniel K. "Fuel and U. S. Naval Operations in the Pacific, 1942," in *The Pacific War Revisited.* op. cit., 57-80.

9. Newman Robert P. "Hiroshima and the Trashing of Henry Stimson." *The New England Quarterly*, March 1998, 5–32.

10. Henry, Michael. "Truman and the Liberal Tradition: A Textbook Survey" in

OAH Magazine of History, vol. 10, no. 4, Summer 1997, 47–49. Stoler, Mark A. *Allies and Adversaries: The Joint Chiefs of Staff, The Grand Alliance, and U. S. Strategy In World War II*. Chapel Hill, The University of North Carolina Press, 2000, 269. Bundy, McGeorge. *Danger and Survival*. op. cit., 93. Sun Tzu wrote about 400 BC. See Sawer, Ralph D. *Sun Tzu: The Art of War*. Boulder, CO, Westview Press, 1994. Neal, Steve. *Eleanor and Harry*. New York, Simon and Schuster, 2002, 262. An exception to a more favorable evaluation of Truman is Arnold A. Offner's *Another Such Victory: President Truman and the Cold War 1945–1953*. Stanford, CA, Stanford University Press, 2002. This heavily documented but one-sided deconstruction of the Truman presidency is in a series whose general editor is Martin Sherwin with Barton J. Bernstein on its advisory board. Russo, Gus. *The Outfit: The Role of Chicago's Underworld in the Shaping of Modern America*. New York. Bloomsbury. 2001, 225. For better or worse, humans must act on what they know. A non-academic made the point well. When Jack Ryan, Tom Clancy's hero of *Red Rabbit*, was musing about critics of Admiral Halsey, he said something that revisionist historians too often ignore: "Halsey had acted rightly where the all-seeing eye of hindsight had castigated him for being wrong. And that was unfair. Halsey could only be judged responsible for the information that was available to him." Clancy, Tom. *Red Rabbit*. G. P. Putnam's Sons, 2002, 182.

11. Beesly, Patrick. *Very Special Intelligence: The Story of the Admiralty's Operational Intelligence Center, 1939–1945*. Garden City, New York, Doubleday & Company, 1978, 132. Deutscher, Isaac. *Stalin: A Political Biography*. New York, Oxford University Press, 1949, 512.

12. Stoler, Mark A. *Allies and Adversaries*. op. cit., 268.

13. Orr, James J. *The Victim as Hero: Ideologies of Peace and National Identity in Postwar Japan*. Honolulu, University of Hawaii Press, 2001, 179. Dower, John. *Days of Destiny*. op. cit., 315. Takaki, Ronald. *Double Victory: A Multicultural History of America in World War II*. op. cit., 71, 95. He confirmed Truman's hatred of the Japanese in 1945 by quoting a letter Truman wrote to his fiancée on June 11, 1911, in which he said that he hated Chinese and Japanese. Takaki, Ronald. "Fifty Years After Hiroshima." *Dissent*, Summer 1995, 328–330. Erikson, Erik H. *Dimensions of a New Identity: The 1973 Jefferson Lectures in the Humanities*. New York, W. W. Norton & Company. Inc., 1974, 12. Albin, Mel, Robert J. Devlin and Gerald Heeger. *New Directions in Psychohistory: The Adelphi Papers in Honor of Erik H. Erikson*. Lexington, MA, Lexington Books, D. C. Heath and Company, 1980, ix.

14. Bernstein, Barton J. "Truman and the A-Bomb: Targeting Noncombatants, Using the Bomb, and His Defending the 'Decision.'" *Journal of Military History*, vol 62, no. 3, July 1998, 8. (Periodical Abstracts Full Text, http.//newfirstsearch.oclc.org.) True leader, in Bernstein, Barton J. "Understanding the Atomic Bomb and the Japanese Surrender: Missed Opportunities, Little-Known Near Disasters, and Modern Memory" in Hogan, Michael J. ed. *Hiroshima in Memory and History*. Cambridge, Cambridge University Press, 1996, 73, 45.

15. Lifton, Robert J. and Greg Mitchell. *Hiroshima in America: Fifty Years of Denial*. New York, G. P. Putnam's Sons, 1995, 331, 332, 338, 199, 274. Gaddis, John Lewis. *We Now Know: Rethinking Cold War History*. Oxford, Clarendon Press, 1997, 90. Gaddis referred readers to Michael Hogan's *Hiroshima in History and Memory* for "various dimensions of the debate," op. cit., 324. Yoneyama, Lisa. "For Transformative Knowledge and Postnationalist Public Spheres: The Smithsonian Enola Gay Controversy" in *Perilous Memories*. op. cit., 329. Dower, John W. *Days of Destiny*. op. cit., 313. In 1995 and 1996 the Internet carried several discussion groups debating the exhibit. As a principal antagonist to the A-Bomb, Gar Alperovitz received considerable attention, and extensive defense from his supporters. How long such material will endure electroni-

cally is questionable, but anyone seriously interested in the topics will find the material rewarding. For an incisive critique of Alperovitz, see Robertson, David. *Sly and Able.* op. cit., 600–601. Reductive and dogmatic, Alperovitz epitomizes the revisionist character.

16. Feis, Herbert. *The Atomic Bomb and the End of World War II.* Op. cit., 200. Kohn, Richard. "History at Risk." *History Wars,* op. cit., 140, 149. McCullagh, C. Behan. *Justifying Historical Descriptions.* Cambridge, Cambridge University Press, 1984, 236.

17. Lasch, Christopher. "Foreword" in Hofstader, Richard. *The American Political Tradition and the Men Who Made It.* New York, Vintage Books, 1974, xx. Posner, Richard A. *Public Intellectuals: A Study in Decline.* Cambridge, MA, Harvard University Press, 2001, 75.

18. Holley, I. B., Jr. "Second Guessing History." *Technology Review.* August/September 1997, vol. 98, no. 6, 53. The distortion of history continued in a book published in 2003 by British historian John Cornwell. After a summary of arguments for first use of the A-Bomb, he recited "equally familiar opposing arguments to the legitimacy of first use, that Japan was on the brink of capitulation, that the Americans saw the Japanese as sub-human, and that Truman was determined to use the bomb to impress Stalin." Noting that prominent American military leaders opposed the use of the bomb, he quoted John Rawls claim that Truman's use of the bomb was due to his lack of statesmanship. As many other writers, Cornwell took no notice of the fact that Japan made no move to *surrender* until the last minute or that although an American military leader like Admiral Leahy had initial questions about the bomb, afterwards he had no qualms about its use. As an accomplished historian Cornwell knows better than to deny readers access to such evidence about the bomb's use, but actual history was trumped by advocacy. Cornwell, John. *Hitler's Scientists: Science, War, and the Devil's Pact.* New York, Viking, 2003, 430–431.

Appendix A

1. *Revisionism Gone Wrong: Analysis of the Enola Gay Controversy.* Arlington, VA, Air Force Association, March 1994.

2. Bernstein, Barton J. "Hiroshima and Nagasaki: The Atomic Bombings Reconsidered." *Current,* no. 372, May 1995, 13–19.

3. For a basic introduction to content analysis, see Riffe, Daniel, Stephen Lacy and Frederick G. Fico. *Analyzing Media Messages: Using Quantitative Content Analysis in Research.* Mahwah, NJ, Lawrence Erlbaum Associates Publishers, 1998.

4. Alperovitz, Gar. *Atomic Diplomacy: Hiroshima and Potsdam, the Use of the Atomic Bomb and the American Confrontation with Soviet Power,* rev. ed. East Haven, CT, Pluto Press, 1994, 158. Although the many citations found in *Atomic Diplomacy* suggest its credibility, one might remember William Appleman Williams' comment: "History is simply not the arithmetic total of footnotes" in his *The Contours of American History.* Cleveland, OH, World Publishing Company, 1966, 491. Leahy, William D. *I Was There: The Personal Story of the Chief of Staff to Presidents Roosevelt and Truman Based on His Notes and Diaries Made at the Time.* New York, McGraw-Hill Book Company, Inc., 1950, 384–385. *The Entry of the Soviet Union Into the War Against Japan Military Plans, 1941–1945.* United States Department of Defense, 1955, 63–64.

5. Bernstein, Barton J. "Understanding the Atomic Bomb and the Japanese Surrender: Missed Opportunities, Little Known Near Disasters and Modern Memory" in Hogan, Michael J. ed. *Hiroshima in History and Memory.* Cambridge, Cambridge University Press, 1996; alternatives, 69. Bernstein, Barton J. "The Alarming Japanese

Buildup on Southern Kyushu, Growing U.S. Fears, and Counterfactual Analysis: Would the Planned November 1945 Invasion of Southern Kyushu Have Occurred?" *Pacific Historical Review*, vol. 68, no. 4, 1999, 561–609.

6. Bernstein, Barton J. "The Alarming Japanese Buildup on Southern Kyushu." op. cit.

7. Bernstein, Barton J. "The Alarming Japanese Buildup on Southern Kyushu," op. cit., 561–609. Bernstein, Barton J. "Reconsidering 'Invasion Most Costly:' Popular-History Scholarship, Publishing Standards, and the Claim of High U.S. Casualty Estimates to Help Legitimize the Atomic Bombings." *Peace & Change*, vol 24, no. 2, April 1999, 220–248. Bernstein, Barton J. "Truman and the A-Bomb: Targeting Noncombatants, Using the Bomb, and His Defending the 'Decision.'" *The Journal of Military History*, vol. 62, July 1998, 547–570. Bernstein, Barton J. "The Atomic Bombings Reconsidered." *Foreign Affairs*, vol. 74, no. 1, 1995, 135–152. Burns, Robert. "To a Louse" (1786).

8. Code of Ethics, Midwest Association of Forensic Scientists, 1991, Section II B, 31.

9. Dower, John W. *War Without Mercy*. op. cit., 301. The background for the idea that "progressives" would help defeat the Axis was described by Heideking and Mauch: "The OSS believed that the labor movement would become the most important ally in the common struggle against the Axis powers. This belief was confirmed by a group of left-wing German immigrants whom Donovan had drafted from the New School of Social Research in New York for the Research and Analysis Branch (R&A) of his new organization. Led by Franz Neumann, Herbert Marcuse and Max Horkheimer, they explained the rise of National Socialism in terms of a historic contradiction between the progressive working classes and the authoritarian German ruling elites, who had enlisted the Nazis to consolidate their threatened position. This interpretation, which combined the Marxist doctrine of class struggle with the egalitarian idealism of the New Deal, not only fixed the ideological point of view of many R&A members but had a considerable impact on the outlook of the OSS and the administration in general" (page 3). Heideking, Jurgen and Mauch, Christof, eds., *American Intelligence and the German Resistance to Hitler*. Boulder, CO, Westview Press, 1996.

10. United States Strategic Bombing Survey. *Summary Report (Pacific War) Washington, D. C. 1 July 1946*. Washington, D.C., United States Government Printing Office, 1946, 21.

Appendix C

1. Talbot, Strobe. *The Master of the Game, Paul Nitze and the Nuclear Peace*. New York, Alfred A. Knopf, 1988, xiv–xv. Alperovitz, Gar. op. cit.

2. Giles, James E. Letter to Editor, *The New York Times*. February 27, 2002, page A-24. Bernstein, Barton J. "Reconsidering 'Invasion Most Costly:' Popular-History Scholarship, Publishing Standards, and the Claim of High U.S. Casualty Estimates to Help Legitimize the Atomic Bombings." *Peace & Change*, vol. 24, no. 2, April 1999, 220–248.

3. Newman, Robert P. and Dale R. Newman. *Evidence*. Boston, Houghton, Mifflin Company, 1969, ix. Williams, William Appleman. *Americans in a Changing World: A History of the United States in the Twentieth Century*. New York, Harper & Row, 1978, xiv. Bosworth, R. J. B. *Explaining Auschwitz and Hiroshima: History Writing and the Second World War 1945–1990*. London, Routledge, 1993. Bernstein, Barton J. Book review, *International History Review*, vol. 19, no. 4, November 1997, 963. The

author was Ross, Steven T. *American War Plans*, 1945–1950. London, Frank Cass., 1996.

4. Zuccotti, Susan. *The Italians and the Holocaust: Persecution, Rescue and Survival.* New York, Basic Books, 1987. Capaso, Aldo. *Idea Chiare Sul Razismo.* Roma, Edizione Augustea, 1942. Andaldo Ugo Giorgio. *Razza, Nazione, Guerra.* Bologna, Edizione SIA, 1940. Tas, Luciano. *Storia degli ebrei italiani.* Roma, Newton Comption editore, 1987, 139–151. It is interesting that the article on Judaism in the 1924 edition of the *Enciclopedia Italian* explicitly denied that Jews were a distinct race.

5. Accusations of "McCarthyism" recall the red baiting of the 1940s and 1950s. Demonizing one's opponents does nothing to advance understanding of genuine issues that need public discourse.

Bibliography

Aldrich, Richard J. *Intelligence and the War Against Japan: Britain, America and the Politics of Secret Service.* Cambridge: Cambridge University Press, 2000.

Allen, Thomas B. and Norman Polmar. *Code-Name DOWNFALL: The Secret Plan to Invade Japan — and Why Truman Dropped the Bomb.* New York: Simon & Schuster, 1995.

Alperovitz, Gar. *Atomic Diplomacy: Hiroshima and Potsdam: The Use of the Atomic Bomb and the American Confrontation with Soviet Power.* 2d ed. East Haven, Conn.: Pluto Press, 1994.

_____. *The Decision to Use the Atomic Bomb and the Architecture of an American Myth.* New York, A. A. Knopf, 1995.

_____. "Hiroshima: Historians Reassess." *Foreign Policy.* Vol. 99, Summer 1995.

_____. "Why the United States Dropped the Bomb." *Technology Review.* Vol. 93, no. 6.

_____ and Kai Bird. "A Theory of Cold War Dynamics: U. S. Policy, Germany and the Bomb." *The History Teacher.* Vol. 29, no. 3, May 1996.

Ambrose, Steven E. *To America: Personal Reflections of an Historian.* New York, Simon & Schuster, 2002.

Ambrose, Stephen E. *Americans at War.* Jackson: University Press of Mississippi, 1997.

Anscombe, G. E. M. *Ethics, Religion and Politics: The Collected Philosophical Papers of G. E. M. Anscombe, Volume III.* Oxford: Basil Blackwell, 1981.

Armstrong, Anne. *Unconditional Surrender: The Impact of the Casablanca Policy Upon World War II.* New Brunswick, NJ: Rutgers University Press, 1961.

Bergerud, Eric. *Touched by Fire: The Land War in the South Pacific.* New York: Viking, 1996.

Bernstein, Barton J. "The Alarming Japanese Buildup on Southern Kyushu, Growing U.S. Fears, and Counterfactual Analysis: Would the Planned November 1945 Invasion of Southern Kyushu have Occurred?" *Pacific Historical Review.* Vol. 68, no. 4, 1999.

_____. "The Atomic Bombings Reconsidered." *Foreign Affairs.* Vol. 74, no. 1, 1995.

_____. "The Dropping of the A-Bomb: How Decisions Are Made When a Nation Is at War." *The Center Magazine.* March-April 1983.

_____. "Hiroshima and Nagasaki: The Atomic Bombings Reconsidered." *Current.* No. 372, May 1995.

_____. "Misconceived Patriotism." *The Bulletin of the Atomic Scientists.* 51, May-June 1995.

_____. "Reconsidering "Invasion Most Costly: Popular-History Scholarship, Publishing Standards, and the Claim of High U.S. Casualty Estimates to Help Legitimize the Atomic Bombings." *Peace & Change.* Vol. 24, no. 2, April 1999.

_____. "Reconsidering Truman's Claim of 'Half a Million American Lives' Saved by the Atomic Bomb: The Construction and Deconstruction of a Myth." *Journal of Strategic Studies*. Vol. 22, no. 1, March 1999.

_____. "Truman and the A-Bomb: Targeting Noncombatants, Using the Bomb, and His Defending the "Decision." *The Journal of Military History*. Vol. 62, July 1998, 547–570.

_____. "Understanding the Atomic Bomb and the Japanese Surrender: Missed Opportunities, Little-Known Disasters and Modern Memory" in Hogan, Michael J., ed. *Hiroshima in History and Memory*. Cambridge: Cambridge University Press, 1996.

Bischof, Gunter and Robert L. Dupont, eds., *The Pacific War Revisited*. Baton Rouge: Louisiana State University Press, 1987.

Bix, Herbert P. *Hirohito and the Making of Modern Japan*. New York: HarperCollins, 2000.

Brooks, Lester. *Behind Japan's Surrender: The Secret Struggle That Ended an Empire*. New York: McGraw-Hill Book Company, 1968.

Bundy, McGeorge. *Danger and Survival: Choices About the Bomb in the First Fifty Years*. New York: Random House, 1988.

Butow, Robert J. C. *Japan's Decision to Surrender*. Stanford: Stanford University Press, 1954.

Capaccio, Tony. "Pentagon A-Bomb Exhibit Includes Suspect Casualty Claims." *Defense Weekly*, August 7, 1995.

Chambers, John Whiteclay and G. Kurt Piehler, eds. *Major Problems in American Military History*. Boston: Houghton Mifflin Company, 1999.

Chappell, John D. *Before The Bomb: How America Approached the End of the Pacific War*. Lexington: University Press of Kentucky, 1997.

Conquest, Robert. *Reflections on a Ravaged Century*. New York, W. W. Norton & Company, 2000.

Craven, Wesley Frank and James Lea Cate. *The Army Air Forces in World War II. The Pacific: Matterhorn to Nagasaki, June 1944 to August 1945*. Washington: Office of Air Force History, 1983.

Cray, Ed. *General of the Army: George C. Marshall Soldier and Statesman*. New York: W. W. Norton,1990.

Crew, Spencer. "Who Owns History? History in the Museum." *The History Teacher*. Vol. 30, no. 1, November 1996.

Davis, Jack E. "New Left, Revisionist, In-Your-Face History" in Toplin, Robert Brent, ed. *Oliver Stone's USA, Film, History, and Controversy*. Lawrence. University Press of Kansas, 2000.

Daws, Gavan. *Prisoners of the Japanese: POWs of World War II in the Pacific*. New York: William Morrow and Company, Inc., 1994.

Dower, John W. *Embracing Defeat: Japan in the Wake of World War II*. New York: W. W. Norton, 1999.

_____. *Japan in War and Peace*. New York: New Press, 1993.

_____. "The Most Terrible Bomb in the History of the World" in McPherson, James M., Alan Brinkley and David Rubel, eds. *Days of Destiny, Crossroads in American History*. New York: Agincourt Press, 2001.

_____. "Triumphal and Tragic Narratives of the War in Asia." *Journal of American History*. Vol. 82, no. 3, 1997.

_____. *War Without Mercy: Race and Power in the Pacific War*. New York: Pantheon Books, 1986.

Drea, Edward J. *MacArthur's Ultra: Codebreaking and the War against Japan, 1942–1945*. Lawrence, Kansas, University Press of Kansas, 1992.

_____. *In the Service of the Emperor: Essays on the Imperial Japanese Army*. Lincoln: University of Nebraska Press, 1998.

Dubin, Steven C. *Displays of Power, Memory and Amnesia in the American Museum*. New York: New York University Press, 1999.

"Enola Gay Archive." http://www/afa.org/media/enolagayu/02–01.html.

Falk, Stanley L. "Burma Memories and the Reality of War." *Army History*. Winter 2003, 12–13.

Feifer, George. *Tenozan; The Battle of Okinawa and the Atomic Bomb*. New York: Ticknor & Fields, 1992.

Feis, Herbert. *The Atomic Bomb and the End of World War II*. rev. ed. Princeton: Princeton University Press, 1966.

_____. *Between War and Peace, The Potsdam Conference*. Princeton: Princeton University Press, 1960.

Fogelman, Edwin. *Hiroshima: The Decision to Use the A-Bomb*. New York: Charles Scribers Sons, 1964.

Foner, Eric. *Who Owns History? Rethinking the Past in a Changing World*. New York: Hill and Wang, 2002.

Frank, Richard B. *Downfall: The End of the Imperial Japanese Empire*. New York: Random House. 1999.

Fujitani, T. Gregory, M. White and Lisa Yoneyama, eds. *Perilous Memories: The Asia-Pacific War(s)*. Durham: Duke University Press, 2001.

Gaddis, John Lewis. *We Now Know: Rethinking Cold War History*. Oxford: Clarendon Press, 1997.

Giangreco, D. M. "Casualty Projections for the U. S. Invasion of Japan, 1945–1946: Planning and Policy Implications." *The Journal of Military History*. Vol. 61, no. 3, July 1997.

Giovenetti, Len and Fred Freed. *The Decision to Drop the Bomb*. New York: Coward-McCann, 1965.

Goldberg Stanley. "The Enola Gay Affair: What Evidence Counts When We Commemorate Historical Events?" *Orbis*. Annual 1999.

_____. "Smithsonian suffers Legionnaire's disease." *Bulletin of the Atomic Scientists*. Vol. 51, no. 3, May 1995.

_____. "What did Truman Know, and when did he know it?" *Bulletin of the Atomic Scientists*. Vol. 54, no. 3, May 1998.

Groves, Leslie B. *Now It Can Be Told: The Story of the Manhattan Project*. New York: Harper Brothers, 1962.

Hare, R. M. *Essays in Ethical Theory*. Oxford: Clarendon Press, 1989.

_____. *Essays on Political Morality*. Oxford: Clarendon Press, 1989.

Harper, Stephen. *Miracle of Deliverance: The Case for the Bombing of Hiroshima and Nagasaki*. New York: Stein and Day Publishers, 1986.

Harwit, Martin. "Academic Freedom in 'The Last Act.'" In *The Journal of American History*. December 1995.

_____. *An Exhibit Denied: Lobbying the History of the Enola Gay*. New York: Springer Verlag, Inc., 1996.

_____. "How Lobbying Changed the History of Enola Gay." *Japan Quarterly*. Vol. 44, no. 3, July-September 1997.

Hein, Laura and Mark Selden, ed. *Living with the Bomb: American and Japanese Cultural Conflicts in the Nuclear Age*. Armonk, NY: M. E. Sharpe, XXXX.

Henderson, Amy and Andrienne L Kappler, eds. *Exhibiting Dilemmas: Issues of Representation at the Smithsonian*. Washington: Smithsonian Institution Press, 1997.

Hogan, Michael J., ed. *Hiroshima in History and Memory*. Cambridge: Cambridge University Press, 1998.

Holdstock, Douglas and Frank Barnaby, eds. *Hiroshima and Nagasaki: Retrospect and Prospect.* London: Frank Cass, 1995.

Holloway, David. *Stalin and the Bomb: The Soviet Union and Atomic Energy 1939–1956.* New Haven: Yale University Press, 1994.

Hubbard, Bryan and Marouf A. Hasian Jr. "The Generic Roots of the Enola Gay Controversy." *Political Communication.* Vol. 15, 4, Oct-Dec. 1998.

Iriye, Akira. *Power and Culture: The Japanese-American War, 1941–1945.* Cambridge: Harvard University Press, 1981.

Johnson, Shelia K. *American Attitudes Toward Japan, 1941–1975.* Washington: American Enterprise Institute, 1975.

Jungk, Robert. *Brighter Than a Thousand Suns.* New York: Harcourt Brace, 1958

Kagan, Donald. "Why America Dropped the Bomb." *Commentary.* Vol. 100, no. 3, September 1995.

Kennan, George F. *Memoirs 1925–1950.* New York: Pantheon Books, 1983.

Kurin, Richard. *Reflections of a Culture Broker: A View From The Smithsonian.* Washington: Smithsonian Institution Press, 1997.

Lanouette, William. "Why We Dropped the Bomb." *Civilization.* Vol. 2, no. 1, Jan-Feb 1995.

Leahy, William D. *I Was There: The Personal Story of the Chief of Staff to Presidents Roosevelt and Truman Based on His Notes and Diaries Made at the Time.* New York: McGraw Hill, Inc., 1950.

Lewin, Ronald. *The American Magic: Codes, Ciphers and the Defeat of Japan.* London: Farrar, Straus and Giroux, 1982.

Lifton, Robert Jay and Greg Mitchell. *Hiroshima in America: Fifty Years of Denial.* New York: G. P. Putnam's Sons, 1995.

Lord, John C. S. J. "The Morality of Obliteration Bombing." *Theological Studies.* vol. 3, September 1944, 308–309.

Lubar, Steven. "Exhibiting Memories" in Henderson, Amy and Adrienne I. Kaeppler. eds. *Exhibiting Dilemmas, Issues of Representation at the Smithsonian.* Washington: Smithsonian Institution Press, 1997.

MacArthur, Douglas. *Reminiscences.* New York: McGraw-Hill Book Company, 1964.

MacEachin, Douglas J. *The Final Months of the War with Japan: Signals Intelligence, U. S. Invasion Planning, and the A-Bomb Decision.* Washington Central Intelligence Agency, Center for the Study of Intelligence, 1998.

Maddox, Robert James. "Casualty Estimates for the Invasion of Japan: The "Postwar Creation" Myth." *Continuity.* Vol. 24, Fall 2000.

_____. *Weapons for Victory: The Hiroshima Decision Fifty Years Later.* Columbia: University of Missouri Press,1995.

Manzo, Louis A. "Morality in War Fighting and Strategic Bombing in World War II." *Air Power History.* Vol. 39, no. 3, Fall 1992.

Marx, Joseph Laurence. *Nagasaki: The Necessary Bomb?* New York: Macmillan, 1971.

Maslowski, Peter. "Truman, the Bomb and the Numbers Game." *Military History Quarterly.* Vol. 7, Spring 1995.

Mayr, Otto. "The Enola Gay Fiasco: History, Politics, and the Museum." *Technology and Culture.* Vol. 39, no. 3, 1998.

McCullagh, C. Behan. *The Truth of History.* London: Routledge, 1998.

Miles, Rufus E. Jr. "Hiroshima: The Strange Myth of Half a Million American Lives Saved." *International Security.* Vol. 10, no. 3, Fall 1985.

Minear, Richard H. "Atomic Holocaust, Nazi Holocaust: Some Reflections." *Diplomatic History.* Vol. 19, no. 2, Spring 1995.

Montgomery, David, ed. *The Cold War and the University: Toward an Intellectual History of the Postwar Years*. New York: The New Press, 1997.

Murakami, Hoye. *Japan: The Years of Trial, 1919–1952*. Tokyo: Kodansha International LTD, 1983.

Nagai, Yonosuke and Akira Iriye, eds. *The Origins of the Cold War in Asia*. New York: Columbia University Press, 1977.

Nash, Gary B., Charlotte Crabtree and Ross E. Dunn. *History on Trial: Culture Wars and the Teaching of the Past*. New York: Alfred A. Knopf, 1997.

Newman, Robert P. "Hiroshima and the Trashing of Henry Stimson." *The New England Quarterly*. March 1998

_____. *Truman and the Hiroshima Cult*. East Lansing: Michigan State University Press, 1995.

Nobile, Philip, ed. *Judgment at the Smithsonian*. New York: Marlowe & Company, 1995.

Offner, Arnold A. *Another Such Victory: President Truman and the Cold War 1945–1953*. Stanford: Stanford University Press, 2002.

Ohl, John K. *Supplying the Troops: General Somervill and American Logistics in World War II*. DeKalb: Northern Illinois Press, 1994.

Orr, James J. *The Victim as Hero: Ideologies of Peace and National Identity in Postwar Japan*. Honolulu: University of Hawaii Press, 2001.

Palmer, Robert R., Bell I. Wiley, and William R. Keat. *The United States Army in World War II: The Army Ground Forces, The Procurement and Training of Ground Combat Troops*. Washington: Historical Division, Department of the Army, 1948.

Piehler, G. Kurt. *Remembering War the American Way*. Washington: Smithsonian Institution Press, 1995.

Pogue, Forrest C. *George C. Marshall: Organizer of Victory, 1943–1945*. New York: The Viking Press, 1973.

Polenberg, Richard. *War and Society, The United States 1941–1945*. Philadelphia: J. B. Lippincott Company, 1972.

Posner, Richard A. *Public Intellectuals: A Study in Decline*. Cambridge: Harvard University Press, 2001.

Quigley, Martin S. *Peace Without Hiroshima: Secret Action at the Vatican in the Spring of 1945*. Lanham, Md.: Madison Books, 1991.

Rawls, John. "Fifty Years After Hiroshima." *Dissent*. Vol. 42, no. 3, 1995, 323–327.

Reischauer, Edwin O. *Japan: The Story of a Nation*. New York: Alfred A. Knopf, 1970.

Reischauer, Edwin O. *The United States and Japan*. 3d ed. Cambridge: Harvard University Press, 1965.

Revisionism Gone Wrong, Part II. Arlington: Air Force Association, 2000.

Revisionism Gone Wrong: Analysis of the Enola Gay Controversy. March 1994 — December 1996. Arlington: Air Force Association.

Revisionism Gone Wrong: Analysis of the Enola Gay Controversy, Part III, Supplementary Documents. Arlington: Air Force Association, 2002.

Revisionism Gone Wrong: Analysis of the Enola Gay Controversy, Part II, Documents and Clippings. Arlington: The Air Force Association, March 2000.

Robertson, David. *Sly and Able: A Political Biography of James F. Byrnes*. New York: W. W. Norton, 1994.

Rose, Lisle. *Dubious Victory: The United States and the End of World War II*. Kent: Kent State University Press, 1973.

Saburo, Ienaga (translation & introduction by Richard H. Minear. *Japan's Past Japan's Future, One Historian's Odyssey*. Lanham, MD: Rowman & Littlefield Publishers, Inc., 2001.

Sadao, Asada. "The Shock of the Atomic Bomb and Japan's Decision to Surrender — A Reconsideration." *Pacific Historical Review.* Vol. 67, 1998.

Sigal, Leon V. *Fighting to a Finish: The Politics of War Termination in the United States and Japan, 1945.* Ithaca: Cornell University Press, 1988..

Sherry, Michael S. *The Rise of American Air Power: The Creation of Armageddon.* New Haven: Yale University Press, 1987.

Sherwin, Martin J. *A World Destroyed: Hiroshima and the Origins of the Arms Race.* New York: Vantage Books, 1987.

Sherrod, Robert. *History of Marine Corps Aviation in World War II.* Washington: Combat Forces Press, 1952.

Skates, John Ray. *The Invasion of Japan: Alternative to the Bomb.* Columbia: University of South Carolina Press, 1994.

Spector, Ronald H. *Eagle Against the Sun: The American War with Japan.* New York: The Free Press, 1985.

Spector, Ronald H., ed. *Listening to the Enemy: Key Documents on the Role of Communications Intelligence in the War with Japan.* Wilmington: Scholarly Resources, 1988.

Takaki, Ronald. "Fifty Years After Hiroshima." *Dissent.* Summer 1995, 328–330.

Tanaka, Yuki. *Hidden Horrors, Japanese War Crimes in World War II.* Boulder: Westview Press, 1996.

The Crossroads: The End of World War II, The Atomic Bomb and the Origins of the Cold War. Washington: National Air and Space Museum, January 12, 1994. (This is the first script for the Enola Gay Exhibit, Courtesy of the Air Force Association)

Thelen, David. "History after the Enola Gay Controversy: An Introduction." *The Journal of American History.* Vol. 82, no. 3, 1995.

Thompson, Robert Smith. *Empires on the Pacific: World War II and the Struggle for the Mastery of Asia.* New York: Basic Books, 2001.

The History of the Medical Department of the United States Navy in World War II: A Narrative and Pictorial Volume. Volume 1. Washington: Division of Medical Statistics, Bureau of Medicine and Surgery, Navy Department, United States Government Printing Office, 1950.

United States Strategic Bombing Survey. *Summary Report (Pacific War) Washington, D. C. 1 July 1946.* Washington: United States Government Printing Office: 1946.

Wallace, Mike. *Mickey Mouse History and Other Essays on American Memory.* Philadelphia: Temple University Press.

Walzer, Michael. *Just And Unjust Wars: A Moral Argument with Historical Illustrations.* 2d Ed. New York: Basic Books, 1992.

Warner, Denis and Peggy Warner with Commander Sadao Seno. *The Sacred Warriors: Japan's Suicide Legions.* New York, Van Nostrand Reinhold Company, 1982

The Entry of the Soviet Union into the War Against Japan Military Plans, 1941–1945. Washington: United States Department of Defense, 1955.

van der Vat, Dan. *The Pacific Campaign, World War II: The U.S.–Japanese Naval War 1941–1945.* New York: Simon & Schuster, 1991.

Walker, J. Samuel. *Prompt & Utter Destruction: Truman and the Use of Atomic Bombs Against Japan.* Chapel Hill: University of North Carolina Press, 1997.

Werrell, Kenneth P. *Blankets of Fire: U. S. Bombers over Japan during World War II.* Washington: Smithsonian Institution Press, 1996.

West, Philip and Steven I. Levine and Jackie Hiltz. eds. *America's Wars in Asia: A Cultural Approach to History and Memory.* Armonk, NY: M. E. Sharpe, 1998.

Wexler, Peter. *Hirohito and War: Imperial Tradition and Military Decision Making in Prewar Japan.* Honolulu: University of Hawaii Press, 1998.

Wilcox, Robert K. *Japan's Secret War*. New York: William Morrow and Company, Inc., 1985.

Yoneyama, Lisa. "For Transformative Knowledge and Postnationalist Public Spheres: The Smithsonian Enola Gay Controversy" in Fujitani, T., Gregory M. White and Lisa Yoneyama, eds. *Perilous Memories, The Asia-Pacific War(s)*. Durham: Duke University Press, 2001.

Index